D0983607

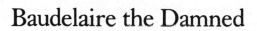

Baudelaire the Damned

BY THE SAME AUTHOR

Culture and Society in France 1848–1898
The Life and Times of Emile Zola
Alexandre Dumas: The King of Romance

Baudelaire
the
Damned
A
Biography

F. W. J. Hemmings

CHARLES SCRIBNER'S SONS · NEW YORK

for Maggi
who helped with the poems

Copyright © 1982 F. W. J. Hemmings

Library of Congress Cataloging in Publication Data

Hemmings, F. W. J. (Frederick William John), 1920–
  Baudelaire the damned.

  Includes bibliographical references and index.
  1. Baudelaire, Charles, 1821–1867—Biography.
2. Authors, French—19th century—Biography.   I. Title.
PQ2191.Z5H4   1982   841'.8   82-10298
ISBN 0-684-17774-9

1 3 5 7 9 11 13 15 17 19 F/C 20 18 16 14 12 10 8 6 4 2

Printed in the United States of America.

CONTENTS

List of Illustrations   vi

Introduction   vii

I   Caroline   1

II   Schooldays   14

III   Wild Oats   27

IV   On the Ile Saint-Louis   43

V   In Chancery   58

VI   The Art Critic   72

VII   The Revolutionary   85

VIII   An Elective Affinity   102

IX   Harpocrates' Forefinger   117

X   Misunderstandings   140

XI   O just, subtle, and mighty Opium!   157

XII   The Widow and her Son   169

XIII   Paris Spleen   186

XIV   Flight into Silence   204

Notes   219

Appendix: French texts of poems and fragments quoted in translation   237

Index   247

ILLUSTRATIONS

Between pages 114 and 115

1a Portrait of Baudelaire's father (Private Collection)
 b Baudelaire as a boy wearing school uniform

2a Baudelaire in his early twenties by Emile Deroy (Musée de Versailles; photo Musées Nationaux, Paris)
 b Sketch by Baudelaire of Jeanne Duval (BBC Hulton Picture Library)

3a Narcisse-Désiré Ancelle
 b Courbet's portrait of Baudelaire in 1847 (Musée Fabre, photo Claude O'Sughrue)

4a Apollonie Sabatier, as painted by Meissonier in 1853
 b Mme Sabatier was the model for Clésinger's statue entitled 'Woman stung by a snake' (Musée Orsay)

5a Marie Daubrun as she appeared in 1854
 b A proof of the dedicatory page of *Les Fleurs du Mal*
 c Self-portrait by Baudelaire under the influence of hashish (photo British Library)

6 Photograph of Baudelaire taken by Carjat around 1860 (BBC Hulton Picture Library)

7a General Aupick, Baudelaire's stepfather (photo British Library)
 b The house at Honfleur built by General Aupick. Baudelaire's mother is at the top of the steps (photo British Library)

8a Photograph of Baudelaire by Charles Neyt
 b The gravestone with inscriptions commemorating Aupick, Baudelaire, and his mother

INTRODUCTION

'En somme, je crois que ma vie a été *damnée* dès le
commencement, et qu'elle l'est *pour toujours*.'
(Letter from Baudelaire to his mother, December 4th, 1854)

Except among a few small and disregarded sects, damnation in the
primitive sense of the word has today become an obsolete concept.
We have to go back to the Elizabethans to find a time when it still kept
its full force and meaning, and it always requires a certain effort to see
things as those distant forefathers of ours saw them. If it were not
that *Hamlet* has now become so familiar and hallowed a text, we
might well think the hero slightly freakish to refrain from despatch-
ing the King when he could, for no other reason than that Claudius
happens to be at his prayers when the Prince comes upon him.
Hamlet wants to be revenged not just here in Denmark but in the
hereafter too; so he will wait a more convenient moment, when his
uncle is

> about some act
> That has no relish of salvation in't:
> Then trip him, that his heels may kick at heaven;
> And that his soul may be as damned, and black,
> As hell, whereto it goes.

Similarly, it is only by a conscious adjustment that we can accept
what Marlowe's contemporaries had no difficulty in believing, which
was that once Faustus had struck his bargain with Mephistopheles
and once the forfeit fell due, nothing could save him from being
'damned perpetually'.

Two centuries of 'progress' and 'enlightenment' supervened
before Goethe turned back to the Faust legend which Marlowe had
presented in all its medieval simplicity. For Goethe, it was too crude,
and he sidestepped the issue of damnation; even though the Devil
wins his wager, Faust is let off having to pay. The notion of a
beneficent Deity allowing eternal torment to be inflicted on His own
creatures, however disobedient and rebellious, was more than
nineteenth-century liberals could stomach.

But Baudelaire was not a nineteenth-century liberal; indeed, to many of his contemporaries, including one suspects Flaubert, he appeared as something of a throwback: regressive in his moral outlook, however modern he may have been in other respects – in his aesthetic insights, for instance. It is impossible not to be struck, as one reads him, by the frequency of his use of the word *damnation* and its cognates; the sentence we have picked as epigraph is simply the most memorable instance that can be found in his writings: 'In short, I believe that my life has been *damned* from the beginning, and that it is damned *for ever.*'

We notice that Baudelaire does not call himself damned, but only his life; his biographer has to explain how this life came to be damned, but need not take into account the possibility that he who lived that life was and is now among the company of the damned. There is little evidence that Baudelaire seriously visualized the afterlife in conventional terms of heaven and hell, and even if he did, it is most unlikely that he would have imagined hell quite as Dante imagined it ... or Wyndham Lewis. As to the kind of existence reserved for humanity beyond the grave, he kept an open mind; he was curious about it, and curiously hopeful; had it been otherwise, had he seriously entertained the notion of a Catholic God sitting in judgement on the souls of the departed, no doubt he would have embraced again, before his death, the faith that he lost in his late teens. But he did believe very firmly that certain lives are damned on this earth and that his was one of these.

In the first of these beliefs he came close to what one imagines must have been, to judge by the tenor of some of his more important tragedies, the viewpoint of Jean Racine, though Racine was not an author whom Baudelaire studied closely or esteemed very highly. For Racine deals in charmed lives – charmed, however, not by some kindly spirit but by a hostile outside force which, irrespective of the struggles of his heroines, Queen Phaedra or Queen Athaliah, to suppress the wayward urgings of their natures or deflect the remorseless course of history, overcomes all their efforts. Some there are that have not grace, and are in this sense damned. The affinities between Baudelaire's philosophy of life and the doctrines of Jansenism that so deeply marked Racine are so remarkable that attempts have even been made to prove that Baudelaire received, through his father, a Jansenist upbringing. The evidence, however, is too tenuous for the theory to be seriously considered.

Damnation in this sense implies predestination, and sometimes there is little that separates the two ideas, except of course that the first always leads to misfortune and misery, whereas the second can lead to greatness and glory. In a passage of his important monograph on the illustrator Constantin Guys, Baudelaire tells a story he claims

viii

to have heard from one of his friends, an artist of repute whom he does not name but who might have been Manet. 'When he was very small, he used to be present when his father was performing his morning ablutions; on these occasions he would contemplate, in stupor mingled with rapture, the muscles in the arms, the gradual shading of the colour of the skin from pink to yellow, and the bluish network of the veins. The images of the external world were already filling him with admiration and taking hold of his mind. Forms were already obsessing and possessing him. Predestination was prematurely showing the tip of its nose. His *damnation* was already accomplished.' It is Baudelaire who italicizes the word.

Here *damnation* can almost be equated with *vocation*, and it might be objected that Baudelaire is straining the meaning of the word, or trivializing it. However, in his century it was almost a commonplace that a vocation for art or poetry was inseparable from moral suffering and only too often entailed desperate material privation as well. The concept of *le poète maudit* was given wide currency by Verlaine in the 1880s but had really been launched fifty years earlier by Alfred de Vigny in a semi-fictional, semi-historical work entitled *Stello*. In this book Vigny tells the life stories of three poets, all of whom died young and in wretched or infamous circumstances: of sickness (Laurent Gilbert), of the fatal dose of laudanum that he took to escape a humiliating fate (Thomas Chatterton), and on the scaffold, sentenced for the political crime of having lampooned the Jacobins (André Chénier). The moral Vigny draws from his triple apologue is that no matter how society is constituted, whether the form of government is an absolute monarchy, an oligarchy, or a revolutionary committee, the poet invariably suffers.

He suffers, however, as Vigny argues, not because he is damned (which would imply persecution on a cosmic scale), but because he is an outcast, a pariah, an object of suspicion to men in power. The romantics thought that society had no room for the poet – although, curiously, there never was a period in France when writers were better represented in the corridors of power; the careers of Chateaubriand, Lamartine, and Hugo go a long way to disproving Vigny's thesis. Whatever the truth of it, and even though he quoted *Stello* approvingly and found in Poe a fourth instance to add to Vigny's trilogy, Baudelaire did not feel that Vigny had got to the heart of the matter. It might be indeed that the poet tended to be misunderstood and undervalued by society, but that was a relatively trivial irritation. The poet was *damned*, with a private damnation that had nothing to do with public reprobation, and Baudelaire needed only to consider his own case to be convinced of this. From the moment of his conception to the hour when he drew his last breath, every circumstance conspired against him: his ancestry was tainted, his birth unlucky, his parents and teachers persecuted him, his mistress betrayed him; he was racked by disease and his neuroticism made him miserable; he lost his money or, worse, it was placed in the hands of a snuffling man of the law who doled him out a starvation allowance; his works, when they appeared, were misunderstood, condemned as pornographic. Finally he had to flee his own country, and in solitary exile was struck down by the paralysis that robbed him of the power of speech and in which he dragged out miserably the few remaining months of his life before dying at the age of forty-six.

As Nicole Ward Jouve has put it with superb understatement, 'Nobody but a lunatic would recommend Baudelaire's life as a pattern to be imitated.' What this observation seems to imply is that the pattern of one's life is to a certain degree a matter of choice. And if Baudelaire's life pattern was so unenviable, could it not be that he consistently made the wrong choices, thus working his own damnation? Was it bad luck or his own folly that led him to contract syphilis at the age of eighteen and at the age of twenty-three to show himself so incapable of handling his own affairs that he was declared legally unfit to remain in charge of them? The idea that he chose his own fate, or perhaps rather that, his fate being what it was, Baudelaire failed to make the choices that would have allowed him to escape from it, has been most persuasively argued by Jean-Paul Sartre, but the charge loses some of its edge in face of the readiness of the accused to admit it. For Baudelaire never regarded himself as an innocent victim; on the contrary, he was paralysed by a sense of guilt, by the consciousness of his own shortcomings. From boyhood through to the last, he was constantly adjuring himself to shake off his lethargy, to overcome the vice of procrastination, to avoid what he regarded as sin, to accomplish his mission. He did accomplish it of course; *Les Fleurs du Mal* was written, unquestionably the most profound and influential single volume of poetry in the French language if not in the whole of world literature, and a corrosive sense of failure on this plane, the artistic, was the one misfortune that Baudelaire was spared. But in no other respect did his efforts allow him to triumph over what he called the 'irremediable' or the 'irreparable'. He could not see himself as having his place among the elect. The nature of his damnation was that he could have said 'yes' to his better promptings, but he could not help constantly saying 'no' or 'not yet'. In this sense, in a purely theological if not Christian sense, he was damned, and he never expressed it more clearly than in the sonnet entitled *The Rebel*.

An Angel pounces like a bird of prey,
Seizes the sinner firmly by the hair,
Shakes him in fury: 'Hear me, and obey!
I'm your good angel, and I'll make you care.

Know then that you must love, and with good grace
The poor, the warped, the mean and dull of mind.
At Jesus' feet a carpet you shall place
Of loving-kindness woven; – for to be kind

Is Love. Let not your heart grow cold,
But to God's glory let the flame take hold
Of lasting bliss, true rapture's steady glow.'

The Angel thus, chastising in Love's name,
With giant talons rends his victim's frame;
But, being damned, the wretch still answers: 'No!'

*   *   *

When the biographer's subject is a poet who wrote in a foreign language, he is faced with a particular difficulty in deciding how he should quote, as he is bound to from time to time, from the poetic works. To reproduce the original poem in the original language and leave it at that is to make unreal and perhaps slightly arrogant assumptions when one's readership is drawn from the English-speaking world. To append prose translations to accompany Baudelaire's French would have been not just cumbersome but wholly inadequate. Poetry is always much more than its mere meaning; the stanzaic form, the metre, the rhythm and the rhymes are quite as much part of the poem as the bare sense of what is being said. The solution I have adopted in this book has been to use verse translations which, while departing as little as can be contrived from the literal meaning of the original, preserve religiously Baudelaire's rhyming schemes, to which he attached such importance (calling rhymes 'the lanterns that light up the pathway of the idea'), and as far as the metre is concerned, to approximate as closely as possible to the original, with one obvious exception: the line of verse most commonly found in French is the dodecasyllable, and I have transposed this everywhere by the most commonly used line in English verse, which is, of course, the pentameter.

Les Fleurs du Mal has of course attracted a great number of translators. I have not studied their work, nor compared my versions with theirs, and any resemblances there may be arise therefore purely from chance.

I

CAROLINE

Every man assumes the day will come when he will be mourner at his mother's funeral, though perhaps only the morbid or the melancholic will give the eventuality much thought beforehand; being so much in the course of nature, it is regarded as scarcely less inevitable than one's own death. The contrary possibility, that once the hazards of infancy are behind him a grown man should none the less be laid in the grave by the same woman as brought him into the world, has always seemed so remote and problematic that a steady mind could never entertain it for more than a fleeting moment. Yet this very possibility, at certain times of his life, haunted Baudelaire; he even discussed it with his mother in agony of spirit; and, in the event, his premonition proved justified. Alone in the death-chamber with him, she held him in her arms and watched him breathe his last, stroking his forehead while he smiled – so she reported – tenderly up at her; in love and gratitude, or with relief that he was at last to be freed from her? We can only guess which it was.

Even though they never lived under the same roof together for more than a few weeks except when he was a child, and were sometimes separated by thousands of miles of land and sea, they were never for long out of touch with one another. Each kept the other's letters and although his mother appears to have destroyed all hers when they came back into her possession at her son's death, she kept all or most of his, and this series of some 360 letters not only represents the fullest single source of information available to us concerning the wretched tribulations of his day-to-day existence, but in addition provides the elements of a case-history, possibly unique in the literature of psychology, of a mother–son relationship of truly monstrous morbidity. Here we have a man of outstandingly, virile genius totally dependent from birth to death, not only financially but emotionally, on a lesser spirit for whom notwithstanding we are bound to feel some sympathy: a puzzled duck that had hatched a black swan, to use Jacques Crépet's trivial but apt comparison.[1] Baudelaire's feelings for his mother ran very deep, and were the more violent because they were contradictory, forming a churning devil's brew in which strong affection conflicted with harsh resentment, while gratitude for her anxious concern for his welfare was poisoned by scalding anger at the limitations of her understanding of his hopes and purposes.

It goes without saying that there were other women in his life who meant more to the sensual and even spiritual side of his nature; it was they who inspired the succession of sombre and radiant cycles of love-poetry in *Les Fleurs du Mal*. As for his mother, the book contained in its first edition only two pieces directly addressed to her and, typically, she failed to notice them when she first read it so that he was obliged to write and point them out to her. But there was another poem, placed immediately after the dedicatory ode 'To the Reader', to which he did not draw her attention but in which he seems to have summed up, obliquely and as it were anonymously, the tragic sense of maternal rejection that ran like a thick black thread through the whole tangled web of his feelings for her. The poem bears the ironical title 'Benediction', and the first five verses run something like this:

When, in obedience to divine decree,
The Poet enters on life's tawdry stage,
His frantic mother, filled with blasphemy
Strikes at the God of Mercy in her rage.

'Rather bring forth a writhing knot of snakes
Than put this freakish monster to my breast!
Curs'd be the night, whose short-lived pleasure makes
Conception penance, and its fruit a jest.

Since of all women Thou hast chosen me
To be dishonoured in my husband's sight;
Since I may not destroy this parody
Like a love-letter that one sets alight,

I will deflect thy wrath that crushes me
On to this damnèd source of my despair.
I shall so twist and nip this wretched tree
That never a bud will burst to foul the air.'

Thus does she spit her rage and swallow her shame,
Ignorant of what was planned from earliest times;
Kindling herself the purgatorial flame
Designed for mothers guilty of her crimes.

*   *   *

Baudelaire's mother was born in London on September 27th, 1793, and given the names Caroline Archenbaut when baptized at St

Pancras Church the following year. Both her parents were refugees from the Terror, seeking safety in England like thousands of others; Caroline's mother, Louise-Julie, *née* Foyot, is said to have been already carrying her when she crossed the Channel. The father was a certain Charles Defayis, about whom nothing is known beyond the fact that he was a royalist officer, which would imply that his family had been ennobled under the *ancien régime*. The Foyots belonged to the upper middle classes, the family fortunes having been founded by Louise-Julie's grandfather, who did well enough in trade to purchase his son (her father) the office of attorney-at-law in the Paris *parlement*.[2] In an undated note written in the latter part of his life, Baudelaire makes a passing reference to 'my ancestors, idiots or madmen, living in gloomy apartments, all of them victims of terrible passions'.[3] Since his own father came of sound peasant stock, and his maternal grandfather, as we have seen, was a respectable lawyer, the remark can only apply to Caroline's father, Charles Defayis, and his forbears, and unless it is pure fantasy must derive from confidences he remembered his mother having made him at some point. But hitherto it has not proved possible to show whether or not he was mistaken in thinking that he had a tainted ancestry; the earlier history of the Defayis family remains shrouded in mystery to this day. His belief that madness ran in his blood is, however, of possibly greater significance than the truth or otherwise of the presumption. It was, to his way of thinking, the first nail in the coffin of his predestined damnation.

Caroline must have remained in England, if not in London, for at least the first few years of her life, since it was only at this time that she could have acquired the knowledge of English that enabled her later on not only to appreciate her son's virtuosity in translating Edgar Allan Poe but to give him lessons in pronunciation.[4] But she may not have been much more than a child when she lost both her parents and, with them, all means of support. Luckily she escaped the charity orphanage that might have been her lot; Pierre Pérignon, a friend of her mother's father and a lawyer like him, adopted her, and until her marriage in 1819 she enjoyed a comfortable home life in the Pérignons' spacious establishment in Paris. Thanks to their care and generosity, she received the kind of education that was given in those days to girls of good family; later, an initiation under their wing into society life helped her acquire the tact and poise that was to stand her in such good stead, many years later, when as the wife of the French ambassador in Constantinople and Madrid she found herself having to entertain travellers of distinction at embassy parties. For her foster-mother Mme Pérignon, the handsome daughter of a West Indies planter who had returned to France shortly before the

3

Revolution, was noted for her *salon*, a magnet during the Empire and under the Restoration for leading political figures and legal luminaries. In her late teens, once she had left the elegant school for young ladies where she had been boarded, Caroline Defayis might have been seen regularly in this drawing-room, handing round orangeade and cakes and possibly called on from time to time to perform on one of the recently popularized pianofortes imported from England.

It may well have been here that she first made the acquaintance of an old friend of her guardian's, a widower in his late fifties called Joseph-François Baudelaire. In addition she saw him on occasions when the Pérignons were invited to dine with him in the charming grace-and-favour house which he had been allocated in consideration of his office as chief curator of the Luxembourg Palace. Caroline enjoyed these visits, particularly after the gates were locked in the evening and she had free run of the gardens. As for their host, although he appeared to the twenty-year-old girl an old man, with his crisply curling grey hair and eyebrows 'black as ebony', she appreciated his cheerful conversation and fund of entertaining stories as much as did the other members of the Pérignon family, who liked to compare him to La Fontaine for his simplicity and good nature.

François Baudelaire and Pierre Pérignon had known one another from their boyhood, when both had studied the classics at the venerable scholastic establishment of Sainte-Barbe. On leaving school, Pérignon had gone in for the law, while Baudelaire had entered the teaching profession, not however as an ill-paid usher but as private tutor to the sons of one of the most powerful nobles of France, the Duc de Choiseul-Praslin. This enviable situation allowed him to mingle on equal terms with many of the leading liberal intellectuals of the reign of Louis XVI, among them Condorcet, the materialist philosopher Cabanis, and Helvétius's widow whose *salon* was frequented, in the years immediately preceding the Revolution, by a number of the more prominent *encyclopédistes*. In this company the young François Baudelaire acquired the polished manners so appreciated later by those of an age to remember the *douceur de vivre* of pre-Revolutionary France. He also formed some useful friendships which not only helped him survive unscathed the turmoil of Jacobin rule but also enabled him to render no small service to the family of his patrons whom, so the story goes, he kept alive during the bread famine by sharing with them the payments in kind he received from a baker to whose daughter he was giving drawing lessons.

For drawing was one of François Baudelaire's many minor talents; he had, indeed, a keen interest in all aspects of the fine arts, a bent inherited, as we shall see, by his son. It was undoubtedly his expertise and taste in artistic matters that led Napoleon to appoint him steward of the Luxembourg Palace (used at that time as the Senate debating chamber), with primary responsibility for commissioning statues for the gardens and pictures for the assembly rooms and galleries. He was a private collector too, on a small scale, specializing in engravings and plaster casts, and, encouraged by his artist friends, had tried his hand at pastels and painting in gouache. A shared love of art was no doubt largely instrumental in creating the bond between him and the amateur painter Jeanne-Justine-Rosalie Janin, whom he married in 1797. The couple had one child born to them and then, in December 1814, his wife's death left him alone in the world apart from his son, Claude-Alphonse, then a boy of nine.

It must have been loneliness, together with the yearning of late middle age for the restorative freshness of nubile youth, that drew him to his friend Pérignon's lively young ward. The offer of marriage, conveyed to her in all probability by Mme Pérignon, would not have struck Caroline as being wildly incongruous; in France at this period it was not at all unusual for men to marry women young enough to be their daughters. The age difference here was 34 years; it had been 32 between Balzac's father and mother. François Baudelaire was a well-preserved sexagenarian, with an easy-going disposition, and she had known him for a good many years. He could offer her a secure future: apart from the quite handsome emoluments attached to his post, he had inherited from his first wife a sizeable acreage of agricultural land situated on the outskirts of Paris which could only appreciate in value and in the meantime brought in a useful rental. Caroline herself had no fortune at all worth speaking of – her dowry was a mere 1000 francs – and even if she had been outstandingly beautiful she could hardly have expected, in her circumstances, to encounter a suitor nearer her own age with means to support her. Young men married to better themselves in those days. The alternative to accepting old Baudelaire's offer would have been to remain an unmarried dependant of her guardian who, she probably thought, had exercised his charity towards her long enough. So she accepted the arrangement with good grace if not with positive alacrity.

They were married on September 9th, 1819, and on April 9th, 1821, the first and only child of the union, Charles-Pierre Baudelaire, was born at no. 13, rue Hautefeuille, a turreted house of antique appearance which consisted inside of a veritable bee-hive of little rooms stuffed with the products of François Baudelaire's mania for collecting *objets d'art*; according to the inventory drawn up after his death, there were no fewer than 27 pieces of sculpture in the house

5

and over 200 pictures, 54 in the library alone, which abutted on to the child's nursery.[5] Many of the oil-paintings had been executed by his first wife; she had had a studio in the Rue de Vaugirard and at her death the widower had transported the greater part of the contents to the establishment where he was to welcome his second wife.[6] Caroline was far from sharing her husband's love of art; she was, besides, prudish enough to feel some embarrassment at being perpetually surrounded by images of naked nymphs and lusty satyrs, which she quietly removed one by one, replacing them by other less indecent pictures stored in the attics. But she was unable to do anything about the prize piece in her husband's collection, a plaster replica of the Graeco-Roman Hermaphrodite, copied from the version in the Louvre, which continued shamelessly to display its swelling buttocks in a place of honour on the mantelpiece.

When in later life Charles Baudelaire tried to trace back to its origins the curse that he was convinced had been laid on him from the very moment he entered the world, he did not forget to mention, half-seriously, that the house of his birth did bear the unlucky number 13. But much more reasonably, he pointed out in talking to the Belgian journalist Georges Barral that he might well have owed his 'execrable temperament' to the fact that he was the offspring of so ill-matched a couple. 'My frayed nerves are due to their disparity. That's what comes of being the unbalanced child of a mother of twenty-seven and a father aged sixty-two.'[7] But it was not simply the advanced age at which his father begot him that had to be taken into account; there was another, far more sinister cause for the evil fate that hung over his life.

So many of the sallies attributed to Baudelaire were clearly designed only to shock or surprise his listeners, that suspicion inevitably attaches to almost any disclosure he made about his family origins. For this reason, the remarks he was overheard to make about his father having worn a priest's cassock, his habit of referring to himself as 'the son of a priest', were for a long time discounted as just one more of the poet's frivolous boasts, inspired perhaps by the indiscreet comments of gossip-column writers on the semi-clerical costume he affected in the 1860s. In recent years, however, quite irrefutable evidence has come to light which shows that François Baudelaire was indeed exercising the functions of a priest in the diocese of Châlons-sur-Marne in 1785, though the exact record, and therefore date, of his ordination has so far not been discovered. It has further been established that only six days after the Convention issued a decree (dated November 13th, 1793) permitting priests to 'abdicate their authority' (i.e. renounce their office), François Baudelaire availed himself of the opportunity. So did, of course, a number of others at the time, but the speed with which he defrocked himself indicates fairly convincingly that he must have lost his faith some time earlier.[8]

In a Roman Catholic country, if not now then certainly in the earlier part of the nineteenth century, to have had as one's father a man who, at a previous point in his life, had taken orders and had subsequently left the Church would be regarded as a matter of extreme gravity. Among the faithful at least it would imply that the child was the issue of a union not just unsanctified but probably accursed. The vow of celibacy taken by the man on ordination could never be lifted by a mere administrative act on the part of the civil authorities, especially when controlled by an atheistic and revolutionary government. The child was thus the living proof of his father's sacrilege, his very presence in the world something unnatural, an offence in the eyes of God. How could this essential stigma ever be erased, how could this original sin ever be redeemed?

But it was his mother rather than his father that the poet blamed when he learned the truth. She must have known the situation before she married; her guardian, or the bridegroom himself, would have had to explain it to her, if only to account for the fact that their wedding could not be celebrated in church. She could have refused to proceed, but instead she sacrificed her religious scruples on the altar of worldly considerations. Yet she continued to pass herself off, hypocritically, as a dutiful daughter of the Church. His father had at least had the decency to abjure his religion.

All through his life, Baudelaire cultivated his father's memory with touching reverence. At the age of seventeen he wrote to Alphonse, his half-brother, asking to be shown a few samples of the poetry he had heard their father had composed. Years later he told his mother he had come across a couple of his father's pictures in a junk shop, but to his annoyance he did not have the money to pay a deposit on them. The terms of his letter make it clear that he was angry she should have sold them, though the descriptions he gives of them also suggest her reasons for having done so: they were both studies of nudes. The one picture he himself never parted with was J. B. Regnault's portrait of his father. He took it with him when he moved to Honfleur to stay with his mother, and he mentions it again in a doleful letter written to her on May 6th, 1861: 'I am alone, with no friends, no mistress, without even a dog or a cat to complain to. I have only the portrait of my father which is for ever mute.' Two years later she sent him all the letters from François Baudelaire that she had kept, and he was overjoyed. 'These old papers have something magical about them,' he wrote. 'You could not have chosen a surer way to touch my heart.'[9]

The portrait referred to was painted around 1810 and showed a younger man than Baudelaire can have remembered. When he was in reminiscent mood he would tell his friends how his father, an old man with long white hair, would take him for walks in the Luxembourg Gardens, shaking his stick at any stray dog that might gambol up, and telling him stories about the gods and heroes which the statues represented. They were not the same statues as one sees there today, but guide-books of the period list them for us; they were all copies or originals of antique figures, several of them no doubt forming part of the booty that Napoleon sent back to France at the conclusion of his Italian campaign of 1796–7. They included a Diane, a Hebe, various Venuses, no fewer than seven Bacchuses, a gladiator, and two groups of wrestlers, besides allegorical figures of Night and Winter.[10] The earliest impact of the classical tradition thus reached the child Baudelaire through works of plastic art, long before he was introduced to the literatures of Greece and Rome.

He lost his father on February 10th, 1827, a little before his sixth birthday. The old man had been under treatment for gout and gravel, but in fact he was suffering from cancer of the bladder which had not even been diagnosed, and he died in considerable pain.[11] For Caroline, who had never been passionately attached to him, it meant a welcome release; towards the end, illness had soured her husband's former good humour and now, an attractive widow of thirty-three reasonably provided for, with only one child to take care of, she could look forward to a life of relative independence with renewed chances of personal fulfilment. She paid for a temporary (five-year) plot in the cemetery of Montparnasse where her husband's remains were interred, but when the renewal date came up she omitted to go through with the necessary formalities to make the concession permanent. So in 1832 the bones of François Baudelaire were dug up for transfer to the catacombs or for reburial in some suburban graveyard, with no stone to mark the spot.[12] Whether this piece of negligence on Caroline's part was deliberate or due to mere forgetfulness matters little; in her son's eyes, when he learned about it at a later age, the insult to his father's memory was one more grievance to add to the score.

It is true that in February 1832 Caroline, now Mme Aupick, was no longer living in Paris, having left the capital the previous month to join her second husband in Lyons. In her default, it was the dead man's elder son, Claude-Alphonse Baudelaire, by now a man of twenty-seven well launched on his career in the magistracy, who might have been expected to concern himself with the business. There were several reasons for the rift that later developed between the two half-brothers, Alphonse and Charles, but this dereliction of

8

duty, as the poet saw it, counted probably for a great deal in the quarrel.

If her first marriage had been a respectable arrangement, Caroline's second was rather more hazardous at the outset though in the end it turned out brilliantly successful. Her new husband had begun life, like her, a penniless orphan, and like her, he owed his education to the kindness of the man who adopted him, a certain Louis Baudard, magistrate and harbour-master at the Channel port of Gravelines, between Calais and Dunkirk.[13] His parents were both of Irish birth or extraction, and he was originally christened James, a name later gallicized to Jacques. His father, an officer in the Catholic Irish brigade which had been formed for service under the French monarchy at the time when the Stuarts had fled to France with their followers, was killed fighting the republican armies in 1793; at that time Jacques Aupick was a child of four. His mother succeeded in reaching Gravelines after the battle and was billeted on Baudard, in whose house she died shortly afterwards in consequence of the privations she had suffered in the retreat. It seemed only natural to the charitable magistrate to take the orphan boy into his home and treat him as though he were his own child; being without natural heirs, he even bequeathed the young man his little property when he died in 1821.

At this date Aupick already had an eventful fighting career behind him, for even as a boy he had never had any thought but to follow the profession of arms like his father before him. After an education at the military academy of Saint-Cyr, he was commissioned in 1809 and took part in several campaigns in central Europe and in the Iberian Peninsula; finally, at the battle of Fleurus, on the eve of Waterloo, he was wounded by a gun-shot in the left leg, from the results of which he was to suffer intermittently for the rest of his life. At the Restoration, he paid for his loyalty to Napoleon by being debarred for a while from army service, but his persistence eventually persuaded the War Ministry to put him back on the active service list at his old rank of captain. When the French invaded Spain in 1823 he distinguished himself in the field and came to the favourable notice of the Prince of Hohenlohe, Marshal of France, the first of a succession of high-placed patrons with whom Aupick succeeded in ingratiating himself.

Since he was residing in Paris more or less permanently after the conclusion of the Franco–Spanish War, the dashing cavalry officer could have made the acquaintance of old Baudelaire's young wife at any time after 1823. But no family letters have so far come to light to show under what circumstances the two might have met, nor when, nor who might have first introduced them. What is certain is that

Caroline availed herself of the greater freedom she enjoyed after her husband's death to see much more of Captain Aupick, and the two must have become lovers within a year or so, at the latest, of her widowhood. In the summer of 1828 she knew she was pregnant; on October 17th Aupick submitted a formal request to the military authorities, as army regulations demanded, for permission to marry her. The Prince of Hohenlohe endorsed the petition, adding that 'for reasons of interest' his aide was anxious to complete the formalities rapidly. Red tape was cut, authority came through within three days, and the ceremony was performed on November 8th, one might say in the nick of time. The newly wedded couple moved to Creil, a small town to the north of Paris on the road to Amiens where Mme Aupick had some discreet friends, and it was in a nearby hamlet, on December 2nd, that she was brought to bed of a daughter who was unfortunately still-born.[14]

It is more than just convention that makes one use the word *unfortunately* here; it might well have made all the difference to Baudelaire's personal happiness in his childhood, and to his relations with women in later life, if he had grown up with this little companion and had had the same kind of charmingly confidential relations with her as Stendhal, Lamartine, Balzac and Flaubert had with their younger sisters. In the account he later gave of De Quincey's childhood, he wrote almost wistfully of the English writer's home life, in a family consisting of a widowed mother and three young sisters, with no 'horrid pugilistic brothers', as De Quincey says. These happy circumstances were, according to Baudelaire, an important factor in the development of De Quincey's poetic sensibility. 'Indeed, men who have been brought up by women and among women differ to some extent from other men, even if one supposes equality in temperament or in spiritual faculties. The nurse who rocks them, the mother who fondles them, the sisters who wheedle them (especially if they are elder sisters, like diminutive mothers), they all transform, as it were by kneading it, the masculine clay. A man who, from the beginning, has been steeped in a gentle feminine atmosphere, in the fragrance of women's hands, breasts, lap, hair, and softly flowing garments,

Dulce balneum suavibus
Unguentatum odoribus,[15]

will have acquired as a result a delicacy of touch and a distinction of tone, a kind of androgynous quality without which the steeliest and most virile genius lacks something when it comes to achieving perfection in art. What I am trying to say is that a precocious taste for the feminine world, for the whole of this vibrant, sparkling, perfumed universe, is what makes for superiority of genius.'[16]

To the extent that Baudelaire had his own experience in mind when writing this passage, it was the 'gentle, feminine atmosphere' his mother provided that he was remembering. The man of forty, indulging in a rare retrospective reverie in one of his letters to her, declared: 'There was a phase in my childhood of passionate love for you; listen, and don't be afraid to read this. I have never opened my heart to you as fully.' And he goes on to recall how she had had to go into a nursing-home for a while and how he was taken to greet her when she was discharged; in the cab that took them home, she showed him the pen-and-ink sketches she had done for him while she was convalescing. He also recalled how they would go for long walks together, in the Bois de Boulogne when they were spending the summer months at Neuilly, and along the embankments of the Seine at a time when they were living as the guests of his half-brother Alphonse in his chambers on the Place Saint-André-des-Arts. This would have been very shortly after François Baudelaire's death, when little Charles had just turned six. 'For me that was,' he goes on to say in the same letter, 'the blissful time of motherly affection. You must forgive me for calling it a *blissful time*, for it was probably a bad time for you. But I was always living in you; you were mine alone, at one and the same time my companion and someone I idolized.'[17]

The little house they rented in the summer of 1828 at Neuilly (3, rue de Seine) is described nostalgically in a short poem included in the first edition of *Les Fleurs du Mal* but given no title, for, as he told his mother at the time of publication, 'I abhor exposing private family matters to public scrutiny.'[18] In it he describes the garden, its plaster statues of Pomona and Venus sheltering in a stunted shrubbery, and evokes the pair of them, his mother and himself, sitting silently over their frugal evening meal while the setting sun poured its golden rays over the table, the plates and the glasses, as though watching them through the windows facing west.

This unassuming little piece is immediately followed, in the collection, by a longer and more characteristic poem about another member of the shrunken household, Caroline's faithful servant Mariette. The life-long impression this girl left on Baudelaire is attested by two separate entries he made in a private notebook kept in the latter part of his life, where her name is linked to that of his father (and, on the first occasion, to that of Poe as well) as 'intercessors' to be invoked at his morning devotions. Her name is also given to an episodic character in his story *La Fanfarlo*, published in 1847, who is shown accompanying the lady the hero has fallen in love with, Mme de Cosmelly; here she is described as 'quite an elegant lady's maid, whose appearance and dress denoted rather the companion and confidant than the servant'.[19]

The real Mariette had certainly died long before *La Fanfarlo* was written, since the poem referred to ('La servante au grand coeur dont vous étiez jalouse . . .') was one of those Baudelaire's friend Prarond remembered hearing him recite no later than 1843, and in this poem she is described as lying beneath some 'lowly turf', lonely and forgotten, the grave untended, the skeleton rotting slowly in the damp earth. He imagines seeing her spectral form seated before the wood fire of an evening in the chair she used to occupy, and asks:

> If, in my chamber, one blue winter's night,
> I were to find her crouched by candlelight,
> Risen from her endless sleep to view the child
> Whom she once tended like a mother mild,
> How could I answer this grave, pious soul,
> Seeing the salt tears from her sockets roll?

One of the unexplained allusions in this poem is to his mother's jealousy of Mariette, which is mentioned in the opening line; the least improbable interpretation is that, particularly when Caroline began seeing a great deal of Jacques Aupick, Mariette came to replace her more and more, and that this usurpation gave rise to angry scenes between the possessive mother and the good-hearted servant.[20] Baudelaire so rarely refers in his writings to events in this early period of his life that one is obliged either to leave the veil unlifted or to resort to some such reasonable conjecture.

There is one further text, the autobiographical nature of which is not so explicit – but then so little of what Baudelaire wrote, other than his literary and art criticism, is free from subjective slant – which can, without straining the evidence, be held to throw some light on the nature of his attachment to Mariette.

In a prose poem, *Les Vocations*, composed in 1862 or possibly a little earlier, Baudelaire describes four boys talking together in a flower garden. Each, by the story he tells, reveals the hidden bent of his own nature, hence his 'vocation'; and it is not difficult to see that each one of these proclivities corresponds to something in Baudelaire himself, which is why we shall need to revert to this text on occasion later. The third boy relates how, on a journey he undertook with his parents, they put up for the night at a crowded inn where there were insufficient beds, so that he was put to sleep with the maid. 'I can tell you, it's a funny feeling being in bed not on your own but with your nanny, in the dark. I was lying there wide awake and to pass the time, while she was asleep, I started touching her arms and neck and shoulders. Her arms and neck are much bigger than other women's, and the skin is so soft, it's like notepaper or tissue paper. It gave me such a thrill I could have gone on for ever, if I hadn't been afraid – afraid of waking her up first of all and afraid of something else, I can't say what. Then I buried my head in her hair which was spread out over her back, as thick as a horse's mane, and it smelt as lovely as the flowers here in the garden do now.'[21]

If there is any precise memory that gave rise to this passage it must date back to some occasion before Baudelaire's eleventh birthday, for it was in January 1832 that he and his mother travelled down to Lyons, she to join her husband who had just been posted there, he to be sent to a boarding-school in the same city. After that, whether or not Mariette was the innocent initiator of this sexually precocious child, he would have seen very little of her. But however sketchy our information about Baudelaire's pre-school days, no detail, however hazily attested, can be glossed over as unimportant; for, as he himself later argued, speaking in general of the artist's creative spirit: 'Every trivial sorrow, every small pleasure in a child's existence, hugely magnified at a later stage in the adult man thanks to his exquisite sensibility, will all unconsciously form the basis of a work of art. In short, and to express my idea more concisely, would it not be easy to prove, by a critical comparison between the works of a mature artist and his psychological condition as a child, that genius is no more than childhood clearly formulated, having subsequently acquired virile and potent organs for its expression?'[22]

II

SCHOOLDAYS

One of the most tenacious legends concerning Baudelaire, and one on which several well-known biographies and biographical essays, including Sartre's, have been based, is that he deeply resented his mother's remarrying and was at loggerheads with his stepfather Aupick from the very beginning. Certain picturesque versions of this legend can be dismissed out of hand as being too absurd to warrant serious consideration, such as for example the story Nadar related[1] of how young Charles, who at the time would have been no more than seven, locked his mother in her bedroom on her wedding-night and threw away the key. (It has already been noted that Captain Aupick and his bride left Paris immediately after the ceremony for Creil, where Caroline could have her confinement far away from gossiping neighbours; her young son would certainly not have accompanied them.) The testimony most often quoted in support of the view that the boy detested his mother's new husband from the moment he came into his life is that provided by Jules Buisson: 'Baudelaire had a very delicate and fine-spun nature, gentle, original, but weak and womanish; it had splintered at the first blow fate dealt him. There was one event in his earlier life that he was never able to come to terms with: his mother's remarriage. On this subject he would discourse endlessly, and the remorseless logic of his arguments could always be summed up as follows: "When a woman has a son like me (*like me* was implied), she doesn't get married again."'[2] But Buisson, a member of the group of young writers who styled themselves the 'Norman School', did not get to know Baudelaire until the poet was in his early twenties. At that stage in his life admittedly, and for reasons to be gone into when the time comes, Baudelaire had developed a violent antipathy towards his stepfather, and it would have been quite natural for him to have blamed his mother for having contracted this marriage some thirteen years earlier. But to suppose the marriage affected him traumatically when it occurred, and that he hated the intruder Aupick from that point on, is to go much further than the known facts warrant.

For a start, Caroline's new status could hardly have brought about any dramatic change in the little boy's normal life; she still remained his 'companion and idol' and he may not have been fully aware that he would have to share her from now on with a newcomer. For on March 23rd, 1830, Aupick was posted overseas, to serve as staff officer at divisional headquarters in Algeria; he thus found himself an active participant in the first wave of the French invasion of North Africa. With his usual vigour he distinguished himself in various engagements with the Arabs, and in October 1830 was promoted lieutenant-colonel. He remained in the field until June 1831, which means that for more than a year, during which time Charles attained his tenth birthday, the boy and his mother were once more living on their own. It is indeed arguable that the 'phase of passionate love' for Caroline, to which Baudelaire alluded in a letter already quoted, extended beyond the period of her widowhood to which it is usually held to refer, and covered additionally the fifteen months of her grass widowhood.

But then there was a change. Aupick returned home for some leave due in the latter part of 1831, and at his next posting away from Paris was able to take his small family with him. While he had been out of France a revolution had brought a new monarch to the throne, but the régime had inherited various problems from its predecessor, among them the pacification of Algeria in which Aupick had played his part. This colonial war was being conducted ruthlessly and on the whole successfully; but Louis-Philippe also found himself facing a potentially dangerous situation inside France as the industrial revolution gathered pace, breaking the old moulds of social organization and creating new risks of civil conflict. Nowhere were these risks more evident than in the ancient city of Lyons, and it says something for the reliance the military authorities placed in Colonel Aupick that their choice should have fallen on him for an important command in this area (he was put in charge of the general staff of the 7th division).

Lyons was then, as now, one of the leading manufacturing towns in France. Silk was the main industry, its products accounting for nearly 30% of all exports. The weavers were no unskilled factory hands, but sober craftsmen who took pride in their work and knew their worth. When the economic depression of the early 1830s caused a contraction in demand, their employers tried to shift the goods by lowering the price, and to do this imposed a cut in the workers' hourly rates of pay. They protested; an orderly demonstration in October 1831 resulted in a meeting between representatives of both sides, at which an agreement was reached for revised payments. Unfortunately not all the employers were prepared to fall into line; a small minority refused to raise their workers' wages and threatened a lock-out. At this, a strike was called; and when the ringleaders were fired on in the streets, with a loss of eight lives, the entire labour force rose as a body, threw up barricades, and drove the military back to their barracks. For a brief period the workers took control of the city; they conducted themselves with exemplary moderation, taking firm measures against looting and against attacks on the persons and property of the manufacturers. Workers' rule was not, however, to the liking of the central government. The army was ordered to reoccupy the city, the status quo was restored, and thereafter there was no question of minimum wage levels for the weavers, who returned to their looms beaten for the time being, but secretly burning with hatred for their masters and for the soldiers who had been used to impose their masters' will.

The rising was quelled before Aupick's arrival in Lyons, but clearly he had to be prepared for a possible renewal of street violence. Nevertheless, by the New Year he must have judged it safe enough for his family to join him. This was the first long journey the ten-year-old Charles had ever undertaken and, judging from the account he sent to brother Alphonse, the experience filled him with rapture and excitement. 'The day now drawing to its close, I saw a most beautiful sight, it was the setting sun; the reddish colour formed a strange contrast with the mountains which were of as deep a blue as the darkest of blue trousers. Having put on my little silk bonnet, I leaned back in the seat of the coach and it passed through my mind that to spend my life travelling would suit me very well . . .'[3] In *Les Vocations*, the prose poem mentioned a few pages back, Baudelaire seems to have remembered this childish thrill, attributing it to one of the four boys that figure in his story, whose opening words are not at all dissimilar to those he had used himself, though by then he would have surely forgotten them: 'It has always seemed to me that what would make me truly happy would be to travel along for ever, not knowing where I was going, with nobody to worry about me, and always seeing new countries. I never feel settled anywhere, and I'm always convinced I shall be better off in some other place than where I am now.'[4] The imaginary voyage, whether along dusty roads or towards the beckoning skyline of the ocean, is a persistent theme in Baudelaire's prose and poetry,[5] even though in reality, once he was a grown man, it was only with the greatest difficulty that he ever brought himself to stir from the familiar streets of Paris.

Lyons, when he got to know the place, was a great disappointment, and it was not long before he was expressing, in a New Year's letter to Alphonse Baudelaire, something like homesickness for Paris. 'I miss the boulevards, and the sweets at Berthellemot's shop, and Giroux's department store, and all those well-stocked emporia where it's so easy to buy presents. Lyons has only one shop where you can buy books with *de luxe* bindings, two only selling pastries and confectionery, and so on ... In this smoke-blackened town there's nothing to be had but fat chestnuts and fine silk.'[6] He soon came to the conclusion that all the inhabitants of Lyons were ill-tempered and dirty in their habits and at his first school the friends he made were drawn exclusively from the set of five 'Parisians' he found there.

The lower orders in Lyons were also, he was given to understand, a riotous and dangerous crowd of roughnecks. As a boy of thirteen he could not have been expected to grasp the reasons for the social discontent that simmered beneath the surface of this 'smoke-blackened town', but he could hardly have remained in total ignorance of the fresh revolt that flared up in 1834, especially since his stepfather was closely involved in suppressing it. At this date, active opposition to the policies of Louis-Philippe's government was concentrated in a small number of secret societies up and down the country devoted to establishing a republic run along socialist lines. The cabinet was sufficiently disturbed by the threat they posed to introduce into the Chamber a bill outlawing all such associations. Their leaders, however, were not prepared tamely to submit to this edict, and fixed on Lyons, where the memory of the events of 1831 was still very much alive, as providing the most promising testing ground for a trial of strength. They enlisted the support of a powerful workers' union, the *Mutuellistes*, and on April 9th a fresh insurrection turned the city into a battlefield. Fighting went on for four days, the working-class districts coming under shell-fire from the forts encircling the town, until finally the troops were able to clear the streets, though only after considerable bloodshed: the dead numbered some three hundred in all, almost as many among the uniformed soldiers as among the ragged weavers.

Confined within the stone walls of his boarding-school, Baudelaire would have known about these dire events only by report. His education had begun in earnest on his first arrival in Lyons,[7] when he was sent for two terms to the Pension Delorme, a preparatory school for the Collège Royal which he joined as a boarder in October 1832. When in 1836 Aupick returned to Paris to take up a new appointment, his stepson was sent to the Lycée Louis-le-Grand, again as a boarder. In both cities it would have been possible for him to live at home and attend school as a day-boy. Why did his parents decide against this arrangement, which almost certainly would have suited him far better?

It was partly a matter of convenience, no doubt, and partly a matter of doing what was best for the boy according to their lights. At Lyons, if he had remained at home, it would have been necessary to have him accompanied by a man-servant on the walk to and from school every day; the streets were not safe for a middle-class child to wander along on his own. Colonel Aupick may have thought too that the discipline of a regulated life where he was under constant supervision could only be beneficial to the lad. In holding this view he was at one with the majority of careful fathers in those days, when it was rather exceptional for the children of well-to-do families to live at home, except in vacations, during their school-years. The *lycées* of the period boarded some 80% of their pupils, most of whom, like Charles Baudelaire, would have had their homes in the vicinity.[8] The Aupicks were merely following the fashion, and there is no reason to suppose they were trying deliberately to rid themselves of the responsibility of looking after a turbulent child.

In any case, to describe Baudelaire as turbulent or even difficult at this age would be unfair. In the lower forms he seems to have been a lively boy, a bit of a chatterbox, occasionally being disciplined for talking in class. As a result he became rather silent and withdrawn. He formed no firm and enduring friendships, of the kind Flaubert made at school with Bouilhet or Zola with Cézanne. His school-fellows' conversations he judged 'often very pointless and very insipid', and occasionally he would go off on his own, rejoining their group only when he feared they might think him stand-offish. 'I much prefer', he told his mother, 'our long spells of silence between six and nine o'clock in the evening, when you are sewing and papa is reading.'[9]

With the onset of puberty, Baudelaire started leading a life apart, deeply tinged with religiosity. He used to hold what he later called 'conversations with God', and he indulged in endless daydreams, imagining himself either a warrior-pope, or else an actor.[10] 'An enthusiast', he was called by one of those who knew him at the Lycée Louis-le-Grand, 'sometimes full of mystical ideas and sometimes expressing – but only in words – the most brazenly immoral opinions which went beyond what was tolerable.'[11] Such affectations of perversity were designed to keep the more conventionally minded of his fellows at a safe distance. Baudelaire felt no need to mix or to share his ideas and aspirations. 'In spite of my family – and particularly among my classmates – I had the feeling my destiny was to remain eternally alone. Yet I had a very pronounced taste for life and pleasure.'[12]

The pleasures, however, were few and found mainly in the occasional reunions with his parents which were less frequent than they might have been, since they were dependent on his winning good reports at school. His letters home, even when he was only twelve, are full of references to the progress he was making in different subjects and of good resolutions to work harder and do better. There is one in particular, written on February 25th, 1834, addressed to his mother and stepfather, in which he pleads with them not to punish him for doing so badly at school by refusing to come and see him on occasions when visits were permitted. The essential passage runs as follows:

When I renewed my promise to you last time not to give you cause to grieve, I meant what I said, I was determined to work and to work hard so that you could say: We have a son who is grateful for the care we have taken. But my thoughtlessness and laziness have made me forget my promises and good resolutions. It's not that I have a froward heart, it's not my heart that needs amendment, it's just that I need a steadier mind, I need to be made to reflect hard enough for the reflections to remain engraved there. You are beginning to think I am ungrateful, perhaps you are convinced I am. How am I to prove the contrary? I know the way: it is to settle down to work now; but whatever I do, this period spent in idleness and in forgetfulness of what I owe you will always be a blot. How can I make you forget in a second my bad behaviour over three months? I have no idea and yet that is what I would like. Give me back your trust and affection, please come to the school and tell me you have done so. It will be the best way too to make me change immediately.
    You have despaired of me as of a son irremediably given up to evil and grown indifferent to everything, who spends his time in idleness, who lacks firmness, is weak and lazy and has not the strength of character to mend his ways. I have been unsteady, I have been weak and lazy, I've let time go past without thinking of anything; but since the heart is unchangeable, my heart, which for all its defects has its good points, is just the same. This made me feel I ought not to despair of myself . . .[13]

Whether this appeal had the effect the boy hoped, we do not know. That he felt he needed to plead in such terms, for fear he should be deprived of the opportunity of a few hours' conversation with his parents, is no doubt what strikes today's reader as especially shocking; it is perhaps less surprising that a twelve-year-old should show himself capable of this kind of moralistic self-analysis in terms of the traditional heart-and-mind dichotomy. This is the age at which children, and boys perhaps more than girls, are much given to examining their own motives, often in a spirit of humility and self-reproach, a tendency if anything reinforced among those of the Catholic faith by the practice of weekly confession (Baudelaire had taken his first communion in August 1832).
    The excuses and explanations were undoubtedly intended more

for his mother's eyes than for the Colonel's. Since these letters from school were rediscovered and published,[14] it has been impossible to see Aupick, as so many of Baudelaire's earlier biographers did, in the light of a kind of military Mr Murdstone. Himself orphaned at an early age, and owing everything to the care taken of him by a kindly and generous foster-father, he may well have felt he owed it to Providence and to his own conscience to extend to Charles the same indulgent affection as had been lavished on him by his own guardian when he was of the same age. Besides, whatever hopes he may have had of a child by Caroline were fast disappearing; the boy was therefore all the more dear to him, as being the nearest to a son and heir he was ever likely to have. Certainly there is not a line in these early letters of Baudelaire to suggest that the youthful writer was aiming to play off a soft-hearted mother against a stern stepfather. The evidence points rather in the opposite direction. Writing to his elder brother, he admits ruefully that he had gained only one prize, a second prize for drawing, at the end of the academic year. On the other hand, he got five honourable mentions (*proxime accessits*), an achievement which, he says, 'delights my father'. He then begs Alphonse not to be 'more difficult to please than he, not to be as difficult as my mother, for instance, who imagines I ought to come first in everything. I can't blame her for her high expectations; her excessive fondness is always making her dream of success for me.'[15]

Caroline, now in her late thirties, saw life smiling on her in a way that made her almost forget the trials and frustrations of her earlier days. Her husband was everything she could wish for; not only did he continue as devoted as he had always shown himself to be, but she could see that, as his career was shaping, there was every chance he would end up occupying some post of great honour in the service of his country. If only her son, by that other man whom she had never passionately loved, might follow his example and not disappoint them all! particularly since her husband was so attached to the boy. So, to leave nothing to chance, she was perpetually nagging him to try and do better; he never seemed able to satisfy her. The dreamy, affectionate younger woman he remembered, in her conventional widow's dress, who used to give him all her time, go for long walks with him and sit with him of an evening over frugal but protracted meals, had turned into a severe, tight-lipped overseer, never relaxing her vigilance, angry whenever he relapsed into one of his spells of *dolce far niente*. By a curious reversal of roles, it was she who had turned into the stepmother, while Aupick had slipped easily into the place of his real father, to the point of almost obliterating for the moment the memory of the old man with his white locks and the walking stick which he used to shake to keep stray curs at bay.

Her motives may have been, if not good, at least understandable; her methods were disastrously ill conceived. Whenever he got bad marks, she flew into a temper and heaped reproaches on him. He reacted, not as another child might, by sulking or rebelling, but by pleading with her. 'My dear mother, You left the school very angry, I know, but in calling me ungrateful you were too harsh, too unjust even. I have pondered too long on all the obligations I have towards my mother not to have realized that, as a schoolboy, my duty is to give her great satisfaction and contentment.' Hypocrisy? Irony? Neither seems likely in a boy of thirteen. In any case, the same note is struck four years later, though by this time it is clear he was beginning to despair of ever discharging all his fancied obligations towards her. 'There is something else that frightens me. When I consider my enormous debt towards you for all the kindnesses you have shown me, I realize there is no other way of repaying you than by giving you cause for pride in my achievements. But, my poor mother, if nature has not given me what is needed to content you, if I haven't the intellectual gifts to satisfy your ambition, then you will die before I have had a chance to repay you even slightly for all the trouble you have taken . . .'[16] One wonders at the brainwashing that lies behind this sense of obligation felt by a boy who had, after all, been virtually banished from his home and shut up in a school which he hated, towards this woman who as he saw only too clearly valued him chiefly as a potential source of gratification for her maternal pride.

But Charles was far too young to realize to the full how the normal relationships between mother and son were becoming distorted, set in an unnatural mould which even at a much later age he was unable to break. The dread of reproaches and recriminations persisted surprisingly long; Baudelaire was well into his forties when he jotted down this revealing comment: 'My mother is a fanciful creature, to be feared and to be courted.'[17] Finally, it is perhaps not altogether absurd to see in this demotion of family affections to a paltry business of bartering services (I pay for your keep, your education, you pay me back later by becoming the successful son every mother hopes to have) the root of Baudelaire's inability to form any kind of love relationship except with the class of woman whose favours were given in return for payment.[18]

The road both of them were travelling to a hell of their own making was no doubt paved with good intentions. For all her tantrums and displays of dissatisfaction, Caroline was secretly delighted at the progress Charles was making; but, she thought, it was essential to keep the boy up to the mark. She concurred with her husband who judged him to be doing extremely well at school, but it was all the more important, in her way of thinking, that he should be encouraged to concentrate on his work so as to do even better. A letter to Alphonse Baudelaire, when Charles was thirteen, shows exactly this mixture of gratification and apprehension:

... We are really overjoyed to hear that Charles has so excelled himself; he has been placed first or second, out of fifty, in all his subjects. He is in a good phase; if he were disposed to carry on like this, we would be very happy, he has such potential that we are right to expect a great deal of him. He is anything but an ordinary child, but he is so lacking in seriousness, so scatter-brained, so fond of play! As for his character, his moral qualities, one couldn't wish for anything better: he has charming manners, an extremely kind and tender heart, and is very affectionate. We really have no complaint to make of him except that he will play in class instead of working and has contracted the bad habit of always putting off doing his prep till the last moment. When you are writing to him, say a word or two about this. Tell him how important it is in life always to do immediately what one has to do, and how serious are the consequences of always deferring things. This defect in your brother reduces me to despair. I do everything I can to correct him.[19]

And so, no doubt, she did, but to no avail; the demon of the dilatory was not one to be conjured by exhortations or punishments, and Baudelaire remained a prey to it all his life. Caroline continued, even after the publication of his master work, to reproach him for his slackness, reminding him that one should never put off till the morrow what can be done today; he accepted her strictures humbly, knowing however that he neither could nor would ever mend his ways. 'You are dinning into me a lesson I already know. I spend my life reading myself sermons which are sublime and irrefutable and have never cured me. I am and always have been full of good sense and riddled with vice. The one thing I need, I fear, is the whipping that children and slaves are given.'[20] What Baudelaire overlooked here, and what Caroline never understood, was that no literary work of real value was ever produced by dread of the consequences of not meeting a deadline.

Early in 1836 Aupick, who by now had been promoted to the rank of full colonel, was transferred to the staff of the 1st division, which meant returning to Paris. Baudelaire was glad enough to leave the rough-and-tumble of the Collège de Lyon, where boredom alternated with violence: playground fights, rows with the teachers, and punishments inflicted for the least sign of rebelliousness. At a later stage, after his stepfather's death, he spoke bitterly of the misery of his school-days, reminding his mother of the 'atrocious education your husband insisted on giving me; at forty, I can't think of schools without a twinge of pain, any more than of the fear my stepfather filled me with. Yet I loved him, and in any case I have enough sense now to recognize his good intentions. But for all that, he was stubborn and misguided . . .'[21] What kind of alternative education Baudelaire thought he should have been given is far from clear; the Aupicks were hardly in a position to afford a private tutor for him. But the little phrase 'yet I loved him' may have more truth in it than the preceding one about 'the fear my stepfather filled me with'; that fear came later. The letters he was writing home around the age of sixteen or seventeen contain expressions of affection for Aupick which go far beyond mere filial dutifulness. About this time the veteran's old injury was causing him a lot of trouble, and one of Charles's letters to his mother starts: 'I would like to have news of papa, whether he is in great pain, whether they are considering closing the wound soon, whether he gets very bored, whether he talks to you about me, anything you can tell me.'[22] In the summer of 1838, Aupick was given sick leave to undergo a cure at Barèges, a Pyrenean health resort, which meant that Baudelaire had to spend the vacation cooped up at school; but he put a brave face on it and in a letter to his stepfather on July 27th he wrote, using as he always did the *tutoiement* which at that period was by no means universal among children addressing their parents:[23] 'I dare not talk to you about your wound; I know you prefer it when we don't show ourselves over-anxious for you; mama seems to think it's taking a long time; if you think you are getting any benefit, then you must stay on till the end of the year if necessary. I had rather do without my holidays than that you should pass up the chance of the slightest relief.' Aupick, it seems, was touched by these words and wrote back sending Charles the money for his fare down south. This time the boy wrote to his mother: 'I would like to thank papa, but how can I? I am in the seventh heaven; to go travelling during the holidays! it's just what I've always wanted to do and now it's happening! . . . I'll be with you in a few days time, the richer for some experiences, travel-stained and mad with joy. Give papa a hearty kiss from me, I would like to hug him for this.'[24] Leaving on August 23rd, he made the journey to Barèges on his own, by stage-coach, and spent a fortnight walking and riding with his stepfather in the neighbourhood. After that the three of them travelled to Bordeaux, where they sailed up the coast to the mouth of the Loire (Caroline suffering sadly from seasickness on the way), and then took the boat up the river, returning to Paris via Blois and Orleans. It was the longest trip Baudelaire had ever made

23

and, it must be said, the only real treat his parents had ever given him.

After that it was back to school. For the past two years he had been a boarder at the Lycée Louis-le-Grand, which had a reputation for strict discipline but was also regarded as academically one of the best in Paris; it counted Victor Hugo, Delacroix, and Jules Janin among its recent alumni. The fees were high, which meant that Baudelaire's schoolfellows were for the most part the scions of the landed aristocracy and the sons of wealthy industrialists or of well-paid members of the legal profession. A number of the boarders came from the families of planters and merchants settled in the French colonies or ex-colonies overseas, Martinique, Guadeloupe, Reunion Island, and Senegal on the west coast of Africa, and it is possible that the stories they had to tell of life at home may have implanted in his imagination the original seeds later to flower in those visions of tropical paradises that enrich some of the most moving poems of the 'Black Venus' cycle.

It had been Aupick's decision that Baudelaire should complete his education at this school where he felt sure his stepson would acquit himself with distinction. He had been genuinely impressed by the progress the boy had been making, 'astonished to the highest degree by this fine intelligence, this inquiring and studious mind, so that he felt more and more deeply attached to him as the days went by', as Mme Aupick testified after her son's death. 'On our return to Paris, when my husband took him along to the Lycée Louis-le-Grand, being full of enthusiasm and confidence about Charles's capabilities and the successes he had won, he said to the principal: "Here is a present I am making you, a pupil who will bring honour to your school."'[25] Aupick was not a man given to idle boasting, but the headmaster, who had had dealings before, no doubt, with proud and doting parents, thought it wise to wait and see. He began by placing Baudelaire in the third form, although at Lyons he had already been moved up to the one above; the great educational establishments of Paris had no unduly high opinion of provincial schools.

Syllabuses at this time were still overwhelmingly humanistic; the study of Latin and Greek occupied most of the scholars' time. A few timid reforms had been made in recent years: the teaching of arithmetic and geometry was introduced in 1828–9; in 1829 provision was made for modern languages to be taught in the schools, but only as an 'optional extra' for those who wanted to learn them. As late as 1836 there was still argument as to whether scientific studies should figure in the syllabus; in a speech on the question in the Chamber, Lamartine urged forcefully that mathematics and physics, if taught at all, should always be subordinate to literary studies which alone conveyed moral truths. However, it never occurred to Baudelaire, then or later, that the exclusion of the exact sciences from the school curriculum constituted a defect in the system. Like nearly everyone in France at the time, he had an unshakeable belief in what he was later to call 'the inestimable advantage of a liberal education. This education', he continues, 'brought to a more or less successful conclusion, leaves its mark, so to speak, on a man, and those who missed it, even the most gifted, are always conscious of a kind of gap which studies undertaken later in life are powerless to fill.'[26]

The subject at which Baudelaire shone, regularly winning first prize, was the composition of Latin verse on set themes. This required, besides a wide command of the classical Latin vocabulary, an intimate knowledge of the various prosodic models that the poets of ancient Rome had taken over from the Greeks; Latin verse has no rhyming system but depends on the manipulation of metre according to intricate and inflexible rules. The years he spent perfecting himself in this apparently useless exercise were not wasted; although Latinisms as such are less evident in his poetry than in Hugo's, for instance, his mastery of the French hexameter, which depends so much for its full effect on rhythmic modulation, the handling of the caesura, the use of alliteration, echoic effects and so forth, derived in large measure from the close study he made at school of the Latin poets of the classical age in order to surprise their secrets and adapt their technique. While anything but classical in his outlook – apart from Molière and the Catholic apologists, Pascal, Bossuet, Bourdaloue, he rarely refers to, let alone quotes, the writers of the French seventeenth century – Baudelaire can be called classical in his aesthetic practice: that is to say, he regarded the business of writing poetry as much more a matter of achieving sublime effects by the application of well-tried rules and conventions than of allowing inspiration to take what form it would. In this sense he can be sharply distinguished from the mellifluous rhetoricians of the romantic period and from the innovatory poets of the symbolist school who came later.

Although they must have recognized they had a gifted pupil, just as his guardian and stepfather had said, the teachers at the Lycée Louis-le-Grand had certain misgivings when it came to assessing Baudelaire's conduct and character.[27] He was thought capricious, unreliable, lacking in the solid virtues that would enable him to make steady progress. He showed himself all too inclined to neglect subjects that made no appeal to him – such as history, for instance. He acquired the reputation of being 'rather an original, sometimes bizarre ... occasionally off-hand, affected ... insubordinate'. He was suspected of having none too good an influence on the other boys, some of whom laughed at him as an eccentric poseur, for ever reciting Hugo and Gautier or uttering outrageously immoral maxims, while others admired his independent spirit to the point of hero-worship.

It was one of the latter who was ultimately responsible for the incident that led to his sudden expulsion from the school a little before he was due to sit his leaving examination, the *baccalauréat*. A class-mate had been seen to pass him a note, which Baudelaire refused at first to let the master see; on being pressed, he tore it up and swallowed the pieces. He was sent to the headmaster, but could not be persuaded to reveal the contents of the note. It was pointed out to him that, by insisting on keeping silence, he risked having the worst construction put on the affair. This struck Baudelaire as so extraordinary, or so he later said, that he burst out laughing, whereupon the indignant principal sent him home on the spot, writing Aupick a brief letter to motivate this extreme measure. The letter concluded by paying tribute to his stepson's gifts, which however were 'spoiled by a very bad disposition which has several times already had a deleterious effect on the internal discipline of the school'.[28]

The incident, naturally, aroused a storm of comment and speculation among the older pupils. The story got around that Baudelaire and the other boy had been carrying on some sort of amorous intrigue; the fact that Baudelaire, in the letter of apology which his mother insisted he should write, referred to the note that he had destroyed as 'a paper which might have caused a schoolfellow to be punished, a paper of no real significance',[29] does not by any means invalidate this interpretation, though it may suggest that Baudelaire was the indifferent recipient, rather than the initiator, of such sexual advances as may have been made. But the true significance of the episode lies elsewhere: this was the first recorded occasion when Baudelaire openly defied authority. The docile child was evolving into a rebellious adolescent.

III

WILD OATS

Baudelaire being already turned eighteen at the time of his expulsion from the Lycée Louis-le-Grand, there was no question of entering him for another school. So for the next few weeks he remained at home, engaged in desultory reading and in pondering his future. His mother, although shocked and pained, said very little; in the discussions she had with her husband about the latest turn of events, she could not fail to be struck by his observation that at least the boy had shown remarkable firmness of character in refusing. to be browbeaten and to betray a comrade. Such loyalty appealed to the soldier in Aupick. In any case the colonel had little enough time, just then, for domestic concerns, being deeply preoccupied with public business of far greater moment. In the spring of 1839 the country was in the grips of a prolonged parliamentary crisis of which advantage was taken by leaders of the anti-monarchist left to stage a rising in Paris on May 13th. Aupick played his part in its suppression, with his usual efficiency and cool-headedness. Marshal Soult, whom Louis-Philippe invited to head a new cabinet after control had been regained, was sufficiently impressed by his qualities to appoint him, when the vacancy arose three years later, to the command of all regular troops stationed in the capital.

His exertions on the day of the insurrection, however, had brought on fresh lesions in Aupick's old wound, and once more he had to apply for sick leave to follow a course of treatment at another watering-place, Bourbonne-les-Bains. His wife accompanied him as previously; and it was decided their son should go into lodgings until the time came for him to take his *baccalauréat*. A suitable *pension* was found; its great recommendation was that the son of the family, Charles Lasègue, a student only a little older than Baudelaire, was well qualified to coach him. It was only during the run-up to his examination that the two had anything to do with one another; then Lasègue went on to lay the foundations of a sound professional reputation in the treatment of nervous disorders and, right at the end of Baudelaire's life, he was one of the specialists whom Mme Aupick called in to treat her son in his final illness.

The Lasègues – father, mother, and son – were the first normal family (for his own could hardly be called normal) that Baudelaire had ever known really well. He observed them closely: the father a soft-spoken, self-effacing man, the mother sensible, active, garrulous, though sometimes caustic in her remarks, and the son combining his mother's cheerfulness with his father's gentleness. But for all their excellent qualities, Baudelaire felt ill at ease among them. Noticing his occasional black moods, they tried to jolly him out of them, and this he resented. 'They are always in good spirits in this house, and that depresses me,' he told his mother. 'To be sure they are happier than we are. At home, I remember tears, father with his worries, you with your bouts of nerves, never mind, I *prefer us* like that.'[1]

The mood of neurotic depression Baudelaire was later to call *spleen* descended on him that summer for the first time in his life; and in describing it to his mother, in the same letter, he can already be observed associating it, in a way that will later become totally characteristic, with a sense of sin and personal guilt. Essentially, spleen was apathy. 'I'm worse than I was at school', he wrote. 'At school I didn't concern myself much with what went on in class, but still I paid some attention; – when I was expelled, that shook me, but still I found a few things to occupy myself with under your roof; – but now *nothing, nothing*, and it's not a sweet poetic indolence but a glum, stupid idleness. I did not dare to explain this fully to my friend,[2] nor show myself to him in my true colours; he would have found the transformation too complete – he had too high an opinion of me. At school I worked from time to time, I read, sometimes I cried, sometimes I fell into a rage; but at least I was alive, which is more than I am now, I'm lower than a snake's belly, and bad, bad, and no longer bad in a pleasant way. If only this painful insight into myself could force me to effect some radical change – but no, instead of that energetic spirit that used to impel me sometimes towards good, sometimes towards evil, there is nothing now but lassitude, glumness, and boredom.'[3]

It was only to his mother that he opened himself up in this way, casting her in the role of a lay confessor from whom he hoped to obtain absolution. Friends of his own age whom he continued to frequent noticed nothing of this inner turmoil. A certain Henri Hignard, who had known him at school in Lyons, reported to his parents that he had spent the previous Sunday (i.e. July 28th, 1839) in the company of Baudelaire 'whom I found as good and warm-hearted as ever . . . We spent the whole afternoon strolling along the boulevards and in the Tuileries Gardens. He's a delightful chap, very friendly with me. Over the past year – for I saw him on my first arrival in Paris – he has turned into a very handsome fellow, but what gave me much more pleasure was that he has become serious-minded, studious, and religiously inclined.'[4] The last epithet is a little surprising; it suggests that the 'conversations with God' of his childhood had not altogether ceased, and perhaps even that Baudelaire was still a communicant member of the Church. One apparently insignificant detail might be adduced in support of this interpretation. Although Baudelaire had a room in the Lasègues' house, he took his meals at a private hotel in the vicinity of Saint-Sulpice owned or at any rate managed by a certain Mlle Céleste Théot. Ernest Renan, who stayed there for a week or so at a slightly later date, called it 'a kind of annex of the seminary [of Saint-Sulpice] where the rules of the seminary were still more or less in force. You were only accepted there on a recommendation of the reverend fathers or of some devout person of consequence.'[5] One may infer from this that Baudelaire's reputation must still have been that of a practising young Catholic, since otherwise he would not have been admitted as a paying guest at Mlle Céleste's establishment.

On August 12th, 1839, he sat his *baccalauréat* and passed, though he very nearly failed in history and geography. The letter in which he announced this success to Alphonse is hardly triumphant; Baudelaire shows himself more concerned about what was to come next and in particular about his choice of career. He felt drawn in no special direction; there were a number of possible fields of activity he would like to explore; his difficulty was to commit himself to any one. A few days after this letter was sent, the Aupicks returned from Bourbonne-les-Bains and the discussions about Charles's future started up in earnest. His stepfather was inclined to take a rosy view of the prospects. He had just been promoted to the rank of brigadier-general and, with his usual luck in finding high-born patrons, was currently basking in the favour of the Duc d'Orléans, heir to the throne. With connections like these, and given a modicum of good will and application on Charles's part, there was no reason why the young man should not fairly quickly work his way to the top of whatever career in the state service attracted him. Baudelaire listened to all this, frowning, silent. Aupick, whose good intentions he could appreciate, was none the less at this moment speaking to him with the voice of Satan tempting Christ in the wilderness: 'all these things will I give thee . . .' Hesitantly, but firmly, Baudelaire pronounced his *Vade retro, Satanas*; he would accept none of his stepfather's well-meant offers of service, he would have no wire-pulling nor would he agree to an office job. Literature would be his career; he would be a writer or nothing.

In making this announcement, Baudelaire may have felt he was rejecting the Devil's third temptation; but he was also sealing his own damnation in another sense, condemning himself ultimately to poverty, ostracism, disgrace and misery; though in fact it would be out of that failed life that he would construct his life's work, it would be on that dunghill of evil that the flowers of his poetry would blossom. He could have had little premonition of this and neither, perhaps, had the others, though in 1839, in spite of the one or two instances of poets who had become men of distinction in the public eye (Lamartine, Hugo), the general view was that writers were somehow marginal to society, since they made no tangible contributions to its welfare. Only four years previously, in his play *Chatterton*, Vigny had exposed and stigmatized this attitude, without probably making the slightest difference to it. The myth persisted that poets were ne'er-do-wells; they were generally pictured, as scruffy bohemians, improvident, dissolute, down-at-heel, and destined to die in a public ward if they did not put an end to their useless lives with an overdose of laudanum.

The consternation, when Baudelaire made his intentions plain, can be imagined. At first Aupick refused to take the young man seriously, then he grew angry; it was the first rift between the two, which never closed and eventually became unbridgeable. Charles saw that he could look for no support from his mother who, indeed, never ceased, till the end of her life, to deplore his obstinate refusal at this crucial point to allow Aupick to arrange his future; in relating the episode to his first biographer, Asselineau, she commented sadly if a little naïvely: 'If Charles had accepted the guidance of his stepfather, his career would have been very different. He would not have won himself a name in literature, it is true, but we should have been all three much happier.'[6]

Eventually a face-saving compromise was reached. Baudelaire would register as a law student for the time being, but in practice would be left to his own devices. Perhaps, in a year or two, he would see things in a more reasonable light. But it was more than Aupick could stand to have him living under the same roof in idleness; he was found — or found himself — lodgings in the Marais district, taking a room in the Rue Culture-Sainte-Catherine not far from the Place Royale. His parents were not washing their hands of him, but they were prepared, for a while, to let him live as he wished and try out his wings.

The first use he made of this new-won freedom was, in that age, and given the streak of recklessness in Baudelaire, almost predictable: he went out and picked some cheap drab from the street and brought her back to his room for the night. The result, equally predictable, was a dose of clap. The only person he could think of to turn to in this predicament was his half-brother, who put him in touch with a Dr Guérin, a specialist in venereal diseases. The treatment prescribed got rid of some of the symptoms, the headaches, the stiffness, but did not immediately stop the discharge. Alphonse does not appear to have berated Charles for his folly or to have suggested he lead a more temperate life in future; venereal disease was so widespread in the first half of the nineteenth century that to contract it was regarded almost as a rite of passage, the contemporary equivalent of the donning of the toga virilis. Certainly Baudelaire himself did not regard the unpleasant experience as in any way a warning or a deterrent to further experiments.

It was some time the following year (1840) that he took up with a girl possibly belonging to the community of poor Jews settled near the synagogue in the Rue du Temple, whom he could have met at one of the dance-halls, such as *La Reine Blanche* or *Le Bal des Acacias*, which at that time were frequented chiefly by artists and their models. Having a cast in one eye, she was known as Sara-la-Louchette (Squint-Eyed Sarah), and, if one takes at face value Baudelaire's own description in an early poem,[7] she was no beauty or rather

'Her beauty flowers only in my sad heart.'

But others who knew her were more charitable; and, certainly, if she did pose as a model, she cannot have been quite as ugly and misshapen as this poem implies. Baudelaire cherished her partly out of pity; he describes her slinking by day along the streets with her head hanging and her eyes fixed on the gutter 'like an injured pigeon', while at night he would listen to the harsh breathing that presaged an early death from consumption or else, when she lay awake quaking with terror at the goblins and ghosts she imagined in the darkness, he would do what he could to comfort her and banish her fears. She would never go to bed without a night-light, and spent more of her hard-earned ha'pence on tallow candles than on good nourishing food.

Sara represented rather more than a passing fancy; his friend Ernest Prarond says that Baudelaire was 'quite mad about her at the time we got to know him', though he adds that 'he was far from lenient towards her when recalling this affair'.[8] Might the reason for the grudge he bore her have been that it was from Sara that he contracted the syphilitic infection which troubled him for the rest of his life and contributed to, if it did not actually cause, his early death? Certainly, by his twentieth or twenty-first year Baudelaire seems to have suspected that he had already signed his own death-warrant and even quoted to his friends the cynical epitaph he had composed for his own gravestone:

> Here lieth one whose weakness for loose ladies
> Cut him off young and sent him down to Hades.[9]

These friends, Prarond in particular, regarded the liaison with Sara as having been altogether disastrous for her infatuated lover. In a sonnet dated October 5th, 1842,[10] Prarond recalls how Baudelaire used to be ingenuous, virtuous, and possessed of every quality an innocent friendship might delight in; then this sister of Judith the slayer of Holophernes and of Jael who murdered Sisera initiated him into 'the monstrous secrets of vice and love' and inspired the 'funereal maxims' that had flowed from his lips ever since. But Baudelaire may have seen things differently. Corrupt she may have been but, as he expressed it in one of his bitter love–hate poems, Nature herself was perhaps using Sara as a 'salutary instrument' to 'mould a genius'.[11]

Ernest Prarond was one of a group of clean-living, idealistic young men with whom Baudelaire struck up an acquaintance in the winter of 1840. It was less for their pretentions to constitute a nursery of budding poets (the so-called 'Norman school') that he appreciated them than for their simplicity and sunny natures which offered some relief from the complications of his own dark and tortured inner life. Their leader was Gustave Le Vavasseur, perhaps the only true poet among them, certainly the only one to whom Baudelaire ever paid tribute in print.[12] As a young man, he was for ever cracking jokes and perpetrating bad puns; his friends never knew what he would get up to next and Baudelaire tells how astonished he was when he entered Le Vavasseur's room one morning to find him stripped to his underpants and struggling to keep his balance on a shaky edifice of tables and chairs. He had been impressed by a team of acrobats seen in a circus and had wanted to prove to himself that he could do as well as they could. He and Prarond were inseparable, and were first introduced to Baudelaire by a mutual friend, Louis de la Genevray, a former class-mate of his at the Lycée Louis-le-Grand. Le Vavasseur shared an apartment with another member of the group, the engraver Jules Buisson, at 31, rue de Beaune, and these rooms served as the headquarters of the 'Norman school' where informal meetings took place most days. No one was too sure why they had chosen this name. Prarond was a native of Abbeville in the province of Picardy; Auguste Dozon came from Lorraine; Buisson from Provence; only Le Vavasseur was a Norman by birth.

According to Le Vavasseur's own statement, it was the 'attraction of opposites' that cemented his friendship with Baudelaire. 'He was dark, I was fair; he of middle height, while I was short of stature; he, thin as a rake, and I, fat as a pig; he kept himself as clean as a cat, while I was as dirty as a stray dog; he dressed as neatly as a secretary at the British embassy, while I looked like a scarecrow. The one reserved, the other noisy; the one driven by curiosity to visit low dives, the other staying chastely at home through indolence; he a pagan out of rebelliousness, myself a Christian by conformity. His caustic sallies contrasted with my indulgent smile; he was for ever tormenting his intelligence to make mock of his affections, while I let my heart and mind trot along together as though harnessed to the same carriage . . .'[3] Le Vavasseur, needless to say, was destined with this happy disposition to a long, contented, and productive life, whereas Baudelaire's fate, once again, was the exact opposite.

Le Vavasseur's reference to his friend dressing 'as neatly as a secretary at the British embassy' serves as a reminder that Baudelaire's famous dandyism dates right back to these early years. Almost as soon as he was able to dispense with the ugly uniform of the Lycée Louis-le-Grand, the blue coat, the chiné stockings and the thick-soled shoes that the boys all had to wear, he emerged like a sable butterfly from the chrysalis. Charles Cousin, another old school-fellow, remembered how struck he was on coming across Baudelaire again in Louis Ménard's rooms on the top floor of a house on the Place Sorbonne. 'Baudelaire at twenty, hesitating between Villon and Ronsard, crazy about old sonnets and the newest painting, with his polished manners and conversation full of paradoxes, leading a bohemian life and a dandy to boot, a dandy above all, with the whole theory of elegance at his finger-tips. Every fold in his jacket was the subject of earnest study. What a miracle that black suit was, always the same, no matter what the season or the time of day! The dress coat, so gracefully and generously cut, its lapels constantly fingered by a carefully manicured hand; the beautifully knotted cravat; the long waistcoat, fastened very high by the top button of the twelve and negligently gaping lower down to reveal a fine white shirt with pleated cuffs, and the corkscrew trousers fitting into a pair of immaculately polished shoes. I shall never forget how many cab fares their varnish cost me!'[4] Prarond's memories corroborate this description. 'I can still see him,' he wrote, 'descending the steps of the Maison Bailly, a slender figure, with a loose fitting collar, a very long waistcoat, spotless shirt cuffs, holding a thin cane with a little gold top and walking with a slow, springy, almost rhythmical movement.'[5] The 'Maison Bailly' that Prarond refers to here was a private hostel for students, situated in the Place du Panthéon and run by a certain Fr. Emmanuel Bailly. Good Catholic families in the provinces boarded their sons here, and Baudelaire used to visit it from time to time to see those of his friends who were in residence, and possibly to sit in at the lectures and seminars that Bailly laid on for his charges.

Since the time he left home under a cloud in the autumn of 1839, he had been seeing very little of his family, though at the end of 1840 he accepted an invitation from his half-brother to stay with him for a few weeks. Alphonse Baudelaire was now a married man, the father of a child, a boy called Edmond, who was to die tragically at the age of twenty-one. He was steadily making his way in his chosen career, the magistracy; eventually, in 1846, he was promoted *juge d'instruction* at Fontainebleau, only to be demoted five years later for having smuggled a few carpenter's tools into prison to oblige a political detainee whose case he was investigating. He was not seriously suspected of favouring anarchists; the general view among his colleagues was that he was a decent, conscientious man, but unmethodical and not always very sensible. Aupick, however, held him in high esteem and consulted him regularly about the best way of handling his scapegrace brother.

We have already seen how Charles had approached Alphonse for advice on the treatment of gonorrhea, advice which the older man gave him without, apparently, seizing the opportunity to read him a lesson on the dangers of consorting with prostitutes. Charles may have concluded that his brother was less stuffy than he had thought, which would explain why he enclosed, in his New Year's letter for 1841, a sonnet of which the best that could be said is that it was a little too frivolous for the eyes of an austere magistrate, let alone for those of his wife to whom Baudelaire suggested he might show it. But if he imagined he had found in Alphonse an indulgent confidant, prepared to concede that every young man should be allowed to sow his wild oats, he was rudely disillusioned a few weeks later when he turned to him for help in dealing with the creditors – his tailor, his bootmaker, his hatter – who were starting to dun him for payment of overdue bills. To go with street-girls was imprudent, perhaps, but to run into debt was quite another matter. Alphonse flatly refused to come to his assistance. He pointed out, in a letter that Charles described as harsh and humiliating, that he, Alphonse Baudelaire, had always taken care not to make inroads on the capital he had inherited from their father. 'You must understand', he went on, 'that when all I earn by dint of eight hours solid work a day, after fifteen years of study and effort, is 1500 francs, I am in no position to hand over to my brother 2370 francs to pay for his extravagances, his mistresses, his follies in a word.'[16] He concluded by suggesting there were only two possible courses of action: either Charles should make a clean breast to his stepfather; or he could leave it to Alphonse to break the news to

Aupick so that between them they could summon the creditors and arrange to pay them by dipping into the trust money.

It is easy to imagine Baudelaire's fury at receiving this ultimatum. If Alphonse considered himself too poor to advance his brother the odd sums needed to pacify the tradesmen, well and good; but he had expressly asked him, in his original letter, not to breathe a word to his parents about the situation, 'as much in order to avoid worrying mama as in my own interests'.[17] And now the fool was insisting it should all come into the open! If only he would keep his mouth shut, Baudelaire could probably pacify his tailor and the rest of them. After all, he was not without 'expectations'; within little more than a year, he was due to come into a property valued at roughly 100,000 francs, so why all this fuss over 2370 francs? He wrote back to Alphonse telling him to forget the whole thing – he would pay his own debts, somehow, only it would take a little time.

Unfortunately Alphonse did not feel he had the right to keep silent. The Aupicks were alerted and, as Baudelaire had foreseen, the General took it badly. What had happened was just what he had feared: left to his own devices, with no aim in view except the vague and chimerical one of becoming a poet, of course Charles was bound to succumb to the temptations of the big city and be led astray by undesirable companions. Alphonse relayed these conclusions to his young brother. 'As a child, you were delightful to deal with, but as soon as you grew up you became difficult, suspicious, always rebellious when your elders tried to check you in your own best interests. The friends you made introduced you to certain women, and you imagined that these women, because they had fallen into the error of yielding to poverty and hankering after the rewards of immorality, were to be regarded as models for the free life. You have fallen into debt in order to maintain, feed and clothe a strumpet, if I may use the term you used yourself and which seems to me exactly right. From the hopeful boy you were, you have changed into a heedless youth.'[18] Outraged middle-class morality was by now gobbling like a turkey-cock.

The letter from Alphonse to Charles is dated April 30th, 1841, by which time certain drastic measures had already been agreed on in order to 'change his way of thinking and above all to put an end to certain evil acquaintances', if we may borrow the words used by Mme Aupick in the account of this crisis that she gave to Asselineau after her son's death.[19] These 'evil acquaintances' did not, of course, include the worthy representatives of the 'Norman school', Prarond, Le Vavasseur and the others, whom Mme Aupick was always glad to see when they called on her and who had apparently taken it on themselves to warn her that 'quite apart from the women he was consorting with, Charles had attached himself to bohemians of the worst sort, to whom he was drawn by a desire to satisfy his curiosity concerning the mysterious haunts of vice in Paris'.[20] The measure eventually decided on to rescue Baudelaire from the life of extravagance and dissipation into which he had plunged was to ship him abroad, for as long a period of time as was thought necessary to 'change his way of thinking'.

The idea of sending him out of France for at least a year may have originated with Aupick, though in broaching the question with Alphonse Baudelaire he said he had consulted with two close friends, Paul Pérignon and Jean Labie,[21] about the desirability of removing Charles from the evil influences of the streets, and that it was they who 'spoke to me about sending him on a long sea-voyage, to India and the East Indies, in the hope that thanks to a change of scene, and having been forcibly separated from the detestable company he has been keeping and confronted with new subjects for reflection, he might return to the true path and come back to us a poet maybe, but a poet who can draw inspiration from purer springs than the sewers of Paris'.[22] The remark would seem to indicate that the General had by now resigned himself to seeing his stepson follow a literary career; all he hoped for, probably, was that the young man should choose 'sound' writers to model himself on; men like Chateaubriand, Lamartine, and Hugo, who hobnobbed with royalty and were to be seen in all the most elegant *salons*. Only so long as he didn't decline into a Grub Street bum, one of those raucous *bousingots* for ever creating disturbances and getting into trouble with the police . . .

The decision to book Baudelaire on a passage to India, instead of letting him tour the Rhineland, Italy, or Switzerland, was explained later by Mme Aupick in terms of her husband's own passionate love of the sea due, she thought, to the circumstances of his birth in a seaport. The considerations that led to this choice originated more probably in a calculation of relative costs; it was also to be feared that he might just as easily succumb to temptation in other European cities as he had in his native country; what was there to choose between the bordellos of Naples and the brothels of Paris? Had the decision been different, we may be sure that his later writings, the poetry and in particular the art criticism, would have been very different too. As matters turned out, among all the major French poets of the nineteenth century, Baudelaire alone knew scarcely anything at first hand of the culture and civilization of Europe outside the frontiers of France.

He himself was purposely debarred from the discussions held at a family council which met at Neuilly in the office of the notary Labie.

It was necessary to hold such a meeting because the expenses of the journey to and from Calcutta were considerable (about 4000 francs) and would need to be raised by a loan on the security of the property that was being held in trust for Charles during his minority. This high-handed decision to use up part of his patrimony, without even consulting him, was possibly the aspect of the whole business that chiefly exasperated Baudelaire. There was certainly a scene between him and his stepfather of a fairly serious nature, though whether one should attach much belief to Du Camp's story that Baudelaire flung himself on Aupick and tried to strangle him at his dinner-table[23] is another question. Whatever it was that occurred (Baudelaire himself referred to it simply as a *vacarme*, a row[24]), his continued presence in his parents' house was judged impossible, and he was sent to stay with the same Mme Hainfray at Creil who had befriended his mother at the time of her confinement in 1828.

What Baudelaire objected to with particular bitterness was no doubt the way he was being treated, at the age of twenty, as a mere child whom grown-ups do not consult over important matters directly affecting him. He was not even to be trusted with his passage-money; that was to be placed in the hands of the shipmaster, a veteran naval officer called Saliz who had impressed Aupick as being a man of integrity. But the chance of visiting the mysterious east must all the same have made a powerful appeal. We have already seen with what excitement, as a boy, he reacted to the prospect of setting out on a long journey; anticipation of all the new sights that would meet his eye had sent him on that occasion into a kind of ecstasy. He had not, in the interval, developed into an incurable stay-at-home, nor was he ever to do so. Some seven years later he wrote to his mother, then in Constantinople, that as soon as he had the necessary cash he would join her there, 'for my passion for travel is as strong as ever',[25] while later still the sight of the 'beautiful tall ships, swaying imperceptibly on the tranquil waters' of the docks at Le Havre seemed to him to be asking 'in a silent language: When shall we be setting forth on our quest for happiness?'[26]

But if his mood, in spite of the earlier unpleasantness, was one of mild elation when on June 9th, 1841, he boarded his vessel, the *Paquebot-des-Mers-du-Sud*, and sailed out of Bordeaux and down the estuary of the Gironde, his spirits rapidly sank again when he realized he was doomed for the next three months to enjoy no society more lively than that of a small group of businessmen and army officers who shared none of his interests and whose observations and comments were of a banality that inevitably invited retorts, coolly and disdainfully delivered as was his wont, of the most outrageous impertinence. The rest of the passengers soon learnt to leave him strictly alone. The captain, who had undertaken to keep an eye on the young man and do what he could to wean him from his exclusive preoccupation with literature, had to confess himself in the end unable to interest Baudelaire in any other subject. With the sailors he had no truck (though he used to pretend, subsequently, to friends he liked to entertain with travellers' yarns, that he was hard put to it to repel their lustful advances). On one occasion, after they had crossed the Equator, he was horrified to see them capture an albatross that had been following the ship, set it on deck and laugh themselves silly at the sight of its unavailing efforts to escape; for the albatross can take flight only from the open sea. Baudelaire saw in this incident an apt symbol of the poet's destiny and there and then composed a short poem on the subject, of which the first three verses present the image while the last states the pathetic correlative:

> The Poet too, lord of the thundercloud,
> Riding the tempest mocks the bowman's aim;
> Earth-bound, in exile, scoffed at by the crowd,
> His giant pinions drag and make him lame.

In the days before the Suez Canal was cut, the only sea-route to India was via the Cape of Good Hope. Even in fair weather, life on board a small sailing ship (the *Mers-du-Sud* displaced only 296 tons) was not only monotonous but attended by discomforts of a kind Baudelaire had never had to endure previously. The cabins for the passengers were tiny and ill-ventilated; especially in the tropics, before they picked up a trade wind, conditions were stifling on deck and intolerable below. The fare consisted of little but salt meat and beans; the very drinking-water was lukewarm and tasted of the barrel it had been stored in; wine was available but it had to be sweet – a dry wine would have deteriorated rapidly in this climate. Baudelaire was afflicted, not surprisingly, with an intestinal disorder for part of the voyage which he tried to cure, in a characteristically eccentric way, by lying on his stomach with his buttocks exposed to the equatorial sun, with the inevitable result that for some time afterwards he found it impossible to sit down.

Some diversion was afforded him by the attentions of an ayah (a coloured nursemaid) who, having accompanied a European family to France, was returning to her native land. She conceived a violent passion for Baudelaire which she did so little to conceal that eventually the captain, on the representations of the other passengers, had her confined to her cabin for the rest of the voyage. Otherwise, the only break in the monotony was a violent storm off the Cape which very nearly caused the vessel to founder. Baudelaire displayed remarkable courage and coolness on this occasion, and it was even in part due to his exertions that complete catastrophe was averted. At the height of the typhoon, when the masts had snapped and the ship was listing dangerously with heavy seas breaking over the deck, he helped the mate execute a tricky manoeuvre which saved them all; together they managed to stretch a tarpaulin against what remained of the guy-ropes, and this was sufficient to catch the fierce wind and so right the ship again. The story, incidentally, was not among those (mostly apocryphal) that Baudelaire related on his return; we know of it through a brief reference in the captain's log, supplemented by a fuller account given by one of the passengers.[27]

The damage sustained by the ship made it necessary to break the journey for a fortnight or so at Mauritius. Captain Saliz was too busy supervising the repair work to pay much attention to his young passenger, once he had made sure he had a room in a hotel in Port-Louis. For the numerous French settlers in this British colony, the arrival of travellers from their home country was always something of an event, and offers of entertainment were readily made and willingly accepted. In this way Baudelaire got to know a local solicitor, a certain Autard de Bragard who, favourably impressed by the young man's charming manners and easy conversation (no one displayed the social graces to better effect than Baudelaire, when he chose), introduced him to his wife, a strikingly handsome woman with a young daughter who, a few years later, was to marry Ferdinand de Lesseps, the creator of the Suez Canal. Thus Baudelaire did not lack for company, and he repaid the hospitality extended him in the way most proper to a poet, by mailing to M. Autard de Bragard from his next port of call a delicate sonnet in praise of his wife's beauty. This poem, under the title *A une Dame créole*, was to figure in the first edition of *Les Fleurs du Mal*, where unfortunately the lady was never able to read it; in the very week the book appeared, she died on board ship on her way back from France to Mauritius.

But in spite of the well-intentioned efforts of the Autard de Bragard family to distract the young traveller, he failed completely to respond at the time to the exotic splendour of this tropical island, so exuberantly celebrated by Bernardin de Saint-Pierre in his popular pre-romantic novel *Paul et Virginie*. It was too remote from civilization and what cultural life it boasted was only a pale reflection of that of Paris; it was no doubt of Mauritius chiefly that Baudelaire was thinking when, in a letter to his mother written six years later, he referred to 'the boredom, the horrible boredom and the intellectual atrophy of hot lands under blue skies.'[28] The one vivid memory he retained of the colony, to judge by what he told his friends on his return, was of seeing a negress publicly flogged in the market-place there.

When the *Paquebot-des-Mers-du-Sud*, refitted and revictualled, was ready to put to sea again, Baudelaire sought out the captain and told him firmly he would go no farther; he had no desire to see Calcutta, so would Saliz kindly let him have the money for his return passage which Aupick had paid him. When Saliz objected that he had no authority to do this, Baudelaire retorted that in that case, he would remain in Mauritius until he had earned the necessary sum himself. The captain pleaded with him to come at least as far as Réunion Island, which was their next port of call, where he promised he would find him a ship bound for France if he was still of a mind to curtail the voyage. Reunion was only a day's sail from Mauritius, so, reluctantly, Baudelaire agreed.

Here Saliz made arrangements with the captain of the *Alcide*, an even smaller vessel than his own, to take his homesick passenger aboard. The *Alcide*, sailing from Sydney with a cargo of horses, had docked at Saint-Denis-de-la-Réunion on August 21st. Baudelaire arrived there aboard the *Mers-du-Sud* on September 9th, but had to wait until November 4th before the *Alcide* was ready for the return voyage. We have no way of telling how he occupied his time on Réunion during these two months, though Théodore de Banville, who met him for the first time shortly after he got back to France, relates how Baudelaire told him over supper that he had lodged 'with a family for whom his parents had given him a letter of introduction'. This is less likely to have happened at Mauritius, an unscheduled stop, than at Réunion or, as it was then called, the Ile Bourbon. The story that Baudelaire went on to tell Banville and Privat d'Anglemont, who was also at the supper party, may however have been pure invention. According to this account, bored with his hosts' insipid conversation, he went off to live in the uplands 'with a tall coloured girl, quite young and knowing no French, who cooked him strangely spiced stews in a great cauldron of polished copper, round which a troop of little blackamoors danced and shrieked'.[29]

The outward journey as far as Mauritius had been accomplished with no stops on the way. The reason was that at that date, barring a few isolated trading posts, the east and west coasts of Africa had not as yet been opened up. Only on the southern tip was there a sizeable white colony, originally Dutch but ceded to the British at the beginning of the century. The *Alcide* put in at Cape Town for provisions on December 4th, 1841, and remained in harbour for four days, during which Baudelaire was free to saunter round this pioneer township perched at the base of a largely unexplored continent. Two features of Cape Town remained in his memory: the style of the domestic architecture, which he characterized as a 'blend of renaissance and moderate rococo', and the pervading smell of sheep, due to the fact that wool and sheepskins were at that time the principal export of the colony.[30]

The last stage of the voyage, up the west coast of southern Africa, across the gulf of Guinea, skirting the reef-strewn littoral of Mauretania (the scene of the shipwreck of the *Medusa* commemorated by Géricault in a celebrated canvas), and so finally into the North Atlantic waters, took two and a half months. Baudelaire saw it later as a great adventure, and he experienced it probably as less vexatious than the journey over; there was only one other passenger, he was not exposed to the homilies of honest Captain Saliz, and above all he was returning home to resume his old life. On February 15th, 1842, he walked across the gangplank at Bordeaux. The following day he wrote two chirpy letters, one to his stepfather and one to his mother, to announce his arrival. 'If I were to write down all I have been thinking and imagining while away from you both, there would not be room enough in an exercise-book; so I will give it you by word of mouth. I think I have come back a wiser man.'[31]

But in fact, when he was reunited with his parents they found he was rather reluctant to talk about his experiences. Possibly the cool reception Aupick gave him, when he learned the young man had cut short the journey he had planned for him, caused Baudelaire to withdraw into himself once more. Or again, it may be that during the few days it took him to make the coach journey up to Paris, ruminating on all that had happened over the past eight months, he reached the conclusion that he was later to enshrine in his long poem *Le Voyage*: the world, so vast and full of promise to those who have never travelled, offers finally no revelation of an objective reality more significant than the subjective truths that only introspection can bring to light. One can see new constellations, strange cities, the gaudily costumed natives of far-away heathen lands, but as the Preacher said of old, there is no new thing under the sun; nor is there anything to be found in a voyage of discovery that cannot be discovered as well or better from the painful scrutiny of one's own soul:

> A bitter truth is all the traveller learns:
> The world's grown small; there is no wild surmise.
> Today as yesterday, where'er he turns,
> A poisoned pool mirrors his own sad eyes.

Henceforth, the fantastic topography of his inner life was to provide Baudelaire with all he needed for study and exploration. He never went to sea again, however he might dream of escape, and came

41

finally to recognize that the only vessel which might bear him across new waters to a new land was Charon's bark, the ship of Death:

> Come, Captain Death, weigh anchor and set sail!
> 'Tis time to quit this shore so drear and grey.
> Though dark both sky and sea with ink-black veil,
> You know our hearts, lit by a brilliant ray.

> Pour out the draught that kills, yet soothes as well!
> This fire so burns our brains, we'll cry adieu,
> Leap o'er the brink – what matter, Heaven or Hell? –
> Brave the Unknown in search of *something new*.

IV

ON THE ILE SAINT-LOUIS

The experiment had failed. For the first time in his life, General Aupick had to admit defeat, and he took it hardly. His stepson had returned home as determined as ever to remain his own master and follow his own star, which necessarily meant that he still refused to be integrated into the ranks of respectable middle-class society, to which he belonged by birth and education, or to enter one branch or another of the civil administration where it would have been so easy for Aupick to establish him. Moreover, within a few brief weeks the general lost even the small measure of authority which control of the purse-strings had given him till then. On April 9th, 1842, Baudelaire came of age and Aupick, who together with the two other guardians appointed by the court (his wife and Paul Pérignon) had been administering his estate during his minority, was obliged to wind up the account. In view of the way Caroline had constantly prodded Charles when he was at school, reminding him tartly of all he 'owed' his parents, it is interesting to note that in the final balance provision was made for expenditure incurred on 'board, clothing, education' to the tune of 1200 francs annually for the period 1828–32, 1500 francs for 1833–5, and 2000 francs for each year thereafter. These expenses almost completely swallowed up the accrued interest on the capital left by François Baudelaire.

The legal documents enabling the young man to enter into possession of his patrimony were signed before the notary at Neuilly on April 30th, 1842, in the presence of the Aupicks and of Alphonse Baudelaire. No doubt all parties behaved with dignity on that occasion, but the general gave his wife plainly to understand afterwards that he would prefer not to have any further contact with her son. She fully sympathized with his attitude and did not attempt, then or later, to make him change his mind, even though it meant that her own meetings with Charles had to be spaced out, since he could visit her only when her husband was not at home. After a while he began to feel these furtive visits to 'that great, gaunt, empty house where the only person I know is my mother'[1] were depressing as well as undignified; he preferred it greatly when she came and called on him – always by prior arrangement – in his bachelor lodgings, where from time to time he would set aside an afternoon for her.

The situation can have given her little satisfaction. She felt it wrong to conceal from her husband that she was continuing to see her son; on the other hand she disliked having to mention it, knowing how deep his disappointment ran. He pretended he had washed his hands of Charles, and she could not blame him for this; but neither could she imitate him and cut herself off from her child completely. So it was tacitly understood between the couple that she remained in touch with Charles but would refrain from mentioning her visits when they took place.

These visits, in any case, posed practical problems. Charles had chosen to go and live in what was then an unfashionable part of Paris, disreputable and difficult of access: the Ile Saint-Louis, the smaller of the two islands in the Seine in the centre of the city. Even in our days it still keeps something of its air of being a world on its own. Anthea Hayter, who tells us she lived there for six years, describes how she experienced 'that feeling of being inside a safe secret privileged retreat which is the magic of the Ile Saint-Louis, whose inhabitants proudly call themselves "les insulaires" and who talk of "visiting Paris" as though the thirty steps across a bridge were a journey to another world'.[2]

Baudelaire started by renting a single ground-floor room in a house on the Quai de Béthune. The furnishing was summary. The chief feature was a large travelling chest with a rounded lid in which he kept the few books he had acquired (chiefly editions of Ronsard and the other poets of the Pléiade). In addition he had a sofa, an old table and chair, and an oak bedstead, with no legs or posts, a sort of 'sculptured coffin' as Charles Cousin described it, where in the daytime two or three cats were usually to be found curled up. Cats – though not kittens – were the only domestic pets Baudelaire ever tolerated; their independence and cleanliness appealed to him, these being virtues he cultivated himself, and besides that he derived considerable sensual satisfaction from smelling their fur and feeling their lithe little bodies underneath. Their eyes too, remote, mysterious, inhuman, seemed to contemplate him with the same wary disdain as did those of his mistress.

It was not only his mother, but also the friends he had made before his voyage, in particular the members of the 'Norman school', who felt that Baudelaire had gone to live at the ends of the earth. 'The Ile Saint-Louis seemed to us even farther from civilization than Mauritius,' commented Prarond. '"You'll get tired of living so far out," I used to say to him. "No," he replied, "the fox is fond of its hole."'[3] He was not trying to avoid his old friends; but he needed his privacy. His mornings were normally spent reading or polishing his poetry in his one-room flat, while in the afternoon, unless he had some amorous assignation, he would set off on a long walk with Prarond, Le Vavasseur and Buisson, sometimes leaving the built-up area behind and heading south to the open country outside the fortifications. A favourite goal for these excursions was the patch of land later converted into the Parc de Montsouris, which at the time was no more than a grassy knoll with a few trees and a windmill, from which one could on a clear day enjoy a splendid view over the city. In the evening they would dine gaily together, either in a country inn or at a vintner's in the Latin Quarter.

However, the attempt to revive the old easy camaraderie was not entirely successful. Baudelaire had changed; the iron had already entered his soul, while the others remained as full of generous illusions as ever. Some of his bitter sallies offended them; there were momentary quarrels, soon made up. In 1843 they invited him to contribute to a collective volume of verse they were preparing for publication, and he agreed, sending Prarond a few pieces and inviting him to make what corrections he thought necessary. Instead of regarding this simply as a polite formula, they took him at his word and suggested various alterations, whereupon Baudelaire, without arguing, took his manuscripts back; the book appeared without his participation.

He was writing a fair amount at this period; Prarond lists fifteen poems, all eventually included in *Les Fleurs du Mal*, of which he says he is certain they were all composed before the end of 1843, and a further dozen of which he cannot be quite so sure, since Baudelaire revised them heavily before publishing them.[4] He never gave these poems to his friends to read but, as Buisson records, 'recited them to us occasionally in an unfinished state, sometimes in our rooms, late at night, while we listened spellbound by his voice and enunciation, sometimes in the open, as we wandered on foot through the Bois de Boulogne or sat in the grass, for it was a real wilderness in those days'.[5] Philippe de Chennevières, a future Minister of Fine Arts, also remembered how in his youth Baudelaire, 'sitting on the sofa in the apartment shared by Le Vavasseur and Buisson, at 31, rue de Beaune, would frequently recite to us strange and powerful sonnets full of spice and energy, the aristocratic verses of a master of colour and description which, in our little group, we felt were superior to those of the *Cariatides*.'[6] He continued these recitations even after the 'Norman school' had dispersed, sometimes after dinner, though only when asked, sometimes over a bowl of punch in a tavern in the Rue Saint-André-des-Arts or in the Rue Dauphine. It was always the more macabre or scandalous poems that were in demand on these occasions, which explains why, long before *Les Fleurs du Mal* were published, Baudelaire had already acquired a sort of underground notoriety as a writer in the morbid and sadistic vein.

Much of the work of composition was done out of doors, in the course of solitary walks round the streets or along the embankments of the Seine. Hatless, wearing an artist's smock, Baudelaire must have presented a curious spectacle as he strode past, paying no attention to his surroundings and stopping every now and then to gesticulate and mutter to himself. In a poem composed at this period, *Le Soleil*,[7] he describes how

> When the fierce sun pours down its radiant heat
> On town and fields, on roofs and ripening wheat,
> Alone I practise my strange rapier play,
> Sniffing out rhymes on every path and way,
> Tripping on words as one might catch one's toe,
> Stumbling on lines imagined long ago.

There is another relevant passage in an article of 1851 where he pictures the rag-picker who has called in at a wine-shop at the end of his day and is now reeling home slightly the worse for drink. 'Here he comes, in the dim light of the street-lamps flickering in the night wind, climbing one of those long winding roads that lead up the Montagne-Sainte-Geneviève. He is wearing his "wicker shawl" and carrying his "number seven".[8] He approaches nodding his head and stumbling on the paving stones, *like young poets who spend their days wandering around searching for rhymes.*'[9] Baudelaire himself must often have been taken for half-tipsy by the uncomprehending, sardonic passer-by when he was engaged on this esoteric exercise.

When, after a year, the lease on the Quai de Béthune apartment expired, Baudelaire moved briefly to an address in the Rue Vaneau, in the Faubourg Saint-Germain; but before long he was back on his beloved Ile Saint-Louis, where in June 1843 he found an ideal set of rooms vacant at the top of a seventeenth-century mansion at no. 17, Quai d'Anjou. This house had originally belonged to the Duc de Lauzun, and had passed in 1779 into the hands of the Marquis de Pimodan; hence it was known indifferently as the Hôtel Lauzun or the Hôtel Pimodan. The building still stands today; it is now the property of the municipality of Paris, and is in a much better state of preservation than it can have been in 1843, after a half-century of neglect. To visualize what it looked like then, one cannot do better than read the opening pages of Gautier's story *Le Club des Hachichins* which is set in the Hôtel Pimodan. Gautier, who later resided in the house for a short while himself, describes how the visitor, once he had persuaded the ancient hag who performed the office of janitor to pull the cord that unlatched the entrance door, found himself in a large, damp courtyard where grass grew rankly between the paving stones; then, having climbed a stately flight of stone steps, he was able to mount the inner stairway, hung with pictures by Le Brun and Patel, which by a gentle gradient led up to the various floors. The general impression was one of spaciousness and decayed magnificence.

The Hôtel Pimodan had been divided up into apartments of different sizes, rented out chiefly to artists or rich amateurs such as Roger de Beauvoir, a noted wit and dandy with his blue coat ablaze with gold buttons, his yellow goatskin waistcoat, his pearl-grey trousers and his cane with its rhinoceros horn handle, and Fernand Boissard who had a princely suite stuffed with art-treasures, among them a piano decorated – allegedly – by Watteau. Joseph-Ferdinand Boissard de Boisdenier, to give him his full name, was a young gentleman who had come to Paris to study art under Devéria, where he developed a passion for the painters of the Cinquecento and strove to imitate them. But painting was only one of his interests; a passable amateur violinist, he got together a chamber ensemble to play Bach, Beethoven and Mendelssohn; he was a fair linguist, he could turn a sonnet, and occasionally put his name to a piece of literary criticism. Boissard was, in short, a brilliant dilettante, attracted to every novelty, but never giving enough of himself to any one art to become outstandingly proficient in it. Eight years older than Baudelaire, he looked the picture of health, with his fair hair cut short and curling crisply, his fresh complexion, red lips, white teeth and grey eyes sparkling with wit and vivacity. But only a few years later he was dead, after a long illness similar in its symptoms if not in its origins to that which was to carry Baudelaire off.

Situated at the top of the house and overlooking the courtyard, the apartment Baudelaire occupied in the Hôtel Pimodan was of far more modest dimensions than Boissard's, and consisted simply of one commodious reception room, a bedroom, and a kitchen-pantry. The rent (315 francs a year) was not excessive, so the new lodger may have felt himself justified in spending lavishly on the furniture and fittings. He had the walls and ceilings covered uniformly with a paper decorated with black foliage on a red background. The drapes were of heavy damask, and at one point Baudelaire had the windowpanes replaced by frosted glass so that he did not risk being distracted at his reading by the sight of the clouds chasing across a blue sky.

His fellow poet Théodore de Banville later recalled how astonished he was, on the first occasion he was admitted to the sanctuary, to see no book-cases anywhere. It was an aspect of Baudelaire's dandyism not to make it obvious that he was plying the trade of a man of letters.

The books which in the Quai de Béthune had been piled into a trunk were here shut away in a cupboard, along with the flagons of Rhenish and the crystal. They were few in number, and were mostly fine old editions of Silver Latin and Renaissance French poets, sumptuously bound. Banville was also struck by the capacious armchairs and by the one huge oval walnut table with irregular kidney-shaped incurvatures, which served Baudelaire equally well to work at and eat off. He was constantly renewing his furniture, replacing what he had with new pieces whenever he saw something that took his fancy in the shops.

He was aiming at a combination of comfort and elegance, to achieve which he had to dig deeply into his capital. One of the luxuries he permitted himself was to have the parquet flooring entirely covered by a carpet which he used to sprinkle with musk, bought in one-franc bottles. But his principal extravagance was buying pictures. A copy of Delacroix's *Women of Algiers* occupied a place of honour, and when in 1843 the thirteen lithographs of scenes from *Hamlet* which his favourite artist had executed nine years earlier were put on the market, Baudelaire acquired the entire set, framed them and hung them along one wall. Shakespeare's master-piece held a special significance for him, for he found it easy to make a flattering self-identification with the Prince of Denmark who like him had a stepfather he hated and a mother he felt had betrayed him. Certain scenes from the third act that Delacroix had illustrated, as when Hamlet chances on Claudius at his prayers and thinks to despatch him there and then ('Now might I do it, pat . . .'), or when, shortly after, he upbraids Gertrude for her second marriage with an almost insane vehemence ('Nay, but to live In the rank sweat of an enseamed bed, Stewed in corruption . . .') – these images particularly exerted a kind of horrid fascination over Baudelaire at certain black moments when he sat in his room alone brooding over his wrongs, real or fancied.

Next to the chimneypiece hung his own portrait done in oils by his friend Emile Deroy. This had been painted in four sittings, in the reception room of his apartment, at night and by lamplight, with Nadar and three other artist friends looking on and making suggestions. The pose, possibly chosen by Baudelaire himself, is very studied, 'to produce a surprise effect, an impression of strangeness and even of satanism',[10] with the lamp casting deep shadows to one side of the head, which is supported on the other by the model's left hand, forefinger pressed against the temple. This is Baudelaire posing as Mephistopheles, with his carefully trimmed beard and moustache and the thick black eyebrows of which one is slightly raised to give a quizzical, sardonic look as he gazes straight at the spectator. Deroy submitted the picture for exhibition at the 1846 *salon*, but it was rejected, and the artist died shortly after, a disappointed and embittered man. Baudelaire himself kept the portrait, taking it with him from one lodging to another after he left the Hôtel Pimodan; but he eventually grew tired of it and gave it to Asselineau, by whom it was bequeathed in due course to the Musée de Versailles.

It was in fact Deroy who introduced Baudelaire to Charles Asselineau, the bibliophile who was to become his first biographer. Asselineau described Deroy as 'remarkably gifted as a painter, a marvellous colourist, withal a man of intelligence and a lucid judge but, like all men of merit struggling against obscurity, somewhat sparing in speech. Poverty and isolation had made him mistrustful and caustic. . . . Baudelaire liked him as much for his qualities as an artist as for his conversation, and the two shared many a meal together.'[11] They were also occasionally to be seen in Banville's chambers in the Rue Monsieur-le-Prince, where one chronicler gives us a glimpse of Deroy sitting in a corner smoking his pipe quietly as if dissociating himself from the discussion and Baudelaire, equally abstracted, 'elbows on knees and head between his hands, adjusting the rhymes of a sonnet'.[12]

Thanks to Deroy, Baudelaire was able to visit the studios of painters and sculptors in the neighbourhood and engage them in talk, imbibing in this way much of the technical information put to good use in his later writings on art; Deroy, it can be said, played the same part in Baudelaire's artistic education between 1843 and 1846 as Cézanne in respect of Zola's between 1863 and 1866. Just as Cézanne took Zola to the Café Guerbois, so Deroy took Baudelaire to the Café Tabourey where he was able to meet and listen to some of the leading art critics of the day. Ever since his childhood Baudelaire had taken a special interest in the fine arts, kindled originally no doubt by his father; he himself later referred to 'the cult of images' as 'my great, unique, and *earliest* passion'.[13] Deroy, however, must be credited with having helped form his taste and open his eyes to certain aspects of pictorial art of which only a practitioner could be aware. At this period of his life, as Prarond testified, Baudelaire 'was as much preoccupied with painting as with poetry. I used to accompany him occasionally to the Louvre which he would seldom pass without paying it a visit.'[14] He already had his likes and dislikes, being a fanatic for Delacroix, for the painters of the Spanish school, and among draughtsmen admiring particularly Daumier but detesting the fashionable Gavarni.

Were it not for his strained relations with his mother, the two years that followed Baudelaire's return from the east might well have counted as supremely happy; certainly he was to experience nothing in the future to compare with it. His health was good, the syphilis being in a dormant stage, he was in a productive vein, experiencing the ever-renewed excitement of creative work which is perhaps the purest joy permitted to man, he had plenty of friends and was constantly making more, he was living in roomy and well-appointed lodgings where he could entertain them, and finally, he had acquired a mistress whom several of these friends might envy him.

If one considers simply her origins, however, she must have seemed an unpromising choice. Jeanne Duval, otherwise known as Jeanne Lemer or Lemaire, sprang from the very lowest stratum of the social underworld, where misery and degradation were in the very air the wretches breathed. Jeanne's ancestry on her mother's side has been traced back to a grandmother who was almost certainly born on the Guinea coast, where she had the misfortune to be taken captive and sold into slavery. In the eighteenth century French traders who for one reason or another found they could not sell a female slave for a satisfactory price in the auctions held in the West Indies, sometimes shipped them to Nantes where they disposed of them to brothel-keepers. Apparently this was the fate of the miserable black girl, Jeanne's grandmother, whose owners had chosen to name her Marie Duval.

On July 25th, 1789, she gave birth to a girl-child, a fact known only because of an entry in the baptismal registry where the baby is described as 'the illegitimate daughter of Marie Duval, prostitute'.[15] This child, named Jeanne-Marie-Marthe, was probably a mulatto, the unwanted offspring of a chance coupling with some white sailor visiting the Nantes brothel. One may surmise that as soon as she was old enough she too was sold into prostitution, and that her daughter Jeanne, about whose father nothing is known, was born as the result of another brief liaison. This would imply that Baudelaire's mistress was a quadroon. Her diluted African ancestry showed chiefly in her rippling black hair and in the dark pigmentation of her skin, though we should not suppose this to have been more than brown. In the nineteenth century, when European women never exposed any part of their bodies to the sun, even protecting their faces with parasols, their skin was paler than we are accustomed to now, and Jeanne's would have appeared quite dark in comparison. When Nadar first saw her, which was before Baudelaire had met her, she struck him as 'a negress, a real negress, or at least a mulatto, incontestably; the packets of powdered chalk she had crushed over her face, neck and hands could not whiten their coppery hue'.[16]

Nadar (or Félix Tournachon as he was then – for it was only later that he adopted the pseudonym used to sign his caricatures and his photographic studies) – saw Jeanne first on the public stage, in December 1838, when she was acting the maid in a farce called *Le Système de mon Oncle*. She was perhaps, Nadar admits, rather tall for the part, and her voice a little too deep, though it carried well and was pleasant to listen to; but it was no doubt her exotic beauty that had persuaded the manager of the Théâtre de la Porte-Saint-Antoine to offer her employment. 'Beneath the wild luxuriance of her ink-black wavy mane her eyes as big as saucers seemed blacker still; she had a small, delicate nose with exquisitely chiselled nostrils, and a mouth that appeared Egyptian, for all that she came from the Caribbean, the mouth of the Isis of Pompeii, with an admirable set of teeth between strong, beautifully sculptured lips. Her whole air was grave, proud, even a little disdainful. From the narrow waist up, her body was long, sinuous like an adder, and particularly remarkable for the exuberant, unbelievable development of her bust, which gave her the appearance of a branch bowed under the burden of its fruit, the total effect being not without grace.'[17]

Other descriptions that have come down to us accord more or less with Nadar's, though Prarond, curiously, remembered Jeanne as flat-chested. She was already visiting Baudelaire when he was living on the Quai de Béthune where his friends noticed her ensconced in a low armchair next to the fireplace, saying very little. Banville, who must have met her for the first time in the Hôtel Pimodan, was particularly impressed by her 'queenly gait, full of a wild grace', which had about it 'something at one and the same time divine and bestial'.[18] This last observation is interesting, confirming as it does what Baudelaire himself wrote about her in more than one of his poems; but it is possible, of course, that Banville had so absorbed his friend and fellow poet's outlook that he saw Jeanne a little through Baudelaire's eyes.

There was only one plane on which the two could meet, since Jeanne, sketchily educated, totally lacking in aesthetic sense,[19] could not possibly have followed the workings of her lover's mind. But being, as Prarond had discerned, an essentially passive creature, she would sit quietly in her usual chair while he recited to her Latin poetry; either the well-known erotic hymns addressed by Catullus to Lesbia or by Propertius to Cynthia, or else odes of his own composition, for Baudelaire, as we have seen, could write verse almost as easily in Latin as in French. The liquid syllables of the antique tongue meant nothing to her, of course, but she was content to be lulled by her lover's ardent accents and to allow her thoughts to wander meanwhile where they would. She must have found it more tiresome when he insisted she should take down at his dictation the poems he had written for her, particularly those in which he sadistically reminded her of the eventual fading of her beauty and its ultimate dissolution. Prarond, to whom he confided all this, mentions that he added caustically: 'Her spelling is elementary, but it does improve the look of my rhymes.'[20] It must be said, however, that a more cultivated woman might not have suited Baudelaire so well. In an early text, a kind of parody of Stendhal's *De l'Amour*,[21] he made a point of denying that a defective education or even defective intelligence in one's mistress constituted a bar to love. 'As for spelling mistakes which are accounted a sign of spiritual deformity in the eyes of certain simpletons, is it necessary to explain how these can constitute a whole artless poem of enjoyment and memory?' – meaning that, when he came across these misspelt transcripts of his own poems, each one recalled to mind some happy hour spent in Jeanne's company.

A little further in the same essay he writes contemptuously of 'people who blush they ever loved a woman as soon as they realize she is stupid. Such men are conceited asses, intended by nature to browse on the thorniest thistles of creation or to enjoy the favours of a bluestocking. Stupidity is often an ornament to beauty; it is that which gives the beloved's eyes the melancholy limpidity of dark woodland pools or the oily calm of tropical seas.'[22] The last phrase in particular is an unmistakable reference to Jeanne. The vaguely African aroma that clung to her was highly evocative of his recent voyage round the Dark Continent and into the Indian Ocean. One does not need to postulate that his reported flirtation with a hot-blooded ayah on board ship or his even more doubtfully attested amours with a native girl up in the hills of Réunion Island had given him a special taste for coloured women. But as many a returned traveller has found, faraway scenes formerly experienced in a mood of depression and mild homesickness will return to the memory later, purged of their distasteful associations and transfigured by the magic of the imagination, so that one can even find oneself yearning for what, at the time, was felt as something merely to be lived through and then forgotten about. So too with Baudelaire. The ocean he traversed and the oceanic islands he visited had bored him; discontented, impatient, he had been consciously aware only of pining for the wet asphalt of Paris. But the sights, the sounds, and above all the smells of the tropics were all the while sinking deep into the lower reaches of his subconscious, where the waters of memory encrusted them with fantastic crystalline ornamentation. And it was this that Jeanne, with the smell of her rippling black hair and coppery skin, had the power to evoke for him.

My head upon your breast, eyes closed, I lie
Breathing the odour of your skin; the while
The dazzling beaches of some indolent isle
Stretch out beneath an equatorial sky.

There in imagination I descry
Strange trees whose fruits the noonday hour beguile,
Lean muscled men, and women whose slow smile
And fearless gaze astound the poet's eye.

Your fragrance guides me back into the past,
Where in a harbour many a sail and mast
All fretted with salt water, sways and dips;

From forest green where blooms the tamarind
Sweet perfume fills my nostrils; while the ships
Scatter the sailors' song upon the wind.[23]

To judge by the poems he wrote for her, and by the occasional hints given by those of his friends who were closest to him at this time, the demands he made on Jeanne were not often sexual in the narrowest connotation of the term. She made a powerful appeal to his senses: to his sense of smell, as in the sonnet just quoted, and to his watching eye, as in the long, lovingly detailed inventory he gives of her physical perfections in another poem, *Les Bijoux*. Naked apart from the barbaric bangles she wore on her wrists and round her neck (the 'Jewels' of the title), she is described in these lines posing for him on the sofa, her limbs and glistening skin lit only by the glow of the coals in the hearth. But it is noteworthy that the role he gives himself here is that of the inactive *voyeur*, full of admiration but sexually unaroused, remaining, as he says, 'on a rock of crystal' where he sits in serene and solitary contemplation. Later on in life he rationalized the deep reluctance to unite his body with Jeanne's – or with any other woman's – using deliberately coarse language to claim that 'the more a man cultivates the arts, the less likely is he to have an erection'. Sexual activity amounting, in his view, to a surrender to animality, the more a man of refinement gives himself up to things of the spirit, the less need he will feel to satisfy himself carnally. 'To fuck is to aspire to enter into another, and the artist never wants to leave himself.'[24]

The term *sublimation*, in the special sense psychologists attach to it nowadays, was not in common use at the time Baudelaire was writing, but the idea it translates was clearly the one he was trying to express. However, the distancing that characterized his relations with Jeanne had other sources, among them an awareness of her basic temperamental frigidity. He saw this in her eyes, which he constantly compares to gems, minerals or precious metals – things that shine and glitter but remain cold in themselves; and he saw it too in her muteness, her inertness in the act of love, as she lay there neither encouraging him nor discouraging him, expressing neither willingness beforehand nor gratitude afterwards. He tried to persuade himself that this passivity only increased his transports, although in reality it denied him the different ecstasy of true communion.

> Your beauty doth outshine the vault of night,
> O sad and silent girl, my soul's delight;
> I treasure you the more, sweet, forasmuch
> As you evade and cheat my loving touch,
> And thus – oh irony! – you multiply
> The leagues that part me from the wide blue sky.
>
> As worms attack a corpse, so I too fight
> Your unresponding body; but in spite
> Of all, implacable and heartless beast,
> Even by your coldness is my love increased.[25]

Beauty is by its nature cold, as marble is cold and the virgin snow sparkling on the mountain-tops. So what reason had he to complain of Jeanne's coldness which could only enhance her beauty for him and so cause the fire of his passion to burn more brightly?

There were, none the less, moments when such seemingly irrefutable arguments appeared the merest casuistry; sick of his unresponsive, undemonstrative mistress, Baudelaire on at least one occasion sought out the poor prostitute Sara whom he had known and, after his fashion, cherished before he left on his voyage to the east. The attempt to drive out the thought of the woman who obsessed him by making love to another was an experiment bound to end in failure, of course, but the failure was not totally unredeemed, since the experience was commemorated in another poem, the untitled sonnet which starts: 'Une nuit que j'étais près d'une affreuse Juive'.[26]

> Last night I slept with a foul Jewish whore
> – One naked corpse beside another laid –
> And, near this venal flesh, my sad thoughts strayed
> To her I had renounced, her I adore,
>
> Picturing her queenly walk, the way she bore
> Herself; her glance direct and unafraid;
> Her helm of perfumed hair, locks disarrayed,
> The thought of which renews love as before.

How fervently would I have shown devotion,
And, from your cool feet to your raven tresses
Poured forth the treasure-house of my caresses,
If but one night, cruel wench! of its own motion

A tear had welled unbidden from your eyes,
Veiling the icy splendour of their skies.

Although by interpreting the poetry fairly literally we can gain some insight into Baudelaire's own feelings in this difficult relationship, when it comes to Jeanne's we are necessarily reduced to guesswork. One reason why he could never, apparently, arouse her might be that she had no great liking for men anyway. In the cycle of poems written about Jeanne, there is a slightly ambiguous sonnet to which he gave the Latin title *Sed non satiata*, a tag deriving from Juvenal's comment on Messalina who, after an orgy, emerged from the embraces of a succession of virile lovers 'tired but not sated'. Superficially, the statement he is making in this poem appears to be that he found himself unable to perform sufficiently frequently to appease Jeanne's desires. 'I cannot,' he writes, 'like the Styx, embrace you nine times', the Styx being the mythical river supposed to encircle Hades by nine separate channels. But in the last line he adds that he cannot either 'in your bed's inferno turn myself into Proserpine.' Now in Greco–Roman mythology Proserpine, or Persephone, was Pluto's consort and thus reigned as queen of the infernal regions; it is easy to see how the name suggested itself to Baudelaire as soon as he used the metaphor 'inferno' of Jeanne's bed. But the expression also suggests very strongly that it needed someone of her own sex to satisfy Jeanne completely.

Apart from this single allusion, and a reference by Nadar to Jeanne's sharing rooms with a pretty fair-haired girl whom he took to be her maid – or so he pretended – there is no positive evidence that she enjoyed herself more with women than with men. It is, however, a fact that Baudelaire originally intended to call his book of verse not *Les Fleurs du Mal* but *Les Lesbiennes*; it was under this title that it was announced as forthcoming on the cover of his *Salon de 1846*. In the event only three poems dealing with lesbianism were included in *Les Fleurs du Mal* (two of which were banned by court order), though more may have been written and at a later stage discarded. How is one to explain this strange interest in female homosexuality on Baudelaire's part? It is true that lesbianism, as a subject for fiction, had attracted 'daring' writers, including Balzac and Gautier,[27] in the past, but by 1846 the topic must have begun to appear a little dated. Rather than a fashionable literary theme, it seems much more likely to have been one of distinct personal interest to Baudelaire. He felt a special affinity with these women, of whom Jeanne may have been one, whose tastes were of course in those days considered to be perverted and unnatural. Like him, they were outcasts, branded from birth, *damned*; indeed, the poem he wrote describing their pleasures is significantly entitled *Femmes damnées* and ends with a lengthy coda evoking their eventual punishment, scourged by an unceasing wind in one of the circles of hell forgotten by Dante:

> Far from the living, for eternity
> Wandering like wolves to expiate your sin,
> O restless souls, follow your destiny
> And flee the infinite you bear within.[28]

The score of poems, of which the majority are sonnets, written for or at least inspired by Jeanne Duval, count among the most exotic and most disturbing in the whole literature of love. This is because, although they do include a few that are brimful of tenderness and gratitude, in the main they show a bitterness and baffled fury that struck a note entirely new at the time and one that has never been and probably never will be surpassed. Jeanne's beauty is celebrated in glowing terms, but she is also denounced as an 'inhuman amazon', as a vampire, as a black witch, as Beelzebub himself.[29] There are poems in which he seems to delight in imagining her not just dead, but rotting disgustingly, as in *Une Charogne (Carrion Flesh)*, one of the very few poems in *Les Fleurs du Mal* which appears to record a specific incident. Walking together through the woods one afternoon, he and his mistress saw, at a turn in the road, the carcass of a dead horse which the carter had not thought it worth his while to drag away to a knacker's yard. The stink, the buzzing of the thousands of bluebottles, the grubs crawling over the spilled and putrid intestines of the animal, are all described in gruesome detail; Baudelaire does not even spare us the stray dog they had disturbed at its beastly meal and which watches them angrily but at a safe distance. Then he turns to Jeanne and bids her remember that this nauseating decomposition is what surely awaits her too, 'after the last sacrament, when you will be left under the grass and the rankly sprouting weeds, to moulder among the skeletons'.

The same macabre idea lies behind another, more solemn, sombre, and touching poem, to which he gave the curious but apt title *Posthumous Remorse*.[30]

> When, my dark beauty, locked in death's embrace,
> Entombed within a sepulchre of stone,
> You lie confined in musty vault alone,
> Your sole domain a coffin's carapace,

When a black slab shall crush your bosom's grace,
And your soft limbs be wasted down to bone,
Your heart be stopped, whence all desire is flown,
Shackled your feet, ended their venturous race,

The grave, that's privy to my infinite dreams
(The grave being ever the poet's partisan),
During those endless wakeful nights, meseems

Will say: 'What boots it, heartless courtesan,
Not to have known what the dead mourn perforce?'
– While the worm gnaws your flesh, as 'twere remorse.

'What the dead mourn' is presumably the warmth and comfort of
human companionship, which he had imagined Mariette yearning
for in her lonely, forgotten grave, but which Jeanne, that remote,
cat-like, sphinx-like creature with the empty black eyes had never
known and had never wanted to know.

V

IN CHANCERY

When he came into his inheritance in 1842 Baudelaire found himself worth slightly over a hundred thousand francs. The capital, prudently invested, gave him an annual income of just under 5000 francs, sufficient for the needs of a young bachelor with no expensive tastes. So long as he stayed unmarried and committed no 'follies' of the kind he had been accused of before he was shipped off to India, there was no pressing need for him to look around for ways and means of earning a living. Such fees as chanced to come his way from publishers or magazine editors might allow him, in time, to afford a slightly less straitened way of life.

But this was only how the situation might have appeared to an uninformed outsider. His relatives, remembering past experience, were extremely doubtful whether young Charles would in fact live within his means; he may have reached what was called 'years of discretion', but they did not suppose the magic dividing-line meant very much in his case, and it became apparent within months that their misgivings were fully justified. From Ancelle, the notary who handled his affairs and who was in close touch with his mother, they learned that he was disposing of certain parcels of the land at Neuilly which constituted the most important portion of the paternal legacy. Questioned about this, he replied that all he was doing was to transfer the capital into investments that would give him a better yield. However, in the course of the visits his mother paid him, especially after he moved into the Hôtel Pimodan, it became clear to her that the money was being diverted into quite other channels. The rent of the apartment may not have been exorbitant, but the antique furniture, the framed pictures, the expensively bound books, the well-schooled valet – these all told their story, and in addition she suspected that her son, always immaculately turned out, was making full use of his line of credit with his tailor, his shirt-maker, his shoemaker. Then there was Jeanne. Mme Aupick had never met her, of course, but she knew about her, and guessed that he was footing the bills for the rent and furnishings of the apartment nearby where he had set her up with her mother as companion-housekeeper.

Nothing struck more terror into the hearts of respectable middle-class families than that spectre, the rapacious mistress. When, ten years later, Alexandre Dumas *fils* wrote his *Lady of the Camellias*, the drama owed a large part of its phenomenal success with bourgeois audiences to his skill in plucking on this particular nerve.

There was more that she discovered only later. Part of the ground floor of the Hôtel Pimodan was let out to a certain Antoine Arondel, a painter specializing in still-lifes who doubled as an art-dealer, using one of his rooms as a curiosity shop. Baudelaire was constantly dropping in to rummage, for he shared with Balzac that passion for bric-à-brac which had played such havoc with the great novelist's always shaky finances. Friends paying him a visit would sometimes find Baudelaire sitting on a low stool in front of a makeshift easel, minutely examining a canvas he had just acquired, which he felt convinced was an authentic work by one of the Bassano family. It turned out to be nothing of the sort, which did not stop him returning to Arondel for more of the same. He gave 1200 francs for a *Mary Magdalene*, said to be the work of Federico – or it might be Taddeo – Zuccari, 1500 francs for a *St Jerome* supposedly by Domenichino, and paid 2000 francs for a Poussin landscape which, like the others, proved to be a copy or a fake. Disappointed, Baudelaire unloaded the merchandise on to other dealers, putting what they gave him into his own pocket.[1] Arondel, knowing he had a small property, was content at this stage to accept Baudelaire's interest-bearing promissory notes; but in years to come, when it became clear these were never likely to be honoured, Arondel was to turn into one of his most pertinacious and troublesome creditors, hounding the unfortunate poet year in year out, and using every form of threat and intimidation open to an unscrupulous debt-collector.

Realizing how worried his mother was getting, Baudelaire tried to reassure her by sending her absurdly optimistic reports of the quantities he was writing, interspersed with stories of lucrative offers which he claimed were being made him by the editors of newspapers and literary periodicals. 'A couple of days ago I had a long interview with the director of the *Bulletin de l'Ami des Arts*. My short story will appear in the first of their January issues. As from now, I am definitely on the staff, and have promised a whole series of short stories. . . . An additional personal interest I have in all this is that the editor of the *Bulletin* is a friend of Jules Janin, who will probably have responsibility for recruiting the staff of *L'Artiste* in its new form (it is up for sale this week); the said editor has made me a formal promise to have me taken on.'[2] It is certain that Baudelaire was in touch with the editor of the *Bulletin de l'Ami des Arts*, Albert de La Fizelière; but equally certain that no story of Baudelaire's ever appeared in its pages, though he does seem to have submitted, probably some time in 1844, a sonnet inspired by Delacroix's painting of Tasso in the madhouse. La Fizelière kept the manuscript for a number of years and then, long after the publication of *Les Fleurs du Mal*, wrote to Baudelaire enclosing a copy of his sonnet, the very existence of which the poet had by then in all probability forgotten. Cannily, La Fizelière held on to the original holograph and was able to dispose of it for a fair sum at an auction in 1878. As for *L'Artiste*, it was Arsène Houssaye, not Janin, who was appointed editor on January 1st, 1844, but it was not until 1846 that Baudelaire's name appeared on the index of contributors, and then only as signatory to a couple of relatively insignificant poems.[3]

With another letter written to his mother in the same year (1843), Baudelaire enclosed an article which he said he had submitted to the left-wing newspaper *La Démocratie pacifique*, but had then withdrawn after certain objections had been raised regarding its morality. 'However,' he went on, 'what is particularly gratifying is that it made such an impression on the people there that they did me the honour of asking me on the spot to write them something else, paying me all kinds of charming compliments.'[4] Here again, there is nothing inherently improbable in the story. *La Démocratie pacifique* had been founded only that year, and the editor was no doubt still looking for promising new talent; moreover, several of Baudelaire's friends, Théodore de Banville, Louis Ménard, and Leconte de Lisle who had recently arrived in Paris from his native Reunion Island, were contributing to the paper or were known to the editorial staff. But Baudelaire never actually published anything in the columns of *La Démocratie pacifique*.

What emerges most clearly from these letters is Baudelaire's anxiety to convince his mother – just as he used to when he was writing to her from school – that he was working hard and would shortly be at the top of the class, or in other words would be shortly taking his rightful place as a respected member of the world of letters. Even more important, in view of her concern about the state of his finances, was that she should be got to believe that he would soon be able to supplement his income by selling the products of his pen. He was not so starry-eyed as to imagine he would find much of a market for his poetry, of which he already had a sizeable portfolio. What the public wanted – as he knew very well – was fiction, preferably of a sensational kind. The New Year letter he wrote her in 1844 starts off with the 'good news' that 'once I have written one or two novels, *I know where I can place them* – it's a matter of a couple of months' work. A novel spread over ten issues of a newspaper fetches on average 500 francs, a novel in ten instalments for a magazine brings in

1000 francs.'[5] Baudelaire omitted to mention that, as an absolute beginner, he would be unlikely to command the average rate.

It is true, however, that if he had really wanted to earn his living by his pen, the serial novel was, at this particular point in time, the best money-spinner of all. Only the previous year a new record had been set by Armand Bertin, editor of the *Journal des Débats*, when he had paid Eugène Sue the princely sum of 26,500 francs for *Les Mystères de Paris*; but this cheque looked small beside the straight 100,000 francs that Dr Véron, the former director of the Opéra who had recently acquired the ailing paper *Le Constitutionnel*, offered Sue for the rights on his next novel. The dramatic increase in the popularity of daily newspapers in the early 1840s was almost entirely due to the discovery, first made by Emile de Girardin, editor of *La Presse*, that the new generation of readers responded more readily to exciting fiction, printed at the bottom of the page, than to the news items or ponderous leaders that filled the upper columns. Previously only a minority of citizens, those who had a vote and so felt they should take an interest in politics, went to the expense of subscribing to a newspaper; now, people of every kind and condition started buying newspapers simply for the sake of the current serial story. Not to take a paper at all was the equivalent in the 1840s of not having a television set today; the *roman-feuilleton* provided family entertainment of a new kind, costing a lot less than an outing to the theatre and, moreover, affording daily amusement instead of being an occasional treat. So, literature (of a kind) had become big business; a new entertainment industry had been created, and the man at the centre of it all, the novelist – or, to be more precise, the writer of good suspense stories – found his situation transformed almost overnight; from being a disregarded hack, he was now seen as a star performer, courted and fêted, wined and dined. No wonder Baudelaire dreamed of climbing on to this particular bandwagon. Sue too had begun as a rich young dandy, had run through a fortune and was now in a fair way to rebuilding it; could he not emulate him? The trouble was, as he secretly knew, that his talents did not lie in the right direction. He could no more compete with Eugène Sue, Alexandre Dumas and Frédéric Soulié than a cat could hope to beat the horses in a steeplechase.

Mme Aupick may have been more reassured when he talked to her about his success in cultivating the acquaintance of leading men of letters of the time. Having the right contacts was, after all, the way to get on in any profession – or so she had always understood, and certainly her second husband's career afforded some support for the idea. Up to a point Baudelaire subscribed to it himself, not yet having come to realize that, as Proust was later to put it, to hope to acquire literary distinction by hobnobbing with those who were commonly thought to possess it was 'as erroneous as to suppose that a man can keep himself in good health merely by dining out frequently in the company of a physician'. There was a bit of the boyish hero-worshipper in Baudelaire, though all his heroes disappointed him in one way or another except those whom – like Poe – he could never hope to meet.

The first great man he approached was Victor Hugo, possibly emboldened by Hugo's reputation for treating idolizing disciples with fatherly kindness. As early as 1840, when he was still at school, he wrote to him, using as a pretext the desire to communicate the emotions that had filled him when he attended a new production of Hugo's romantic drama *Marion Delorme*.[6] It is a curiously awkward letter; Baudelaire says nothing of his own literary aspirations, nor does he work in any of the expected compliments on Hugo's other books or plays with which, even at this date, he was very familiar; but he is clearly angling for an invitation: 'having been young yourself, you will understand how a book can make us love its author and feel the need to thank him personally and humbly kiss his hand.'[7] Hugo, always grateful for incense from whatever quarter it was wafted, gave him leave to call. The meeting proved rather disconcerting; the only suggestion Hugo made was that Baudelaire should shake the dust of Paris from his feet as soon as he could and try working on his own somewhere in the country. This was curious advice, coming from Hugo, being directly contrary to what he was both practising and preaching at this time. One has only to look at the opening poem, entitled straightforwardly 'Fonction du poète', of the new collection, *Les Rayons et les Ombres*, which he published that very year (1840), to see that in Hugo's opinion the poet's function was not to write hymns to nature, nor, when there is strife in the city, to put on his sandals and walk out through the gates into the fields and woods. He should remain behind to guide the people, to prophesy, illuminate, and point the way to the promised land; his gift being to discern, in the dark womb of time, the still dormant seeds of an unimaginable future. But Hugo, one must suppose, judged Baudelaire a little young to be indoctrinated with the principles of social commitment; and besides, looking at this pale, overwrought adolescent, he may have thought quite simply that a breath of country air and some wholesome country food would probably do the boy a world of good.

It was some three years later, this time through the good offices of Prarond, that Baudelaire met Hugo's one-time friend, the already influential critic Sainte-Beuve. He had read and admired, rather more than it is fashionable to do today, the two collections of poetry that Sainte-Beuve had published in 1829–30, and also his long, pallid, introspective novel *Volupté* which excited him inordinately when he was in his teens, but it may well have been Sainte-Beuve's earlier treatise on the forgotten French poets of the sixteenth century that Baudelaire valued more than any of his subsequent writings; we have seen already how the works of Ronsard and his school formed his favourite reading matter on the Ile Saint-Louis.

His friendship with Sainte-Beuve lasted for the rest of his life, but it can hardly be said to have helped him in his struggle to win the esteem of the literary establishment. There was no critic at the time whose word carried more weight, and yet Sainte-Beuve always had private reservations about Baudelaire, and never once responded to the poet's reiterated pleas that he should favour one of his works with a review. Not that Sainte-Beuve ignored him systematically; thus in 1860, in an open letter to the editor of *Le Moniteur*, he mentioned Baudelaire in passing as 'the one, among those I call my young friends, whom I have known longest; he knows how highly I prize the subtlety of his intelligence, his clever, curious talent'.[8] This was all very well (though, applied to Baudelaire, the expression *talent habile et curieux* comes close to damning with faint praise), but it would have been more helpful if Sainte-Beuve had thought fit to devote even one of his numerous critical articles, which appeared regularly week after week in *Le Constitutionnel* and *Le Moniteur*, to some aspect of the work of his 'young friend'. But as Baudelaire said, with respect precisely to this oblique and unsatisfactory tribute, 'one is never praised as one would like to be, even by the acutest of minds. There are friends one can never steer in the right direction.'[9]

When in 1865 Sainte-Beuve was appointed a member of the Senate – in part an act of public recognition, though the nomination was also due to the government's desire to provide him with a sinecure, since his health was failing and his earning capacity in consequence reduced – Baudelaire told his mother he felt he should write and congratulate him, though, given the powers and constitution of the Senate under the Second Empire, neither he nor Sainte-Beuve could be under any illusions as to what this public honour really amounted to. Nervously, she wrote back to urge him to send a letter couched in more respectful terms than he had indicated, whereupon Baudelaire told her roundly to mind her own business. 'Do you think I should seriously act the part of the prudent, foxy courtier with a man who, in spite of my relative youth, has always considered me as his equal? There have been ten occasions already when we have quarrelled; for although so much older he is more petulant than I am. Do you really imagine that this new distinction is going to increase his literary influence? How can you make so egregious an error? Now I who know him inside out, I can assure you that even if I run counter to all his cherished ideas, he will always do for me everything I ask him to, within the bounds of possibility.'[10] This was generous, if Baudelaire really believed what he was saying; but it is more likely that he could not bring himself to face the fact that a lifetime's friendship with Sainte-Beuve had in the end brought him no tangible benefits whatsoever.

However much he may have thought it politic to ingratiate himself with his seniors, in order to secure the introductions and recommendations so necessary to a young man trying to make his way, Baudelaire's irrepressible independence of spirit, the eccentricity both of his appearance and of the turn of his conversation, had the unfortunate effect of arousing mistrust and apprehension among his elders whenever he appeared; was this young man not trying to take a rise out of them? He lacked that indispensable quality the French call *bonhomie*, cheerful, unaffected simplicity of manners and speech. It was not that he failed to display ordinary politeness, on the contrary, but his politeness seemed just a trifle overdone, especially in the free-and-easy society of bohemian artists in which he moved, and could be construed as having ironical overtones. This was something that struck Théophile Gautier very forcibly, when he first met him at the Hôtel Pimodan in the company of Fernand Boissard, the sculptor Jean Feuchères, and two young women of easy virtue.

He talked in measured terms, used, in conversation, the choicest vocabulary, and articulated certain words in a special way as though to emphasize them and as though he attributed to them some mysterious significance. One could almost hear the italics and capital letters in the modulations of his voice. Tall stories, very popular in the Hôtel Pimodan, he disdained as being crude, the kind of thing only art students went in for; but he permitted himself paradox and hyperbole. Speaking simply and naturally, with an air of complete detachment, as though he were making some trite remark about the weather, he would come out with some diabolically monstrous axiom or would coolly advance this or that wild and yet mathematically deduced theory, for he used rigorous logic in the development of his crazy ideas. As a conversationalist, he did not go in for witty remarks or verbal humour, but he looked at everything from a particular point of view which altered the perspective, as if taking a bird's eye view or a worm's eye view of the world, and he picked up connections which no one else would have noticed and which struck everybody by their irrational rationality. The few gestures he made, never flinging his arms about, were slow and sober, for he hated the violent gesticulations of the southerner. Nor was he particularly voluble in speech, thinking it in better taste to imitate the phlegmatic deliberation of an English gentleman. The impression he gave was of a dandy obliged to consort with bohemian artists, but retaining his distinction, his fine manners, and that cult of the person which characterizes a man imbued with the principles of Beau Brummel.[11]

By the summer of 1845, which was when Gautier made these observations,[12] Baudelaire had already acquired, in certain restricted circles, the reputation of a rum customer who could be relied on to provide entertainment of a rather special nature. Some of the poetry he was writing was expressly composed, apparently, to shock, startle, or amuse the company in which he found himself, though we know of only one such composition dating back to this period, and that only by the synopsis provided much later by a member of the audience who had heard it more than once.[13] The starting-point was suggested, probably, by the lines Othello speaks, referring to Desdemona:

> I had been happy, if the general camp,
> Pioneers and all, had tasted her sweet body,
> So I had nothing known.

Baudelaire imagined a tyrant (modelled on Louis-Philippe) who, smitten with the charms of the poet's mistress, requests him to 'lend her' for a night. The poet indignantly refuses, whereupon the king threatens him with an unheard-of vengeance, which duly takes place: the royal troops receive the order the following night to carry out a collective rape. The narrative ends with the poet, now raving mad, babbling meaningless verses.

The sort of notoriety Baudelaire enjoyed thanks to these performances was not, unfortunately, one which would predispose a magazine editor, in the stuffy climate of the July Monarchy, to commission articles from him, nor would it encourage any of the influential people whose support he was trying to win to recommend that he be given a trial. He had written a great deal, but had still published nothing under his own name, and consequently had earned not a penny by his literary endeavours. Due note was taken by the Aupicks and by Alphonse Baudelaire; they had in any case been warned by Ancelle that the young man had already run through half his fortune in two years. It was left to his mother to break it to him that her husband – with her full agreement – had decided to set in motion the procedure authorized by the law in such cases; control of his financial affairs would be taken out of his hands and put into those of a 'judicial counsellor' whose duties would be to ensure that the remainder of the capital would be kept intact, the interest only being paid to Baudelaire month by month.

Since none of Mme Aupick's letters to her son have come down to us, we have to deduce what she wrote to him from the reply he sent, in which he was at pains to refute her various arguments. She had tried to soften the blow by telling him that there was really no cause for resentment, since the step the family was proposing to take was prompted solely by their concern that he should not be reduced to complete destitution. He had shown he had no head for business, but there was nothing discreditable about that. This might be true, he replied, for most people, but 'unluckily for me, I am not made like other men. What you look on as an unfortunate measure rendered necessary by the circumstances, is something I cannot, just cannot accept. ... I am adamant in rejecting anything that limits my freedom. Is it not unbelievably inhuman to submit me to the judgement of a handful of men who have no interest in the matter and who do not know me? Between you and me, is there anyone who can boast he knows me, or knows where I want to go, what I want to do, and what patience I am capable of displaying?'[14]

Baudelaire than alluded to the aspect of the whole business that must have made him feel most uncomfortable – the sums his mother had been lending him to allow him to meet immediate liabilities. He reminded her how 'it had been agreed between us that after a given lapse of time you would have the right to a certain proportion of my future earnings'. What he feared now, he said, was that the disgrace he was threatened with would make it impossible for him to settle down to work of any kind. If the calculation had been that a sudden reduction in his income would provide the necessary stimulus to start earning, then she would be disappointed. 'The result will be the exact reverse of what you expected – that is to say, I shall be utterly discouraged. ... I would prefer to have no fortune at all, and to become totally dependent on you, rather than to be made the subject of some court-order – the first would still leave me free, the alternative would place limits on my freedom.'[15]

The process was seen by Baudelaire, not incorrectly, as an attempt on his mother's part to force him to revert to the status of a child whose pocket-money is doled out to him and whose fortune is held in trust by his elders. This remained, in fact, his real status in law for the rest of his life; inevitably he felt it as a humiliation preying on his mind all the time and hampering him at every turn. He had absorbed the middle-class prejudices of his family at least to the extent that he felt his private financial situation to be nobody's business but his own. Of what use was it to tell him that he had only to prove himself – that is, to prove he could earn a living in his chosen career – for the interdiction to be raised? It was precisely the affront of the legal interdiction, the denial of his right, enjoyed as a matter of course by all adult citizens, to call his own his own, the forcible limitation of his freedom of action, which in his view would frustrate all his efforts. How could he be expected to engage in creative work when all the time he knew he was tied to his mother's apron-strings?

If she did not see it in quite the same light, she cannot be altogether blamed. Unless Charles were to give up the idea of becoming a writer and embrace some recognized profession, he would continue as he had begun until he had run through his entire fortune, in two or three years, perhaps, at most. And after that, what? Destitution? a debtors' prison? Would he not drag them all down, herself, her husband, in his disgrace? Far better to make sure that the remaining 50,000 francs were placed where he could not touch them, so that at least he would remain solvent and be obliged to cut his coat according to his cloth.

The normal course in such cases was for the court to order the convocation of representatives of the family, and to pronounce after hearing what they had to report and after listening to any representations the defendant might care to make – if indeed he was in a fit state to plead; the procedure was more commonly invoked when there was clear evidence of insanity or at least feeble-mindedness rendering the defendant incapable of handling his own affairs. The family council duly met on August 24th, 1844, and produced a damning report on Baudelaire's record of prodigality as demonstrated since he attained his majority; their plea concluded with a request that the court should appoint a legal guardian to administer and control his affairs, adding that this should be 'some person other than the mother . . . having in mind the state of her health and a mother's weakness where her children are concerned'.[16] Baudelaire, probably too depressed to do otherwise, did not trouble to exercise his right to plead his case before the court, which accordingly granted the petition, appointing Narcisse-Désiré Ancelle to administer the estate.

Ancelle at this time was a man of forty-three, married, with five children. Having started life as a notary's clerk, he had worked as assistant to Jean Labie, the notary at Neuilly-sur-Seine who had been one of the witnesses at Mme Aupick's second marriage and had helped hatch the plan to send Baudelaire to India in 1841.[17] Labie had long ago retired; Ancelle had succeeded to his office in 1832. Especially in a rich town like Neuilly, the notary was a person of some consequence. His main duties were to keep records of the ownership of properties in his area, to attend to the transfer of title-deeds, and to arrange sales and mortgages. Though drawing no salary from the state, a notary held a quasi-official position and needed to be a man of scrupulous honesty, since large sums of money passed regularly through his hands. 'It is the notary,' as one of them wrote, 'who in the marriage contract establishes the first bases and the first links of the family; it is he whom the dying man summons to his bedside, to confide to him his final wishes. As guardian of every kind of interest, as a confidant of the most secret thoughts, as arbiter in most business deals, as an almost necessary intermediary in the movement of property and capital, he becomes the friend, the judge, the protector of families.'[18] Ancelle was, as the phrase went, 'an ornament to his profession'; the authorities held him in high enough esteem to appoint him mayor of Neuilly in 1851, an office he continued to hold until his retirement in 1868.

The care of Baudelaire's estate was only one of a large number of similar trusts he was called on to administer, though it may have given him rather more trouble than most. Prudence required that he should keep the remnants of the poet's fortune in secure investments, paying over no more than the modest interest these earned. He was obliged to resist, as far as he could, Baudelaire's frequent demands to be allowed to anticipate his income; this he would consent to do only if the advance was approved by Mme Aupick. He steadfastly refused to settle the outstanding claims of Baudelaire's creditors, who were forced to wait until after the poet's death, when his affairs were wound up.

There may have been some justice in the complaints Baudelaire later made that Ancelle took an indiscreet interest in his private affairs. He suspected, as he told his mother, that for a time 'my person, my opinions and my affections were a subject for perpetual jests on the part of his horrible female, his hideous daughter, and his squalid brood of urchins'.[19] He hated, when he was in urgent need of renewing his wardrobe, having to go along to Ancelle's tailor with a note authorizing him to purchase clothes up to a given sum. He could not prevent Ancelle coming to see him, however inconvenient the visit might be; on one occasion, some time in May, 1861, the old man stayed so long that Baudelaire found himself obliged to take him out to dinner, and was on tenterhooks throughout the meal, knowing that the notary had no sense of social decorum; and sure enough, to his intense embarrassment Ancelle sent for the proprietor at the end of dinner 'to ask him – guess what! – if he was German or English, if he had been in business long, if the restaurant was showing a good profit, etc.'[20] One can imagine Baudelaire toying with what was left of his wine and staring fixedly at the ceiling while this indiscreet interrogation was in progress. He dreaded above all meeting any of his friends when he was in Ancelle's company and being obliged to effect an introduction; indeed, it is remarkable that the man nearest

68

to him in the latter part of his life, his publisher Poulet-Malassis, only discovered the truth, that Ancelle all those years had been his legal guardian, after Baudelaire suffered a cerebral haemorrhage in Brussels and the old notary arrived to take charge.

Undoubtedly Baudelaire misjudged Ancelle during the earlier stages of his dealings with him; this was inevitable, given the position each one found himself in with regard to the other. Ancelle may have been ill-educated – most notaries were at the time – and something of a philistine, but he was not the boor Baudelaire sometimes made him out to be, and he was certainly not his 'principal enemy' as the poet once called him, writing the words in capital letters for greater emphasis, though he did add: 'not out of malice, I know'.[21] Particularly after Baudelaire started having books published, Ancelle developed a keen interest in his career as a writer and even, towards the end, took to acting as a kind of unpaid literary agent – without much success, it must be admitted, but his honest efforts did finally cause Baudelaire to appreciate him at his true worth. When, a year before Baudelaire's death, Asselineau was invited to dinner by Ancelle to meet Mme Aupick and the widow of Alphonse Baudelaire, he reported to Poulet-Malassis that 'these good folk [the two women] have no inkling that the one person who confers lustre on the family name is our own dear Baudelaire, nor that he has one of the most remarkable minds of our age. They appeared to gawp at hearing me speak of him in the terms we use among ourselves. I wouldn't be surprised if they didn't think I was having them on. In the whole company there was only one who showed true affection for Charles, and that was the good old man Ancelle, a stout fellow. He has some strange ideas about our friend, but he really does love him. He speaks of him every day and in the warmest terms.'[22]

But many years had to pass before Baudelaire became reconciled to, or rather resigned to, the status of permanent minor to which the court judgement of 1844 had reduced him. Initially, he felt it as a deep shame, a certificate of incompetence, and as the months went by, his dejection and despair grew even blacker. His income, now slashed to a mere pittance, made it impractical to go on living in the Hôtel Pimodan much longer; and indeed, the idea had crossed his mind, even before disaster struck, that he should move in with Jeanne, whom he had set up in rooms in a little street on the Ile Saint-Louis which bore the picturesque name Rue de la Femme-sans-Tête. As the storm-clouds gathered over his head, and in particular as his relations with his mother worsened, he drew nearer to his dark-skinned mistress who he came to realize was the only creature in the world to whom he could turn for support and solace. Even so, he baulked at the idea of setting up house with her, and it was only after his attempt at suicide that he stayed for a short while under her roof, and then only because he was in need of nursing and Jeanne was the only person at hand.

There is no need to suppose any reason for this botched attempt to take his own life other than that Baudelaire found it impossible to recover from the blow to his pride and had in consequence lost all interest in further struggle. The letter he wrote to Ancelle on June 30th, 1845, gives a rather confused account of his motives. His debts, he said, had nothing to do with it. 'I am killing myself because I cannot go on living, because I find it unbearably wearisome to go to sleep and wake up again. I am killing myself because I am of no use to anyone and *dangerous to myself.* – I am killing myself because I believe myself to be immortal and because I hope.'[23] The mixture here of a profession of religious faith ('I believe myself to be immortal') and a declaration of intent to commit the one act which that faith prohibits above all others may suggest that the balance of his mind was truly disturbed. Everything depends on the interpretation one puts on the words he underlined: 'because I am ... *dangerous to myself.*' It may be that Baudelaire had a premonition of the spiritual decay that lay ahead, if he went on living a life deprived of hope, and that it was to avoid the danger of slipping into a slough of despond from which he might find it impossible to extricate himself, that he decided to escape now, while he was relatively innocent and unpolluted, into the hereafter.

On the other hand, remembering how often a prior announcement of an intention to do away with oneself is to be interpreted as a cry for help, one can question how seriously Baudelaire proposed to put his plan into effect. Everything suggests that he wanted to be saved. The weapon he used was a knife, which he drove into his side while he was in a restaurant with Jeanne. Earlier he had run into Louis Ménard, one of whose hobbies was chemistry, and asked him to procure him some prussic acid. Ménard had fobbed him off with some excuse, and Baudelaire had left in high dudgeon. A few days later, when another friend of Baudelaire's, Privat d'Anglemont, visited Ménard and mentioned that Baudelaire was no longer to be seen in his usual haunts, Ménard remembered the previous incident and the two of them called on Jeanne to see if she had any information. Summoned by her mother, she sauntered up to the door and, having first made sure the two visitors were not creditors trying to trace Baudelaire's whereabouts, told them that her lover, 'wishing to get back at his mother and compel his stepfather, General Aupick, to settle his debts, had staged a suicide in the neighbourhood where they lived; he had inflicted a minor injury on himself, and was being looked after by his parents'.[24]

During the few weeks he spent convalescing under their roof, the Aupicks made one last attempt to persuade him to lead a more regular life, and he complied to the extent at least of registering as a student at the Ecole des Chartes, though he never actually signed on for any courses at that institution. When he finally decided to leave the house in the Place Vendôme it was, as he told his mother, in part because he felt he needed to be on his own to recover his balance, and also because 'it is impossible for me to turn myself into the sort of person your husband would like me to be; consequently I should be robbing him if I were to go on living at his expense; finally, I don't think it is *decent* that I should be treated by him in the way he appears to want to treat me henceforth. It is probable that I shall be obliged to lead a life of great hardship, but it will be better for me so.'[25] Aupick, if he was shown this letter, will have shrugged his shoulders, while privately wondering, no doubt, what would be the next scrape from which his incorrigible stepson would need to be rescued.

VI

THE ART CRITIC

The decision to leave his parents' home was taken hurriedly and without prior arrangement. Baudelaire booked a room in the first hotel that appeared suitable and then sent for the trunk containing his books and personal effects. In the letter to his mother announcing this move, he explained that he did not intend to stay in the hotel any longer than necessary; just as soon as he was repossessed of his furniture he would start looking around for more permanent lodgings. To pay to get the furniture out of store, he was counting on the proceeds of a few articles due at the end of the month. In the meantime, he hoped his mother would be kind enough to settle with the hotel and also let him have a little extra money for himself, since he had come away practically penniless.

In the event, the idea of setting up again in an apartment of his own remained a dream; Baudelaire spent the rest of his life moving from one cheap hotel or lodging-house to another, when he was not literally homeless. The articles for which he was expecting payment were, needless to say, a myth, at best a way of softening the brusqueness of a begging letter which was only one in a series addressed to his perpetual creditor, his mother. She may, however, have felt she could place a little more reliance than before on these optimistic forecasts, since at this time Baudelaire was no longer a would-be author but had at last burst into print. Shortly before the suicide attempt he had published – at his own expense, admittedly – a review of the spring art exhibition, a slim pamphlet entitled simply *Salon de 1845*. This was, at all events, a start, however modest.

It was under the July Monarchy that France finally achieved world supremacy in the production of works of pictorial art, retaining this pre-eminence until well into the twentieth century. As Lamartine declared, his breast swelling with patriotic pride, in a speech in the Chamber of Deputies on March 30th, 1841: 'Paris has become one vast artists' studio. Europe visits, admires, purchases, and we export our output everywhere. . . . "Painted in Paris" is a title of honour for a work of art, a certificate of good taste, a guarantee of origin that is, in itself, a mark of the highest distinction.'[1]

Every spring the galleries of the Palais du Louvre were temporarily cleared of the old masters which normally adorned the walls, so as to leave room to hang the best products of the Paris studios over the previous year – or what passed as the best. The tradition went right back to the seventeenth century, when the custom grew up of exhibiting works by members of the Academy of Fine Arts in the Salon d'Apollon in the Louvre; hence the exhibition itself came to be known as the *Salon*. After the French Revolution the right to exhibit ceased to be restricted to academicians, so that the annual or biennial display was turned into a great popular bazaar. To have even one of one's works accepted by the jury of selectors was considered a signal honour; it was an essential stepping-stone in an artist's career, marking the end of his probation. Unless he passed this test, he knew he had no future; we have already seen how Baudelaire's friend Deroy, discouraged by a series of refusals, fell into a decline and met a premature death.

The curiosity aroused by the *Salon*, held earlier in the century at irregular intervals but since 1834 an annual event, was immeasurably greater than in our days, since it provided the general public with a unique opportunity to assess the latest developments in the world of art. It was the only exhibition there was – private shows were as yet undreamed of – and it attracted not just connoisseurs and would-be purchasers, nor even just the art loving, cultivated stratum of society, but a multitude of quite humble, uneducated folk who at that time were offered little in the way of cultural stimulus and who crowded into the Louvre as soon as the exhibition opened in March; in 1846 well over a million visitors were estimated to have viewed it over the three months it lasted. The fact that entry was free except on Saturdays meant that every class of society was represented, butchers' wives and guardsmen rubbing shoulders with bankers and ladies of fashion.

Once inside, the viewers were confronted by a bewildering array of canvases of all sorts and sizes and of very varying interest. To guide them through the labyrinth, almost every newspaper and periodical of any standing published reviews of the exhibition, such reviews being known also as *salons*. They were not written necessarily by specialists; if Gautier, who had attended an art school in his youth, could claim to be one, others, like Jules Janin and Gustave Planche, were primarily literary critics or, like Musset and Barbier, creative writers; others again – Thiers and Guizot, Eugène Pelletan and Félix Pyat – were professional politicians who plumed themselves on their discrimination in matters of art. Right from the start, Baudelaire was better qualified as a *salonnier* than most of these; as we have seen, his interest in art had been fostered by his father while he was still a child

73

and, as he grew up, it was with artists that he associated quite as much as with writers. Frequent visits to art galleries, beginning with a school trip in 1838 to view the royal collection at Versailles, and the knowledge of art history he had picked up from his reading (especially of Stendhal's *Histoire de la peinture en Italie*), imbued everything he wrote on the subject with an air of quiet authority. Reading Baudelaire's first *salon*, one is struck again and again by the breadth and surety of his references not just to the great masters of the past but also to the earlier achievements of a number of the contemporary painters he is discussing; it is clear that he had been touring the annual exhibitions for some years, noting, appreciating, and remembering what he had seen.

Nevertheless it was not an auspicious moment he had chosen to make his début in this field. In comparison with what had gone before and what was to come after, French art in the mid-1840s was passing through a dull and uneventful phase. The great days of romanticism lay well in the past, and the new realism of Courbet had yet to manifest itself. Large-scale historical painting was still much in evidence, kept alive by commissions from the Ministry of the Interior, but conservative critics lamented the passing of the 'great tradition'. The landscapists of the Barbizon school were undervalued by officialdom – Théodore Rousseau, notably, saw his submissions regularly rejected, including even, in 1842, his magnificent *Allée des châtaigniers* painted in Brittany the previous summer. Corot was deemed acceptable, and was commonly regarded as being 'at the head of the modern school of landscape painters', as Baudelaire noted in his *Salon*, adding however that 'if M. Théodore Rousseau chose to exhibit, there would be some doubt as to which of the two was supreme.'[2] In fact Rousseau, known as *le grand refusé*, would no doubt have been only too happy to exhibit; but in respect of his inability to please the selectors he could almost be called the Cézanne of the July Monarchy.

Throughout the reign of Louis-Philippe and indeed under the Second Empire as well, nothing caused more angry comment and more furious controversy than the capricious judgements of the committee, made up of senior members of the Academy of Fine Arts, whose task it was to pick and choose among an avalanche of entries and to decide which works should have the honour to be exhibited and which should be rejected. Baudelaire expressly declared, in the opening pages of his brochure, that he had nothing to contribute to this ongoing debate. As for the other great subject of discussion in those years, that is, the deleterious effect of middle-class taste on the general standard of painting, the line he took was that it was pointless to kick against the pricks. Like literature, the fine arts were subject nowadays to commercial pressure; a new class of purchasers had entered the market, looking for pictures suitable for hanging on the walls of their low-ceilinged houses and apartments. The grandiose compositions meant for the embellishment of palaces and cathedrals were quite unsuitable for their purposes; what they required were small easel pictures, representing scenes easily recognized and understood. Anecdotal painting was much in favour, and of course there were hundreds of shopkeepers and small factory owners who were prepared to pay to have their portraits done in oils. To satisfy this new demand, a large, undistinguished group of popular artists had come into being whose compositions were intelligible at the lowest level and posed no problems. Objects in their pictures were always clearly recognizable, given sharp outlines and coloured in accordance with prevailing assumptions (an orange is orange, what the devil!). Devoid of style or individuality, such art had only ingenuity and slickness to commend it. Painters chose their subjects with scrupulous care so as to avoid offending or upsetting their middle-class patrons, and their pictures were worked over to the point where a prospective purchaser would consider them 'finished'; the result was a well-groomed, well-behaved, and totally emasculated art.

Not surprisingly, it was the last kind of art to appeal to Baudelaire. Its most popular representative, Horace Vernet, whose inflated reputation was chiefly based on his patriotic pictures of battle-scenes from the colonial war in Algeria, was cuttingly dismissed in two brief paragraphs in this first *salon*; Baudelaire reserved it for his second (written the following year) to launch a truly devastating attack on Vernet. In regard to most of the other exhibitors, he judged the general level of technical competence to be high, but made no secret of his disappointment at the lack of imagination and almost complete absence of originality. Of Adolphe and Armand Leleux, two brothers who worked in collaboration, he comments: 'All their pictures are very well executed, very well painted, and very monotonous in manner and choice of subjects.' Of Eugène Le Poittevin: 'Genre pictures, true genre pictures too well painted. Actually, everybody these days paints too well.' Of Jules Joyant: 'There is nothing so embarrassing as to report on works which year after year show the same dispiriting perfections.'[3]

To account for this dismal state of affairs, nothing would have been simpler for Baudelaire than to follow the line of his fellow critics and put the blame on the corrupt taste of the middle-class art purchaser which encouraged these timid, mediocre, but conscientious hacks. In fact, he refuses from the outset to do this; he has no intention, he writes in the preface to the *Salon de 1845*, of making a scapegoat of the bourgeois client, of imitating those of his colleagues 'who for several years now have been devoting their energies to anathematizing that harmless creature who would like nothing better than to appreciate good painting, if these gentlemen could only make him understand what it was, and if the artists would show him specimens of it more frequently'. To despise the bourgeois as blind and stupid, to castigate him for his lack of culture, is absurd: 'the bourgeois – since we are on the subject – is an eminently respectable person; for if your income depends on him, you have to please him. ... Whatever pleases, has a reason for pleasing, and to draw back disdainfully from the ignorant masses is no way to shepherd them on to the right path.'[4] The critic who contents himself with throwing his ink-pot in the faces of the public is not doing his job. 'Any public undeniably has a sense for the truth and a willingness to recognize it; but it is necessary to turn people's faces in the right direction and give them the right push.'[5] Thus the answer to the question – posed as the title of the first chapter of Baudelaire's second *Salon* – 'What is the point of criticism?' – is implicitly answered already; by expatiating on the merits of good art, even more than by wasting time damning bad art, gradually and over the course of time the critic will be able to improve standards by improving the taste of a public new to art.

Baudelaire tends, in the *Salon de 1845*, to spend most time on artists with established reputations, Delacroix, Corot, Decamps, and to pass over the others rapidly unless he can find something good to say about them. As he strolled round the galleries, making pencil notes in his catalogue, he kept his eye open for any sign of new talent, anything that might denote a strong and original personality. The only one he thought he discovered was the now almost forgotten painter William Haussoulier, a newcomer whose *Fountain of Youth*, previously exhibited at the London Royal Academy, gave him the cue for a lengthy, detailed, and enthusiastic analysis, which may not have been entirely unjustified; unfortunately, Haussoulier never repeated this first success.[6] It is in any case curious that Baudelaire should have singled out a semi-mythological, semi-allegorical picture, whatever its 'elegance and distinction', as the one exhibit by an unknown artist that seemed to hold out some promise for the future. For in general, to judge by the concluding remarks not just of the *Salon de 1845* but of the *Salon de 1846* also, what Baudelaire was looking for was a new, 'heroic' art drawing its themes from modern times. 'He alone will be the painter, the true painter, who proves himself capable of distilling the epic qualities of contemporary life, and of showing us and making us understand, by his colouring and draughtsmanship, how great we are, how poetic we are, in our cravats and our polished boots.'[7] However bizarrely formulated, this prediction amounts to a plea for what Baudelaire later called 'modernity' in art; something he was oddly unable to discover in Courbet, whose work displeased him for other reasons, and did not sufficiently recognize in Manet. Perhaps he would have found it in the Impressionists, had he lived long enough to see their work, or perhaps again not; the nineteenth century undoubtedly had its 'epic qualities', but they were not of the kind that could readily be translated into works of pictorial art.

In spite of – or perhaps because of – its unusual qualities, the *Salon de 1845* aroused little attention when it was published. Henri de La Madelène, writing long after the event, claimed that at the time Baudelaire's brochure 'provoked a storm, on account of the boldness of his criticism and the daring standpoint he adopted, but struck everybody by its solidity of doctrine and maturity of style.'[8] But there is little evidence for this popular reaction in the press at the time. Le Vavasseur sent a glowing review of the *Salon* for the local paper at Abbeville to print, which Baudelaire called 'ravishing'[9] but which can have had little effect on public opinion in the capital. Other friends, Champfleury, Vitu, wrote obliging notices in the papers for which they worked, but these papers had small circulations. Baudelaire must have felt disappointed, though whether his disappointment was sufficiently acute to have contributed to the suicidal depression into which he fell a few weeks after his essay appeared, is rather doubtful.[10] It is true that at a later date he had all the unsold copies of the *Salon de 1845* destroyed; but this may simply have been because he felt the ideas he expressed in it were, on the whole, much better presented in his later art criticism, and particularly in the *Salon de 1846*.

However slight the immediate impact of the *Salon de 1845*, and whatever reservations he may have had later about its value, Baudelaire had at least appeared in print, he had crossed that particular Rubicon. It was a moment of triumph which he was later to recall sardonically, noting that 'the day the young writer corrects his first proof, he is as proud as a schoolboy who has caught his first dose of pox.'[11] From now on, authorship would be a virus from which he would no more be able to rid himself than he would be able to cure himself of the other disease.

The next step was to look for an opening on some newspaper or other, and here the obvious choice was *Le Corsaire-Satan*, for which several of his old friends wrote: Prarond, Le Vavasseur, Chennevières and Champfleury. The title of this gossip-sheet, hinting as it did at a combination of piracy and diabolism, gives sufficient indication of the sort of scurrility the paper might be prepared to stoop to. In the absence of any effective laws of libel, the Paris

77

gutter-press of the time specialized in retailing scandal and drew its revenues in part from the hush-money extorted from those who were prepared to pay up rather than have their indiscretions made public property. Protests and threats were of little avail; any injured parties who presented themselves at the offices of *Le Corsaire-Satan*, horsewhip in hand, were disconcerted to find themselves confronted by the editor, a certain M. Lepoitevin Saint-Alme, 'a dignified old man, a retired cavalry officer to go by appearances, who swept off his hat majestically to reveal a shock of white hair'.[12] Age has its privileges . . .

Baudelaire's contributions to *Le Corsaire-Satan* in 1845–6 consisted of a few reviews, a libellous piece of tittle-tattle about Balzac,[13] a half-serious, half-frivolous essay on love from which we have already had occasion to quote,[14] and a more serious article on an exhibition of neoclassical French artists which opened that winter and was currently attracting a great deal of interest.[15] It was held in premises above a department store, the Bazar Bonne-Nouvelle; there was a charge for admission, the profits going to a charity club that had been formed to provide pensions for veteran artists fallen on evil days. Here, in quiet surroundings, so different, wrote Baudelaire, from the 'turbulent, garish, noisy, crowded annual exhibitions,'[16] the visitor could admire, alongside rarely seen masterpieces by the group that had come into prominence during the Revolution and the First Empire (David, Guérin, Girodet and Prudhon), an interesting selection of paintings by living artists whose work was seldom encountered in the annual spring exhibitions; either because, like Ingres, they were too proud to compete or because, like Théodore Rousseau, they could not satisfy the exacting but peculiar standards of the jury. Seen in the perspective of history, the 1846 Bazar Bonne-Nouvelle exhibition ranks as the first serious attempt to challenge the monopolistic stranglehold of the official *salon de peinture*; the tradition it inaugurated continued under the Second Empire with the one-man shows of Ingres, Courbet and Manet, and can be said to have culminated in the sensational and hotly discussed *Salons des Indépendants* of the 1870s.

None of this, of course, could have been foreseen by Baudelaire or indeed by anyone else at the time. What is of particular interest today in his brief review of the exhibition is the evidence it provides that Baudelaire, the champion of Delacroix and romanticism, had yet a sufficiently catholic taste to respond with equal discernment to the neoclassical school of an earlier age, 'the austere ancestors of romanticism' as he calls them. His article includes – and, indeed, chiefly consists of – an eloquent tribute to the art of the French Revolution, 'that painting which deliberately dispenses with charm and morbid allurement, which draws its vitality above all from the soul and intellect – an art as harsh and despotic as the revolution from which it sprang'.[17] To illustrate his point, Baudelaire devotes most space to David's masterpiece, the portrait of Marat assassinated.

In 1846, for political reasons as much as because of changes in popular taste, this picture would have been coolly regarded by most of those who viewed it at the exhibition; in praising it, Baudelaire was well aware that he was flying in the face of received opinion. Today, of course, the unpopular view he put forward is the generally accepted one; for many critics, the *Marat* represents the purest achievement of David's art; at the very least, one must allow it to be supremely effective in its own terms as a piece of political iconography, unsurpassed until Picasso painted his *Guernica*. The details, and possibly even their disposition, give the impression of being photographically observed; as Baudelaire says: 'all these particulars are historical, and as real as a Balzac novel; the drama has been caught, still living in all its lamentable horror, and by a strange feat that makes of this painting David's true masterpiece and one of the great curiosities of modern art, it has nothing trivial or ignoble about it'. If we study the picture today, in the Musées royaux at Brussels where it is housed, we can see precisely what Baudelaire meant in calling it 'the sustenance of the strong and the triumph of spiritualism' and in maintaining that 'as cruel as nature, this picture exhales the perfume of the ideal'. The legendary ugliness of Marat's face has been smoothed away, transfigured perhaps in death, but the gash in his chest and the pool of blood on the sheet are faithfully rendered. Marat's nickname, and the title of his newspaper, was 'l'Ami du Peuple', and David has unobtrusively stressed the dead man's solidarity with the poorer classes whose cause he espoused, by such touches as the patched blanket and the crude, unplaned wood of the packing-case that served him as a desk; the inkwell is utilitarian and the turban wound round the journalist's head is of unbleached cotton. These details proclaim Marat's humility, while the bare muscular arms and the composure of his face speak of strength and goodness. The words of Charlotte Corday's letter, clearly legible, are at once a tribute to Marat's reputation for disinterestedness and an implicit denunciation of the treachery of his enemies: 'That I am most unhappy suffices to give me a claim on your benevolence.' The saintly philanthropist wantonly butchered – this is how the picture shows us Marat, and this is how Baudelaire shows us the picture. 'There is something in this work that melts the heart and wrings it too; in the chilly air of this chamber, on these cold walls, around this cold bath-tub that is also a coffin, there hovers a soul.'[18]

With the exception of this short essay on the neoclassical

exhibition, the pieces Baudelaire published in *Le Corsaire-Satan* did little to enhance his reputation as a serious writer, nor could they have done very much to restore his finances; for the normal payment made to contributors to this paper was $7\frac{1}{2}$ centimes a line, rather less than the proverbial penny. Baudelaire succeeded quite well in catching the tone of light-hearted banter characteristic of this kind of popular journalism, but he must have regarded it as a great waste of time and his colleagues soon came to realize that he used the editorial office above all as a *salon de conversation*,[19] a place he could visit whenever he felt the need to exchange ideas and pleasantries with his friends and occasionally, if the moment seemed opportune, to touch them for the odd loan. He continued to send his mother optimistic bulletins; thus, in March 1846: 'Thanks to a series of approaches – some successful, others less so – I find myself in a position to earn a great deal in a short time – but I am *burdened by the debts you know about*, which grow daily more and more shameful. I have to write five pieces for *L'Esprit public, commissioned* – two for *L'Epoque*, two for *La Presse*, and an article for *La Revue Nouvelle*. All that adds up to an immense sum. I have never entertained such bright hopes.'[20] No doubt Baudelaire had paid visits to the offices of all the newspapers and periodicals he names and had talked to the people he met there, who, seeing he was empty-handed, were happy to make him vague promises, if he would kindly let them see what he had to offer next time he called ... But in the end nothing, or almost nothing, got written. The only one of the newspapers he names in his letter that ever published anything of his was *L'Esprit public*, which on April 15th, 1846, found room for an essay entitled 'Conseils aux jeunes littérateurs' which offers in a flippant form some very sound advice to would-be writers, advice from which Baudelaire himself could have greatly profited, had he but been disposed to follow his own maxims: 'In our day, it is necessary to produce quantities; therefore one has to go fast; therefore one has to hasten slowly.' – 'Inspiration is decidedly dependent on regular work.' – 'Never have any creditors; if you like, you may pretend to be in debt, that's the most I will allow you.'[21]

In April 1846 Baudelaire applied for membership of the Société des Gens de Lettres, signing himself 'Baudelaire-Dufays, journalist on the staff of *L'Esprit public* and *Le Corsaire-Satan*, author of two brochures on the 1845 and 1846 art exhibitions'.[22] It was not until May that the second of these two brochures was published, which is perhaps why his admission to the Society was delayed until June. Baudelaire's motives in joining can only have been to tap a useful source of cash loans on the security of works supposedly in process of being composed.[23]

Before writing his *Salon de 1846* Baudelaire had managed, after long delay, to make personal contact with Delacroix. He may have hoped that his flattering reference to the artist, at the beginning of his *Salon de 1845*, as 'decidedly the most original painter of all times, ancient and modern', would have resulted in an invitation to visit from Delacroix; but Delacroix was suspicious of flatterers and, besides, was of a retiring disposition. So his admirer had to wait until February or March 1846 when, using perhaps as an excuse that he needed to talk with the artist before writing his next *Salon*, Baudelaire finally obtained permission to cross the threshold of the studio. Of this first meeting, there is no record in the portions that have survived of Delacroix's diary, but Baudelaire gives some account of it in his third and last *Salon*, that of 1859. He was very civilly received, and probably made a good impression since he was content to listen quietly and take note of what Delacroix had to say. On visits he made the following year (1847) Baudelaire, according to Delacroix's diary entries, talked more freely, expressing views that the master did not always share; moreover the poet embarrassed him on one occasion by asking him to speak to the editor of the *Revue des Deux Mondes* on his behalf, and vexed him on another by borrowing 150 francs.[24] The two men, despite the one's unrivalled insight into the nature of the other's art, had little in common; Delacroix did not think much of several of the writers and musicians Baudelaire admired, privately despised certain artists Baudelaire had praised, and was not always happy about Baudelaire's comments on his own work, complimentary though these were meant to be. Since Delacroix was unquestionably, among all the members of the romantic generation, the man whose genius Baudelaire rated most highly – far more highly than Hugo's, as a passage in the *Salon de 1846* shows very clearly[25] – his failure to break down the artist's reserve must have constituted one of the great disappointments of his life.[26]

When composing his first *Salon* Baudelaire had followed a traditional formula popularized originally by Diderot and by this time almost universally applied. The various exhibits were dealt with according to their categories: religious paintings, portraits, landscapes and so forth; the *salonnier* discussed what he felt were the outstanding achievements of the year in each division. The *Salon de 1846* breaks completely with this convention. Pursuing the same aim as before, to provide the untutored art lover with a useful guide to help him develop his own feeling for art, Baudelaire set himself to compose a concise treatise on the nature of the aesthetic experience and the reasons why the work of certain artists can be seen to have permanent value while others, whatever transitory popularity they may enjoy, will eventually be discovered to lack the qualities that might have allowed their works to endure. The points he makes and the arguments he develops are illustrated, where appropriate, with reference to the pictures in the 1846 exhibition; but essentially the exhibition itself was no more than a pretext for Baudelaire to outline, however sketchily, his own aesthetic system. In his later writings on art he was able to elaborate certain aspects and introduce a few new concepts, but basically he never departed from the general lines he laid down in 1846. Moreover, the conclusions he reached at this stage were applicable, *mutatis mutandis*, not just to the fine arts but equally to literature and music, so that the method he adopted in evaluating painting served him just as well to judge the work of writers and composers.

The first question he suggested the apprentice art lover should ask himself, when faced with any new picture, is not: does this strike me as a faithful replica of reality as I know it? Nor should he try and assess it in accordance with whatever preconceived notions of aesthetic beauty he may have adopted or absorbed. The first question to ask is always: does the picture impress me as the work of a strong individuality, of a powerful *temperament*? The critic's business is 'to require of the artist a fresh, honest expression of his temperament, assisted by whatever aid his mastery of technique can give him. Whoever lacks temperament has no business painting pictures and . . . should accept direction from a painter who can give proof of temperament.'[27]

The term *temperament*, which Zola later fastened on and turned into a catchword, was occasionally replaced, elsewhere in Baudelaire's critical writing, by such near-synonyms as *originality*, or *dominating faculty (faculté maîtresse)*. What he meant was perhaps never better expressed than in the 1861 essay on Wagner: 'An artist, a man truly worthy of this great name, must possess something essentially his own, thanks to which he is what he is and no one else.'[28] What Baudelaire first looks for in an artist and what he implicitly requires the critic to look for, is then neither the skill and care with which he reproduces what he sees, even if it is a portrait that he is painting; nor the charm or dramatic interest he manages to impart to his composition; nor his skill in overcoming the difficulties inherent in his subject; nor, finally, should the critic concentrate on assessing the purely aesthetic qualities of the work, balance, harmony, simplicity, etc. Each and every one of these questions can be raised, but at a later stage. What the critic should start by looking for is some overriding quality or combination of qualities peculiar to the artist himself, which will distinguish his paintings from those of any other artist.

The cardinal importance of this criterion had been recognized by

Baudelaire from the beginning, as can be seen from the way he praised Delacroix in the first of his *Salons* as being 'decidedly the most original painter of all times', and concluded his review of the 1845 exhibition by remarking wryly: 'Everyone paints better and better, sad to say – but as for invention, ideas, temperament, there is no more than there has ever been.'[29] He used the same touchstone when judging literature; in the brief review he published, between the two Salons, of Chennevières's *Contes normands*, he commented: 'While all our modern authors do their best to compose themselves a second-hand soul and temperament, Jean de la Falaise gives us his own, his true self, his definitive self, and has quietly composed an original work.'[30]

The most important sections of the *Salon de 1846* are the first three, in which Baudelaire distinguishes the three elements that go to make up an artist's 'temperament': historical, geographical, and psychological.

Each age, he suggests, has its own general concept of aesthetic beauty, to which no artist can remain indifferent. Not only is it bound to condition him, but he should not try to resist it; he would be untrue to his own nature if he attempted, out of affectation or nostalgia, to escape into the past. And yet how many modern artists commit this treason! Baudelaire had ended his review of the 1845 exhibition with a plea for some painter to arise who could 'show us how great we are, how poetic we are, in our cravats and our polished boots', and he ended his review of the 1846 exhibition with a similar appeal. Balzac had shown how the heroic and epic aspects of modern life could be portrayed in the novel; how long do we have to wait, he asks, before a painter comes along who will do the same thing, working in his own medium? 'Pictorial art has methods and motifs which are as numerous as they are varied; but there is a new element, which is the beauty of modern times.'[31]

Drawing on theories popularized by Mme de Stael at the beginning of the century, Baudelaire analyses in the second chapter of the *Salon de 1846* the difference between artists of the south (those of Italy in particular) and those of the north, a difference due above all to the influence of climate. The great colourists originate in northern Europe, in the Netherlands, England, and that part of France that lies nearer the Channel than the Mediterranean; this is because the sunlight in these regions is all too often filtered through a blanket of mist and cloud. In reaction, or else to compensate for the muted tonalities they find in nature, northern artists cover their canvases with brilliant colour; they *romanticize*; whereas in Italy, nature is so beautiful in itself that painters are content to reproduce what they see, which makes them naturalists.[32]

Finally, there is the psychological element; here, generalizations become more difficult. Given that an individual artist is attuned to his time, given too that he is a colourist, how does one recognize 'temperament' of a high order? Baudelaire gives no direct answer to this question. The nearest he comes to doing so is when, writing about Delacroix and possibly quoting something Delacroix had said to him in the course of their first conversation, he lays it down as a basic principle 'that a picture must above all convey the artist's inmost thought, which dominates his model, as the Creator dominates creation'. This dominant thought will communicate itself through the work of art to the spectator. Thus, Delacroix's *Dante and Virgil crossing the Styx* of 1822 'always leaves a deep impression, the intensity of which increases the farther one stands away from it. Always ready to sacrifice details for the sake of the general effect, and fearing to diminish the vigour of his thought by the effort that would be involved in producing a more distinct, calligraphic outline, he makes fully manifest an elusive originality which is the heart and soul of the subject.'[33]

This is, no doubt, the best that rational discourse can do in delimiting the essence of what we call the greatness or the genius of a particular artist. But Baudelaire himself admitted, towards the beginning of his essay, that rational discourse was perhaps, in the last resort, of little use in this exercise, and that a sonnet or an elegy might serve the purpose better. In other words, it may be that one can only convey the essential quality and quiddity of a work of art by transposing it into another medium, as his friend and master Gautier had occasionally tried to do and as he himself was to do, much more effectively than Gautier, in a number of the poems later included in *Les Fleurs du Mal*; most brilliantly of all, perhaps, in *Les Phares*, which is an ambitious attempt to evoke, stanza by stanza, the style of painting and most characteristic themes of seven outstanding artists, the last of them Delacroix:

> Delacroix, blood-red lake where demons dwell,
> And dark green fir-trees cast a dark green shade;
> Beneath a sullen sky strange fanfares swell
> And die, a stifled Weber serenade.[34]

84

VII

THE REVOLUTIONARY

Over the six months following the publication of his *Salon de 1846*
Baudelaire seems to have been principally occupied with putting the
finishing touches to the one and only work of fiction he ever
completed, the story entitled *La Fanfarlo*. We do not know for
certain when he started work on it, but there are good reasons for
supposing that he drafted a preliminary version as early as 1843–4. If
it is true, as was stated by Baudelaire's first editors, that he originally
offered the story to the *Revue de Paris*, then *La Fanfarlo* must have
been completed and ready for publication in 1845, since the *Revue de
Paris* ceased publication after its issue of June 14th, 1845. *La
Fanfarlo* may well have been one of the three 'books' he alludes to in a
letter to his mother written at the beginning of 1845, as being almost
completed, and needing only twelve days' uninterrupted work to be
in a state to be sent to a publisher or a magazine editor. 'To be sure,'
he added, 'I would not boast of such a *tour de force* if the said volumes
had not been started ages ago, so much so that the paper has yellowed
. . .'[1] In the end he had to wait until January 1847 before seeing *La
Fanfarlo* in print, in the *Bulletin de la Société des Gens de Lettres*.

   La Fanfarlo belongs to that hybrid variety, the long short story:
longer than the average Maupassant *conte*, shorter even than a short
novel like Constant's *Adolphe*. Its dimensions are comparable to
those of the various component tales in the collection entitled *Scènes
de la vie privée* with which Balzac had inaugurated his career as a
serious writer in 1830. In other respects too *La Fanfarlo* betrays the
influence of Balzac, which is hardly surprising, given Baudelaire's
well-attested admiration for the only nineteenth-century novelist he
appears to have read with unalloyed pleasure.[2] The leisurely
presentation of the main characters, the readiness with which he
seizes on opportunities to interrupt the narrative in order to
intercalate some general observation, the strictly contemporary
setting, his attitude to the war between the sexes, even the mildly
amused tone with which the events are related – all this could have
been imitated directly from Balzac; at the very least it provides
evidence of the attentiveness with which the disciple observed the

master's example and absorbed his method. In addition, the plot of
La Fanfarlo bears a superficial resemblance to the third part of
Balzac's novel *Béatrix* which Baudelaire could have read, under the
title *Les Petits manèges d'une femme vertueuse*, in *Le Messager*
where it appeared in instalments between December 24th, 1844, and
January 23rd, 1845. In both stories a young man undertakes to
seduce the mistress of the heroine's husband (Béatrix in Balzac's
novel, the actress-dancer La Fanfarlo in Baudelaire's story) as a
means of effecting a reconciliation between erring husband and
betrayed wife. The differences between the two situations, not to
speak of the two sequels, are however at least as striking as the
resemblances, and it is by no means certain that Baudelaire drew on
Balzac's novel to construct the scenario of his own story;[3] at the very
most, *Béatrix* might have provided Baudelaire with a starting-point.

From the point of view of the biographer, what gives *La Fanfarlo*
its chief interest is the self-portrait Baudelaire offers us in his
description of the appearance and character of the hero of the story,
Samuel Cramer. The physical similarities are unmistakable.
'Samuel's brow is noble, unlined, his eyes gleam like two drops of
black coffee, his nose twitches in a teasing, sarcastic manner, his
sensuous lips curl impudently, his square chin is borne arrogantly,
and he wears his hair in a pretentiously Raphaelesque style.'[4] By the
time Baudelaire came to publish *La Fanfarlo*, the floating,
'raphaelesque' hair that the portraitist Deroy had shown gracing his
head was no longer to be seen. The onset of alopecia, a side-effect of
syphilis, had caused him to have it all cut short to disguise the fact
that much of it was falling out, a shaven skull being less unsightly
than bald patches. This was how Gautier remembered him at their
first meeting: 'his glossy black hair was very closely cropped; this
hair, combed forward in regular points over the dazzlingly white
brow, gave him the appearance of wearing a Saracen's helmet.'[5]

After this complacent physical description we are given a moral
portrait, somewhat less flattering, in fact quite merciless, but equally
valid for the author as he saw himself.

He was at once a great do-nothing, a melancholy seeker after fame,
and a man of merit dogged by ill-luck; for rarely has he had in the
course of his life any ideas that were not half-baked. The sun of
idleness, for ever radiating inside his brain, vaporizes and
incinerates that half portion of talent that God has allotted him.
Among all the semi-geniuses that I have known in our exhausting
Paris life, Samuel was more than any other the man to muff his
finest conceptions; a morbid, whimsical creature, whose poetic
gift shone much more in his person than in his works and who, in

the small hours, brooding over a blazing coal fire with the clock ticking on the mantelpiece, always appeared to me as the god of impotence – a modern, hermaphroditic god, whose impotence is of such enormous, colossal proportions as to be truly epic![6]

Baudelaire's attitude to Samuel Cramer, his own reflection in the distorting mirror of his own self-doubt, is, as one of the critics of *La Fanfarlo* has said, 'ambiguous and complex – distant, amused, critical, mocking, indulgent, uneasy, condemnatory',[7] and even after this introductory sketch, the deflationary confession continues with countless little ironical brush-strokes: 'His ardour when he had been a believer was matched only by the passion he put into his atheism.' – 'When he discovered he owed a paltry 20,000 francs,' he said to himself delightedly: "How sad, how lamentable the fate of a genius in debt to the tune of a million!" '[8]

As the story progresses, Samuel is deservedly humiliated by the woman he set out to trick; she takes her revenge by enslaving him. 'His punishment was the fruit of his sin. He had feigned passion often enough; now he was compelled to make acquaintance with it; but it was not the calm, gentle, strong love one may feel for an honest girl, rather it was the terrible, devastating, shameful love, the unhealthy passion a courtesan can inspire. Samuel came to know all the tortures of jealousy and the grief and depression we sink into when we realize we are the victim of an incurable, constitutional disease – in short, all the horrors of that marriage of vice called concubinage.'[9] Here again, right at the end of the story, the confessional note cannot be missed. La Fanfarlo in her final incarnation has taken on the alluring, demonic form of Jeanne Duval.

But in spite of this sombre dénouement, one has the impression that for the most part, the autobiographical elements in this sketch are more applicable to Baudelaire as he was before 1844, leading a carefree life and taking little thought for the future, than to Baudelaire as he was in 1847 when *La Fanfarlo* was published. By this time the spruce dandy of yore had lost most of his fine feathers. Charles Toubin, first introduced to him by Champfleury in the Café de la Rotonde at a time when 'he had published nothing, I think, but his *Salon* and a few scattered articles in *Le Corsaire*', noticed little of the fussy dresser left in Baudelaire, though his linen was still spotless and his boots clean. He was wearing, Toubin remembered, 'a red cravat – though he was not a republican – rather loosely tied, and one of those sack overcoats that had been in fashion some while back, which he found useful to dissemble the gauntness of his frame'.[10] After 1846 he could be observed in the streets wearing a workman's overall on top of a pair of still elegant black trousers with shoe-straps;

a peculiar costume which might have been taken as a sign of a partial conversion to populism ('artisan above, dandy below', as one wit put it[11]), though it is unlikely to have been adopted for any other reason than that Baudelaire could not afford to replace his worn-out clothes with anything more elegant.

The year 1847 was one of increasing hardship and deepening despondency for Baudelaire. He had almost given up writing, apart, of course, from the occasional poem he was still adding to the hoard from which, in due course, he would extract the jewels that now glitter in *Les Fleurs du Mal*. His debts continued to mount and, following in this respect the example of Balzac, he was constantly on the move in the hope of throwing his creditors off the scent; sometimes, on days when bills fell due that he could not pay, he avoided the debt-collectors by begging a few nights' hospitality from one or other of his large circle of acquaintances. Toubin, who was sharing rooms with his brother at this time, was called on occasionally to render him this service, and records that 'more than one of the pieces in *Les Fleurs du Mal* were, if not composed, at least put on paper in our lodgings. The poems were habitually made up by Baudelaire in cafés or while walking down the street.'[12] Toubin goes on to say that he never ordered anything but white wine in a café, and would never accept anything stronger. His circumstances were such that often enough he found himself without the price of a meal. In this extremity, he would ask Toubin solicitously whether he had anyone dining with him that evening. If the answer was no, Baudelaire would generously offer to 'keep him company'. However, Toubin never took this polite sponging amiss since, going around with Baudelaire, he found himself introduced to a host of illustrious figures whom he would never have met socially otherwise: Gérard de Nerval, Théophile Gautier, the sculptor Préault and Frédérick Lemaître, the actor, with whom Baudelaire would sometimes have a game of dominoes in the café adjoining the Théâtre de la Porte-Saint-Martin.

This bohemian, hand-to-mouth existence continued through the year, with little or nothing achieved that might rescue him from the morass of petty debts into which he was sliding. He spoke to his mother, in a letter written on December 4th, 1847, of two important studies, commissioned eight months previously, which he had still not completed. One was a history of the development of sculpture, the other a history of the art of caricature; the latter had in fact been announced as forthcoming on a fly-sheet of the *Salon de 1845*. These two treatises, which he could write, he says, off the top of his head, would bring in 600 francs, enough to meet his most pressing obligations, but no more. Then he returns to an old pipedream.

'Come the New Year, I shall start on a new line, that is, the creation of works of pure imagination – the Novel. This is neither the time nor the place to expatiate to you on the gravity, the beauty, the infinite ramifications of that art, but since we are on the subject of earnings, I will content myself with saying that, *good or bad, there's a market for everything*; all one needs is assiduity.'[3]

No doubt Baudelaire was speaking in all seriousness here; only by turning to the novel could he hope to retrieve his financial situation. And after all, why not? His friends – Gautier, Champfleury – had shown it could be done; and whatever one might think of the current best-selling writers of fiction, the great Balzac, still active, still adding to his long list of masterpieces, provided an irrefutable argument in favour of 'the gravity, the beauty, the infinite ramifications of that art'. Baudelaire was well aware of the disdain with which so many of his colleagues – including Sainte-Beuve – regarded the productions of the popular novelists of the hour, like Eugène Sue and Paul Féval; but he did not entirely share it. Such writers had a certain talent, as he pointed out in his *Conseils aux jeunes littérateurs*, which, however superficial, could not be sneered away; it worked, since people bought and read their books in vast numbers, and to inveigh against it was a waste of time. If his friends thought that their writings, being superior to these pulp novels, ought to be accorded more attention, all they needed to do was to prove they had as much talent in their sphere as Sue displayed in his. 'Arouse as much interest, using new methods; deploy an equal or superior force in the opposite direction; double, triple, quadruple the dose till you reach as strong a concentration; then you'll lose the right to complain about the bourgeois, because the bourgeois will be right behind you. Until that happens, *vae victis!*, woe to the vanquished; for in strength, which is the supreme justice, lies truth.'[4]

This passage, which he was to echo a little later in the notorious dedication of his *Salon de 1846* 'to the bourgeois' ('You are the majority, both in numbers and intelligence; therefore you represent strength, which is justice') shows Baudelaire in an unexpected light, as a defender of market values, even where literature was concerned. His argument was that there was no point in writing for a non-existent public; and, if one had one's eye on the 'glittering prizes', very little point in writing for a strictly limited elite. Popularity, with the financial rewards that went with it, was proof enough that one was writing 'for one's time'; those who cannot impose their works on the new public, by educating it to want something better than cheap thrills and empty entertainment, are in no position to complain that the purveyors of 'commercialized literature' are hogging the market.

In time, Baudelaire was to change his mind on this question, and presented a directly contrary view in one of the prose poems he published in *La Presse* in August 1862. The poet gives his dog an exquisite perfume to sniff; the animal recoils, barking, and his master reproaches him, saying: 'Ah! miserable dog, if I had offered you a shovelful of dung, you would have nuzzled it delightedly, perhaps even devoured it. In this, unworthy companion of my sad life, you resemble the public, to whom one should never present delicate essences which exasperate it, but instead, choice scraps of ordure.'[15] But in the 1840s, before disillusion set in, he was still persuaded that a writer could become a power in the land, rich and respected, while making no concessions to the corrupt taste of the time, simply by the force of his personality conveyed through his works. Could this be true even of a poet? Could poetry ever prove as lucrative as the *roman-feuilleton*? Baudelaire maintained (in the same essay, *Conseils aux jeunes littérateurs*) that it could, *given time*. 'Poetry is one of the arts that yields the highest return; only it is the kind of investment that pays dividends only in the long term — though they are magnificent when they fall due.'[16] Even in a purely material sense, one cannot fault Baudelaire here. *Les Fleurs du Mal* must have earned far more for its various publishers, down to the present day, than *Les Mystères de Paris*. But Sue was able to enjoy the proceeds of his work during his lifetime; Baudelaire's efforts profited only his heirs, distant collateral relatives whom he never even knew.

In any case his New Year resolution, to start writing novels, would have been better made at the beginning of almost any year rather than 1848; but how was he to know that 1848, a year of revolution, class conflict, election campaigns and street-battles, would kill the market for every kind of literature except political journalism? he would have needed better powers of divination than most of his contemporaries. To be sure, he was responsive enough to the current unease in the last year of the 'bourgeois monarchy' to sense that changes were on the way. Delacroix, recording a visit from him on March 2nd, 1847, noted that the conversation had touched on 'the necessity of a revolution. He (Baudelaire) is struck by the prevalent immorality. He believes the time is coming when the rascals will be held in check by honest folk.'[17] Whether this could be interpreted as a prognostication of the events of the following year depends entirely on who Baudelaire judged were the 'rascals' and who the 'honest folk'; Delacroix does not specify.

Hardly anyone in France, in reality, expected the kind of revolution that was accomplished in February 1848, nor that it should occur at precisely that time. Experience had shown, for one thing, that revolutions never happened in mid-winter. For another, the political crisis did not seem all that dangerous. The parliamentary opposition was hoping to get rid of Guizot's ministry and to effect some reform of the electoral law; few could have supposed that the action of the Minister of the Interior in prohibiting a reformist banquet due to be held in the Champs-Elysées would precipitate the downfall of the monarchy. There was an angry exchange in the Chamber between the minister and Odilon Barrot, leader of the opposition, following which Barrot summoned a meeting of left-wing deputies at his house. Lamartine, one of the principal anti-government orators, could not be present, but when informed that the majority had voted timidly in favour of abandoning the demonstration, he proclaimed that even if the Place de la Concorde, where the rally was to take place, was empty the following day and all his fellow deputies stayed away, he would march on his own, 'taking my shadow behind me'.

In fact, he was far from finding himself alone. The great square, where the guillotine had stood during the First Revolution, was packed with angry workers and excited students, among whom rode mounted police to prevent the formation of compact gatherings. This was on Tuesday, February 22nd. Baudelaire, scenting battle, had gone along as an observer, and had stationed himself, together with Courbet and two other friends, behind the parapet of a little garden adjoining the square. Suddenly a group of rioters debouched hurriedly from a side-street, hotly pursued by a detachment of municipal guardsmen with fixed bayonets. One of the fugitives, who was unarmed, dodged round a tree, slipped up, fell, and was immediately pinned to the ground with a bayonet through his chest. Horrified, Baudelaire and Courbet set off for the offices of Girardin's newspaper *La Presse* to report the atrocity.

Baudelaire and Courbet had not known one another very long. Charles Toubin, a fellow countryman of Courbet (they both came from the Franche-Comté) claimed to have introduced the two some time in 1847 in the Café de la Rotonde, a favourite spot for the artist to meet his friends. It was from this same café near the Ecole de Médecine in the Latin Quarter that on the second day of the revolution (February 23rd), Baudelaire joined up with Toubin and Champfleury to find out what was happening. There was a rumour that fighting was going on in the Saint-Denis district, so they crossed the Seine and then, hearing sounds of firing coming from the Place du Châtelet, hastened in that direction. The barricades they kept encountering forced them to follow a circuitous route, but eventually they reached the Boulevard du Temple, where they learned that the King had dismissed Guizot and that a new ministry was being formed. Everyone seemed delighted, as though the main objective had been reached, and joined in singing the Marseillaise and the Hymne des Girondins. Thinking the commotion would now die down, the friends dispersed, though not before Baudelaire had, once again, invited himself to supper that evening with Toubin. The latter found him, as he later reported, 'enchanted with what he had seen over the past two days. The opening act in the drama he had found most interesting, though he felt dissatisfied with the conclusion, reckoning that the curtain had fallen too soon. I had never seen him so cheerful and, for a man unused to walking, so lightfoot and tireless. His eyes were sparkling.'[18]

The curtain, as we know, had fallen only on the first act, and was to be raised almost immediately. In the interval, Baudelaire had made up his mind to abandon the passive role of spectator and to take an active part as a militant. The following day (February 24th) Toubin saw him again standing behind a half-built barricade, armed with a double-barrelled gun and wearing round his waist a cartridge belt of yellow leather; he had joined with the insurgents in raiding a gunsmith's shop. Nor was Toubin the only one to see him thus accoutred. Another was his old friend Jules Buisson, who hailed him across the street to know the meaning of this martial panoply. Baudelaire walked over in great excitement. '"I've just fired my first shot!" he exclaimed. I smiled, looking at his brand-new gun. "Not for the republic, surely?" He did not vouchsafe an answer, but went on shouting his refrain: "General Aupick must be shot!"'[19] The name would not have meant anything to the majority of the insurgents who surrounded him, but since Aupick held an important army command in Paris, the suggestion, though wild, was not totally pointless; incipient revolutions before now had been crushed by the use of the regular troops. One may safely assume, however, that Baudelaire saw the disturbance as a heaven-sent opportunity for Hamlet to be revenged at last on Claudius.

Buisson's ironic remark: 'Not for the republic, surely?' shows he felt the same astonishment as all his friends that Baudelaire should suddenly have plunged into the fray on the side of the revolutionaries. Ernest Prarond was just as taken aback as Buisson, remembering how, in the days when the 'Norman school' was flourishing, 'Baudelaire did not simply disdain politics, he professed a positive contempt for it; neither he, nor any of us, felt anything but pity for the inferior art practised by demagogues. Consequently the excitement my friend exhibited amazed us all.'[20] The volte-face has continued to puzzle all those who have written on Baudelaire's political evolution, and who never fail to draw attention to the passage at the start of the *Salon de 1846* where Baudelaire declared that whenever he saw a policeman beating up a republican in the street he was filled with profound satisfaction and felt like urging the guardian of the law to even greater brutality. How is it possible to reconcile such retrograde sentiments with Baudelaire's behaviour less than two years later, when he joined the republicans on the barricades in their struggle against the forces of law and order?

Was it from sheer irresponsibility, which would argue a profound political nihilism? Certain reflections he put on paper at a rather later date can be cited in support of this view: 'I can well understand a man's abandoning one cause to find out what it was like to serve a different one'; and again: 'Among the rights of man about which there has been such a lot of talk recently, one right has been forgotten – and yet its establishment is in everybody's interest: the right to contradict oneself.'[21] There was that in Baudelaire which drove him always to swim against the current. In the years immediately preceding the 1848 Revolution, when sympathy for the downtrodden proletariat was much in fashion, to flaunt such reactionary opinions as he did was little short of scandalous, and Baudelaire took great delight in scandalizing his contemporaries. Maurice Barrès tells how, when Leconte de Lisle, brimming with utopian schemes for a juster social order, first met Baudelaire in 1846 he was puzzled and not a little shocked; Baudelaire's 'aristocratic prejudices were bound to offend the members of the little set where Leconte de Lisle, Ménard and Thalès Bernard communed in the generous and absurd spirit abroad during the closing years of Louis-Philippe's reign, when Paris was seething with revolutionary fervour'.[22] At a time when all the earnest pink-cheeked intellectuals were busy denouncing the soulless reign of the bankers and captains of industry, the 'imp of the perverse' in Baudelaire drove him to proclaim exactly contrary opinions.

There may be some truth in this, but at the same time it would be a mistake to exaggerate Baudelaire's political inconsistency. In February 1848 he joined a people in arms; this was a working-class revolution, whereas before there had been nothing but half-hearted talk and half-baked theories, and Baudelaire had no time for armchair socialists. In the same year as he met Leconte de Lisle and shocked his genteel left-wing sentiments with his 'aristocratic prejudices', he was also reading Pierre Dupont's newly published *Chant des ouvriers* which still had the power to move him when he re-read it five years later:

We had been waiting so long for a little vigorous, authentic poetry! Whatever party one belongs to, whatever prejudices one has imbibed from early years, it is impossible not to be moved by the spectacle of these disease-ridden masses who breathe the dust of the factory floor, who choke down fibres of cotton, are contaminated with white-lead, mercury, and all the other poisonous chemicals necessary for the manufacture of luxury articles, who sleep in verminous hovels where the humblest and loftiest virtues coexist with the most hardened vices and the worst that our prisons can spew; these sighing, languishing multitudes to whom 'earth owes its wonders'; who feel 'a red, impetuous blood course through their veins', who cast a long, melancholy look at the dappled shade in the great parks, and who, for consolation and sufficient comfort, intone at the top of their voices the heartening chorus: 'Let us love each other, brothers!'[23]

At no point in his life did Baudelaire despise the working class; they were the damned of the earth and from the depths of his different damnation he could feel a profound affinity. But of the self-appointed 'leaders of the people' he was for the most part deeply suspicious; for such men (and women, for they included George Sand) his aversion predated the revolution and remained as strong as ever as it followed its ill-fated course, as he watched them argue and prevaricate until the high hopes of February foundered in the blood-bath of June.

The indispensable key to his attitude is to be found in a text which no magazine editor would consent to publish during his lifetime and which consequently remained unknown until it appeared in the posthumous (1869) edition of his *Petits poèmes en prose*. The opening lines of *Assommons les pauvres!* (*Let's beat up the poor!*) run as follows:

I had shut myself up in my room for a fortnight, surrounded by the kind of books that were popular at that time (this was some sixteen or seventeen years ago): treatises on the art of making the nations healthy, wealthy and wise in ten easy lessons. I had in this manner digested – ingurgitated would be a better word – all the elucubrations of those contractors for the public weal, including those whose remedy is that the poor should all accept slavery and those who preach to them that they are monarchs unjustly deprived of their kingdom. It is scarcely surprising that I had reached a condition bordering on vertigo or addle-headedness.[24]

The implied sneer at the works of the doctrinaire socialists who provided the shaky theoretical foundations of the 1848 Revolution cannot be missed; if Baudelaire's account of their teachings is deliberately distorted, it is still recognizable and, besides, the clue provided by the dating ('some sixteen or seventeen years ago') is in itself sufficient, for *Assommons les pauvres!* was written probably about 1864–5.

The rest of the prose poem tells how, consumed with a raging thirst, 'for inordinate indulgence in bad books engenders a proportionate craving for fresh air and cool drinks', Baudelaire left his lodgings and was about to turn into a tavern when, dumbly importuned by a decrepit pauper standing outside, he acted on a sudden impulse and instead of giving the fellow the few pence he expected, threw himself on him without warning and began cudgelling him mercilessly. To his delight and relief the beggar retaliated with spirit, blacked both the poet's eyes and knocked out several of his teeth. The fable ends with Baudelaire scrambling to his feet, pulling out his purse and dividing the contents with his assailant, satisfied in his own mind at having established, if in so outrageous a fashion, that the poor are capable of securing justice for themselves without any help from utopian dreamers whose remedies, if applied, would prove more devitalizing than the social evils they are proposing to abolish.

Baudelaire's scepticism of the efficacy of middle-class do-goodism was reinforced by what he saw and heard at the election meetings preceding the vote for the Constituent Assembly in April. One of the socialist candidates – actually an old friend, Alphonse Esquiros – began his speech by mouthing the customary tirades against 'the infamous Guizot and the infamous Louis-Philippe', and continued by 'painting an eloquent, dismal picture of the sad condition of the workers'. His audience was choking with emotion by this time; then suddenly Baudelaire rose to his feet to ask Esquiros, 'with the grimace habitual to him at such moments, whether the rights of small traders did not appear to him just as sacred as those of the working class'. Knowing that his audience almost certainly included a number of the local shopkeepers, Esquiros felt obliged to assent, and was about to pick up the thread of his discourse when Baudelaire interrupted again. 'Since we are on the subject of commercial interests', he asked, 'may I seek your views on free trade, that extremely important question which must be regarded as the keystone of the social edifice?' This time Esquiros was completely floored, turned red and stammered that 'he had not had the time to study this question, the importance of which he fully appreciated, but that if he was returned by the electors he would devote to it all the attention the problem demanded'; after which, thoroughly discomfited, he stepped down from the platform, leaving Baudelaire free to exercise his deflationary tactics on the next speaker.[25]

The only prominent socialist active in Paris during the Revolution for whom Baudelaire felt any respect was Pierre-Joseph Proudhon, who attracted him precisely because Proudhon differed radically from the flock of cloudy-minded utopians who were darkening the intellectual sky at the time. The questions he is reported having put to Esquiros indicate a close acquaintance with Proudhon's *Système des contradictions économiques* of 1846, and some of the socio-religious poems that Baudelaire was writing in 1848–9 (notably *Les Litanies de Satan* and *La Rançon*) show signs of being based on ideas found in Proudhon's book.[26] He had some limited personal contact with Proudhon during the months of revolutionary turmoil, having first met him by pure chance in the offices of *Le Représentant du Peuple* where he had gone in search of someone else. Intrigued by Proudhon's manner, and having for once a few francs in his pocket, Baudelaire suggested they should dine together that same evening in a restaurant in the Rue Vivienne. 'Proudhon chattered away incessantly, amplifying his ideas in quite violent language, confiding to me, a complete stranger, all his plans and projects, and firing off, apparently impromptu, salvo after salvo of amusing comments.' He ate the plain though copious meal at great speed and, as though to apologize for his greediness, observed gaily to Baudelaire: 'You are surprised to see me eat so heartily, citizen; my appetite functions in accordance with the great things I mean to achieve.' Baudelaire could not be quite sure whether, in saying this, Proudhon was speaking jocularly or in all seriousness.[27] When their dinner was over Baudelaire, as host, rang for the waiter, but Proudhon pulled out his own purse to settle the bill, paying, however, much to Baudelaire's astonishment, only for his own share. 'Going Dutch' was a novelty at the time; perhaps Proudhon judged that for one man to treat another was undemocratic.

Baudelaire's enthusiasm for the revolutionary cause evaporated very quickly, as soon, in fact, as he realized how unlikely it was that the nation as a whole would ratify any radical change in the status quo. All that had happened was that a monarchy had been replaced by a republic; but, once the dust had settled, the men of property would regain their hold, and those who might have founded a new social order, like Proudhon or Blanqui, would find themselves in prison or in exile. Nevertheless he did what he could in the early months to help the men of the left in their struggle to stay in power. He persuaded Champfleury and Toubin to join with him in founding a republican news-sheet, to be called *Le Salut public*. Toubin did not much like the name but Baudelaire insisted on having it because it recalled the famous or infamous but all-powerful Comité de Salut public of 1793–4. 'Baudelaire admired the (French) Revolution as he admired everything that was violent and abnormal and for that reason,' Toubin later confessed, 'I felt more fear than affection for him.'[28] They printed 400 copies of the first issue on February 27th. Criers were easily found among the hundreds of unemployed, but with one accord they decamped with the proceeds. There was just enough money in the kitty for a second issue, dated March 1st. This time Baudelaire, wearing his workman's overalls, walked the Rue Saint-André-des-Arts selling the paper, while a woman supporter, disguised as a working girl, did her best to dispose of the rest of the issue in another neighbourhood. They returned to the 'offices' (a rented room on the second floor of the Café Turlot) with 15 francs between them – not enough for a third issue, so it was decided to spend it all on a banquet to commemorate the launching and almost simultaneous demise of *Le Salut public*.

With the abrogation of the old laws requiring official registration of new press titles, a great variety of newspapers were now in circulation, many of which lasted little longer than *Le Salut public*. In April Baudelaire got himself appointed secretary to *La Tribune nationale*, a relatively long-lived paper edited by an economist, Jules Schmeltz, who was well thought of by Proudhon and Girardin. It had been founded, like so many others, as a propaganda sheet in view of the approaching elections, and even if there was some wavering in its political line at the start, it finally came down in favour of left-wing candidates, proposing in its issue of June 2nd a list that included Proudhon, Leroux, and several members of the working class. The view once taken that *La Tribune nationale* was essentially a conservative paper is no longer tenable,[29] and there is consequently no need to suppose that Baudelaire's collaboration with it implies that at this date he had already shifted his political allegiances.

In any case his activity during the ultimate workers' insurrection of June 23rd–24th, crushed with much bloodshed by troops led by General Cavaignac, proves conclusively not merely that his sympathies lay with the poorer classes but that he was prepared to risk his own skin in defending their cause. Our knowledge of his personal participation in the fighting derives from the narrative of his friend Le Vavasseur who, together with Chennevières, had been detailed to help guard the Louvre during the emergency. They were allowed to leave once the news of the 'pacification' of the Faubourg Saint-Antoine came through, and set off together in search of further information. Heading first for the Café de Foy, they saw coming towards them down the street an oddly assorted couple: Baudelaire, in a state of feverish excitement, and the worker-poet Pierre Dupont, who in contrast seemed phlegmatic and almost jaunty. Having met, they all entered the café together. 'I had never seen Baudelaire in such a mood,' Le Vavasseur relates. 'He was perorating, declaiming, boasting, fidgeting to rush off to martyrdom. "They have just arrested De Flotte,'[30] he said. "Was it because they could smell gunpowder on his hands? Smell mine!" And then socialist tirades, the apotheosis of the bankruptcy of society, etc.'[31] His friends, including Dupont, were seriously alarmed, not that Baudelaire was losing his reason, but that he might lose his liberty; at this point in the game, to indulge in loud expressions of revolutionary fervour in a public place was almost to invite arrest and court martial.

The 'June days' effectively ended whatever chance there might have been of establishing a different social order in France. On November 4th the new constitution was promulgated, and on December 10th Louis-Napoleon Bonaparte was elected first President of the Republic by an overwhelming majority of votes. Three years later he overthrew the constitution by force. Once more Baudelaire took to the barricades, but this time the fighting was on a small scale; the workers had no more stomach for it, and the middle-class republicans were few in number and soon rounded up. The only evidence we have that he participated in the brief struggle is an entry in the autobiographical *Mon coeur mis à nu* (*My Heart Laid Bare*) for which he began making notes in 1859: 'My fury at the *coup d'état*. How many shots were fired at me! Another Bonaparte, the shame of it!'[32] The ease with which the Second Republic was overthrown strengthened Baudelaire's contempt for the passive mass of the people (an attitude which needs to be carefully distinguished from the solidarity he felt with the struggling proletariat, the revolutionary in arms). 'All in all, at the bar of history and of the French people, it must be accounted one of Napoleon III's great glories that he demonstrated how anyone who chooses can, by making sure of the telegraphic service and the state printing press, govern a great nation. They are fools who think that such things can be accomplished without the consent of the people.'[33]

Outstanding among such 'fools' would have been Hugo, no doubt. But although Baudelaire judged Hugo to be quite wrong in supposing Louis-Napoleon to have seized power against the will of the majority, he did not entirely condemn the stand he took in opposing the usurper on December 2nd, 1851, and in maintaining this opposition subsequently from safe refuges in Brussels and the Channel Islands. When in 1860 Baudelaire was preparing his important essay on the exiled poet for Eugène Crépet's series *Les Poètes français*, he warned the editor that he would not be touching on political issues. 'For one thing,' he went on, 'I doubt if it is possible to mention the political satires [*Napoléon-le-Petit* and *Les Châtiments*] even in a derogatory way; and the fact is that if I were to speak of them, whatever my views on the stupidity of political diatribes, I would have to side with Hugo rather than with the Bonaparte of the *coup d'état*.'[34]

The abrupt extinction of the Second Republic by this *coup d'état* left Baudelaire disillusioned and disinclined to take any further interest in matters of public policy. Writing to Ancelle on March 5th, 1852, he mentioned that he had deliberately abstained from voting in the elections for the Legislative Chamber a week previously, and explained his decision somewhat cryptically as follows: 'December 2nd had the effect of *physically depoliticizing* me. . . . Had I cast my vote, it could only have been for myself. Perhaps the future belongs to the *déclassés*?'[35] Nevertheless, Baudelaire did not entirely shut his eyes to political developments under the Second Empire. 'I have convinced myself a score of times,' he told Nadar, 'that I had no further interest in politics, and whenever a crisis arises, I am consumed with passion and curiosity.'[36] But the passion and curiosity remained a private matter. Never again was he to be a militant; and he scrupulously avoided all public pronouncements on political or social issues, except in so far as he allowed his ideas to percolate, heavily disguised, in a few allegorical prose poems.[37]

However, he did intend there to be a chapter in *Mon coeur mis à nu* on what he calls his 'intoxication of 1848', and in the jottings that survive we have some hints as to what conclusions he might have drawn had he ever written the book. In the cold light of reason, he asks himself what motives he may have had to have acted as he did, and lists them thus:

> 'The thirst for vengeance.
> 'The *natural* pleasure taken in acts of destruction.
> 'Literary intoxication (reminiscences of my reading).'

Referring to the great working-class demonstration of May 15th, which came near to inaugurating a form of communist rule, he comments: 'Still the appetite for destruction; a lawful appetite, if all that is natural is lawful.' As for the street battles in June, what did they prove? 'The madness of the common people and the madness of the middle classes. The natural love of crime.'[38]

Interpreting these admittedly ambiguous and truncated reflections, one cannot help being struck by the threefold repetition of the word *natural*, underlined on its first occurrence. Quite recently, Baudelaire had 'discovered' the early nineteenth-century political philosopher Joseph de Maistre and had conceived a violent admiration for his teaching, considering him 'the greatest genius of our time – a seer'.[39] Following De Maistre, Baudelaire saw nature as being opposed not just to art, but to civilization also and to the working of the Divine Spirit on earth. Thus, the proposition advanced here dubitatively: 'if all that is natural is lawful', is not one that he would subscribe to without serious reservations. 'Woman is natural, that is to say abominable,' is one of the many outrageous anti-feminist sallies to be found in *Mon coeur mis à nu*; the sentence continues: 'that is why she is always vulgar, the contrary of the Dandy.'[40] The notorious 'eulogy of make-up' which he included in his essay on Constantin Guys of 1863 amounts to an expression of approval for any and every artifice designed to disguise and metamorphose the natural woman.[41] As for dandyism, it was precisely because it was an unnatural ethic, a controlled and disciplined suppression of natural impulses, that Baudelaire made it the core of his personal philosophy. 'Can the Dandy be imagined addressing the people,' he asked elsewhere in *Mon coeur mis à nu*, 'save to insult it?'[42] The dandy yields to no natural emotion, however generous.

Revolt is natural, therefore abominable even though generous; hence its origins are satanic. The three poems Baudelaire included in *Les Fleurs du Mal* under the title *Révolte* are, besides being blasphemous attacks on established religion, all susceptible to fairly precise political interpretations: they are either a plea for revolutionary action (*Le Reniement de Saint-Pierre*), a dramatization of the class war (*Abel et Caïn*), or else a celebration of Lucifer as the patron of outlaws, conspirators, and terrorists (*Les Litanies de Satan*, which Swinburne thought 'one of the noblest lyrics ever written; the sound of it between wailing and triumph, as it were the blast blown by the trumpets of a brave army in irretrievable retreat'[43]). The implication is that behind every attempt to overthrow the established order there is always the Serpent that whispered to Eve, the Anti-Christ, the Devil.

But that does not mean one should not side with the Devil. The unique dipolarity of Baudelaire's thought means that what is damnable, considered from one viewpoint, becomes hallowed, seen from another, and that these two viewpoints can be adopted by the poet practically simultaneously. Baudelaire wondered about his 'intoxication' in 1848, analysed it, but did not condemn it outright, even when reconsidering it in the light of his reading of the arch-reactionary Joseph de Maistre. Along with thousands of others he had been able to give rein, for a few months, to his 'lawful', natural, satanic lust for revenge, revolt, and destruction. The *coup d'état* meant the enthronement of 'unlawful', unnatural but divine authority, and Baudelaire does not hesitate to speak of the 'providentiality' of Napoleon III.

By the zest with which he flung himself into public disorder in the name of democracy, as well as by the masochistic fervour with which he acquiesced in the re-establishment of order under an autocracy, Baudelaire presents, in schematic, exaggerated, almost caricatural form, the spiritual history of the men of his generation to which Leconte de Lisle and Flaubert also belonged, among many less well remembered. After 1851, republicanism acquired for a period the stigma of criminality, and Baudelaire acquiesced in this too. 'Myself', he wrote proudly, 'when I consent to be a republican, I commit evil knowingly.' He was not far from regarding republicanism as an aspect of original sin. 'We have all of us got the spirit of republicanism in our veins, as we have the pox in our bones; we are democratized and syphilized.'[44] Just as syphilis was the punishment for the sin of sexual promiscuity, so republicanism, an infection equally incurable, was to be regarded as punishment for the crime of social promiscuity, of prostituting oneself to the masses.

In 1871 there was a fresh working-class revolt, crushed even more mercilessly by the forces of reaction. How would Baudelaire have reacted to the Commune, had he lived to the age of fifty, retaining health and strength? There are at least even chances that he would have joined with Courbet in lending it his active support and with Vallès in manning the barricades in its defence.

VIII

AN ELECTIVE AFFINITY

Exactly three weeks after the crushing of the working-class insurrection of June 1848 in which Baudelaire played an active though ineffective part, he published, in an ephemeral journal called *La Liberté de penser*, the first of his many translations of the tales of Edgar Allan Poe. Purporting to be a vision of the transcendental universe, related by a dying man under the influence of hypnosis, the particular story he chose to inaugurate the series was a strangely inappropriate offering, one would think, to the readers of *La Liberté de penser* at this particular moment in history when most of them would have been more concerned with the present crisis than with speculations on the hereafter.

Moreover Poe's *Mesmeric Revelation*, with its talk of 'unparticled matter', 'luminiferous ether' and the like, cannot have been the easiest text to render into French, especially for an apprentice translator such as Baudelaire was at this point; and it is hardly surprising that a comparison between his version and the original brings to light some strange misunderstandings. But few, if any, of his readers were equipped to detect such flaws. Educated Frenchmen at the time were far more at home with Latin than with any modern foreign language, and his friends were therefore quite impressed to discover Baudelaire could read English, though when one of them complimented him on his linguistic prowess he is said to have answered airily: 'English? but I've always known English.'[1] They nodded; of course, his mother had been brought up in England; he must have heard it in the cradle.

In fact, there is no evidence at all that she took the trouble to teach him the language that she herself had learned in her infancy; he did not begin to study it until he was eleven, when he started taking English lessons at school.[2] Lacking incentive and encouragement, he seems not to have progressed very far, but after the move to Paris he began again and in 1837 came second in English at the Lycée Louis-le-Grand. However, the class was probably a small one; the school inspector's report for that year shows that no more than 100 out of the thousand boys at Louis-le-Grand had opted to learn one or the other of the two modern languages (English and German) taught there. The English master, a certain Charles James Wilkin, was unpopular, and besides, it was not until the following year (1838) that modern languages were made part of the basic curriculum at state schools; previously, they were classed with music, dancing, swimming, and fencing as 'extras' that could be taken by those who applied to do so during recreational periods.

All in all, having done one year of English at the Collège royal in Lyons and, after a long interval, another year at the Lycée Louis-le-Grand, it is doubtful whether Baudelaire managed to pick up more than an elementary knowledge of the language while at school, though he felt confident enough even so to undertake to give English lessons to a thirteen-year-old boy in the year after he left school, when he was staying with the Lasègues.

Although we lack precise information on the point, it can be assumed that he continued his private study of the language and literature, in a desultory fashion, over the succeeding years. For a generation or so, some acquaintance with English had been considered almost obligatory among the young romantics. It had started with the extraordinary interest aroused by Byron, an edition of whose complete works was put on the Paris market in 1818 by the enterprising publisher and bookseller Galigniani. At that time Byron was still untranslated, and Galigniani had probably counted on selling his edition to British tourists in Paris who were particularly numerous during the years following Napoleon's downfall; but rumours of the brilliance of Byron's verse and the audacity of his thought soon spread among the small number of Frenchmen sufficiently conversant with English to read his works in the original. They formed a phalanx of initiates whose enthusiasm communicated itself to others, and young men like Jean-Jacques Ampère, the son of the celebrated physicist who gave his name to the unit of electric current, Pierre Lebrun, who was to win fame a couple of years later with his highly successful adaptation of Schiller's *Maria Stuart*, and Prosper Mérimée, the polyglot who in due course was to introduce Pushkin to the French – these three among others taught themselves English for the primary purpose of gaining access to Byron's works. Etienne Delécluze organized his Sunday 'matinées britanniques' in the early 1820s, chiefly as seminars for the study of *The Corsair*, *The Giaour*, *Manfred* and the other poems. It was Delécluze who commented that to read Byron was to risk becoming addicted as to opium; and it is certainly true that the impact of this volcanic poetry was quite traumatic in many cases. One of his visitors, Jules Michelet, recorded in his diary how he took away a volume of Byron from Delécluze's shelf and 'devoured it' that same night. 'I was like those who become enslaved to strong drink; everything else seems tasteless to them.'[3]

Next to Byron it was Shakespeare, among the English poets, who chiefly stirred the imagination of the French romantics. Both Stendhal and Delacroix, English speakers up to a point, made trips across the Channel expressly to see Shakespeare performed in the London theatres. When, in 1827, a British company visited Paris to put on a Shakespeare season at the Odéon, they found themselves playing to attentive and appreciative audiences, in the midst of which several earnest young men could be observed, night after night, following the text from copies they had brought along in their pockets. Shakespeare's language, of course, confronted his French devotees with bigger problems than did Byron's. One of those whose passion for the great dramatist became eventually quite obsessional, an architect named Jules Vabre, left Paris to settle in London with the object of perfecting his knowledge of English so that in the fullness of time he would be equipped to provide his compatriots with a truly flawless translation of Shakespeare's works. After a while his friends lost touch with him completely, since in order to immerse himself in his new environment he refused to read a word of French and consequently never opened the letters he received from France. One day in 1843 or 1844 Gautier, who had known him well in former times, ran into him again in a tavern in High Holborn, surrounded by hearty early Victorians washing down their helpings of roast beef with draughts of strong ale. Instead of embracing Gautier *à la française*, Vabre shook him warmly by the hand and began to talk with so strong an English accent that the other could scarcely understand what he was saying and quipped: 'All you need to do now, my dear Vabre, in order to translate Shakespeare, is to learn French!'; whereupon the ex-architect, with a naïveté worthy of one of Balzac's monomaniacs, exclaimed: 'I must start doing just that, you're quite right!'[4] But the ideal translation of Shakespeare that he dreamed of remained, for all that, just a dream.

Coming late on the scene, Baudelaire escaped the full blast of the cultural anglomania of the 1820s and 1830s, but it can hardly be doubted that, with little guidance, he was making his own voyages of discovery among the English and American poets in vogue at the time. One of the poems in *Les Fleurs du Mal*[5] oddly conflates a version of a stanza from Gray's *Elegy in a Country Churchyard*

('Full many a gem of purest ray serene
The dark unfathomed caves of ocean bear . . .')

with a quatrain from Longfellow's *Resignation*:

'Art is long, and Time is fleeting,
And our hearts, though stout and brave,
Still, like muffled drums, are beating
Funeral marches to the grave.'

Tennyson was another poet whose works he must have perused, though perhaps at a slightly later date; a quotation from *The Lotus-Eaters* is discoverable embedded in the seventh section of his long, allusive poem *Le Voyage*, written in 1859. On more than one occasion he linked Tennyson with Byron and Poe as a trinity of poets of equal brilliance.[6] His preferences may not accord with our modern canon, but it remains true that among the major French creative writers of his century, if one excludes Mallarmé, none showed greater interest than Baudelaire in the work being produced concurrently by fellow poets across the Channel and on the other side of the Atlantic.

Anyone who, like Baudelaire, tries to learn a foreign language without proper tuition and without living in the country in which it is spoken is obliged to invent his own methods, and translation exercises are no doubt as good as any. It is hard to imagine that he had any other aim in view when, some time in 1845, he set himself to turn into French a short story, *The Young Enchanter*, which he had found in one of those prettily produced annuals called keepsakes which were so popular, both in England and in France, in the 1830s and 1840s. Readers of *Madame Bovary* will remember how the heroine, at her convent school, pores enraptured over the keepsakes smuggled into the dormitory by girls who had been given them as New Year presents, admiring as she handled them their 'fine satin bindings' and the illustrations protected by tissue paper which lifted lightly off the page as she blew on it. The steel engravings were what chiefly fascinated Emma, Flaubert tells us; but keepsakes also included poems, historical and biographical anecdotes, improving essays and of course fiction, usually of the sentimental kind and of unassailable propriety. *The Young Enchanter* is not untypical of the keepsake literature: a tale of true love rewarded, set in Naples and Athens in ancient times, and seasoned with a dash of the adventure story – suitable for boys as well as girls, then, but likely to strike the sophisticated adult reader as pointless and insipid. It in no way connects with Baudelaire's private preoccupations and normal literary themes, and the only reason he could have had for translating it was to improve his knowledge of English. But having finished it, he signed it (the original had been published anonymously) and succeeded in selling it to *L'Esprit public* where it was published in three parts between February 20th and 22nd, 1846. A comparison with the original shows that Baudelaire's understanding of English was still imperfect at this date, but that as a translator he had promise; it reads fluently, and gives no impression of having been turned into French from a foreign language. The best proof of this is that until comparatively recently, in spite of its uncharacteristic setting, and subject, *Le Jeune Enchanteur* was assumed by all Baudelaire's biographers and editors to be a story of his own invention.[7]

La Révélation magnétique, which was what Baudelaire called his version of Poe's *Mesmeric Revelation*, thus counts as the second of his translations from the English. He published the story with a prefatory note in which he categorized Poe as a 'philosophical' novelist along with an oddly assorted group of others: Diderot and Laclos, Hoffmann, Goethe, and Jean Paul, Maturin and Balzac. There is no common denominator to which these eight authors can be reduced; Laclos, in particular, seems to have been added quite arbitrarily, and perhaps only because of Baudelaire's profound and lasting admiration for Laclos's one and only novel, *Dangerous Acquaintances*. Among the others, if one assumes that Goethe is included either for his *Elective Affinities* or because Baudelaire imagined *Faust* was a novel, the link seems to be that they were all using fiction to present some sort of metaphysical system. 'It is certain,' Baudelaire writes, 'that these specifically literary minds make curious forays, when the whim takes them, into philosophy. They dive into it suddenly and escape from it abruptly by paths that only they have discovered.'[8]

Nebulous though the argument is in this preface, it is clear that Baudelaire undertook the translation of *Mesmeric Revelation* for reasons very different from those that prompted him to attempt a version of the unpretentious anonymous story *The Young Enchanter*. This time he is writing with some knowledge of the author he is translating; moreover, he has chosen this particular story for what he takes to be its philosophical content rather than for its purely literary merits or for its entertainment value.

How, when, and where could he have come across the work of Edgar Allan Poe? Although he could have read French adaptations of one or two of the tales published in Paris newspapers in 1846, it could only have been the series of translations by Isabelle Meunier, appearing in *La Démocratie pacifique* between January 1847 and May 1848, that gave Baudelaire his first inkling of the American story-writer's range and ingenuity. *La Démocratie pacifique* was a paper primarily devoted to propagating Fourier's brand of socialism, which in itself would hardly have caused Baudelaire to take out a subscription; but Leconte de Lisle worked on its staff and it is very likely that Baudelaire spent some of his time in the newspaper office, chatting to Louis Ménard, Thalès Bernard, and Théodore de Banville, all friends of Leconte de Lisle and apt to foregather there. He may even have been introduced to Isabelle Meunier on one of these visits; she was in fact the English wife of one of the members of the staff of *La Démocratie pacifique*.

The five stories she translated were *The Black Cat*, *The Murders in the Rue Morgue*, *The Conversation of Eiros and Charmion*, *A Descent into the Maelstrom*, and *The Gold Bug*. All five were taken from the 1845 Wiley and Putnam collection, entitled simply *Tales*, which at the time was the only volume of Poe's works obtainable in Paris. The selection had been made not by the author himself but by 'a gentleman whose taste does not coincide with my own', as Poe later remarked in a letter to George Eveleth;[9] even so, among the twelve stories the volume contained there were, apart from those already translated by Isabelle Meunier, several others (*The Fall of the House of Usher*, *The Mystery of Marie Roget*, *The Purloined Letter*, *The Man of the Crowd*) which one might think would have commended themselves more readily to Baudelaire than *Mesmeric Revelation*. Probably he chose it simply because it accorded best with his preconceived view of Poe as a 'philosophical novelist'. He might have intended to follow it up with further translations, but if so, the project was soon forgotten in the vicissitudes of his troubled life. In October 1848 he left Paris to travel down to Châteauroux, taking Jeanne with him; some well-disposed person had persuaded the local conservatives that he was the man they needed to take over the editorship of their newspaper, *Le Représentant de la Loire*. How long he stayed in the provinces is uncertain, one reason being that the flow of letters to his mother, one of our principal sources of biographical information, dwindled to a sporadic trickle after she left France in May 1848 to accompany her husband to Constantinople.

Towards the latter part of 1849, news of Poe's death at Baltimore on October 7th reached France, and with it the information that an edition of his complete works in three volumes, published by Redfield of New York, was to be put on the market in the course of the following year. Thinking that Amédée Pichot, editor of the *Revue Britannique*, might have been sent a set for review, Baudelaire applied to him in the hope of borrowing it, but to no avail; Pichot was away at the time. Judging from a note to his bookseller, written in October 1851, Baudelaire was particularly anxious to get hold of an edition of the works that included a biographical study, 'if there is one';[10] which suggests that it was Poe's life, quite as much as his works, that interested Baudelaire at this stage. Having drawn blanks in every direction, he took the desperate course of calling on any

American citizen temporarily resident in Paris who might be thought to have information to impart on the subject. Charles Asselineau relates amusingly how he accompanied his friend on one of these expeditions. The address Baudelaire had been given was that of a hotel in the Boulevard des Capucines at which an American man of letters 'who must have known Poe' had just booked in. 'We found him in shirts and underpants, in the midst of a flotilla of shoes of all sorts that he was trying on, helped by the shoemaker. But the circumstance did not deter Baudelaire; the man was forced willy-nilly to undergo questioning, in between taking off a pair of half-boots and trying on a pair of pumps. Our host turned out to have a poor opinion of the author of *The Black Cat*. I remember in particular that he told us Mr Poe was an eccentric whose conversation was not at all 'consecutive'. Going downstairs, Baudelaire said to me as he pulled his hat violently on to his head: "The damned Yankee!"'[11]

Finally his efforts were crowned with success, when he tracked down an American journalist, William Wilberforce Mann, who it is true did not possess the invaluable Redfield edition of the works, but did have in his rooms a file of the *Southern Literary Messenger* which he allowed Baudelaire to consult; it covered the entire period of Poe's editorship of that magazine (1834–8), and thus included several of the earlier stories as well as specimens of his poetry and literary criticism. In addition, in the volumes for 1849 and 1850, Baudelaire found two articles which were precisely what he was looking for: an obituary of Poe by the then editor of the *Messenger*, John R. Thompson, and a long review article by John Moncure Daniel of the Redfield edition which included a great deal of information (and misinformation) about Poe's life and career.

It was on the basis of these two monographs that Baudelaire wrote his celebrated essay, *Edgar Allan Poe, sa vie et ses ouvrages*, which was published in the *Revue de Paris* in March and April 1852 and later reissued, in a revised and abridged version, as the introduction to his first volume of translations of Poe's stories, brought out by Michel Lévy in 1856 under the title *Histoires extraordinaires*.[12] By far the greater part – perhaps as much as three quarters – of Baudelaire's 1852 essay is directly lifted from one or other of his two sources; and when he departs from them, or brings in additional matter, it is either to give Poe a more dignified image, or else to make him more closely resemble Baudelaire as he saw himself, that is, the foredoomed victim of a cruelly hostile external Power.

One can express this best by saying that Baudelaire's portrait of the dead Poe effected the same kind of transfiguration as he had described David achieving when he painted the portrait of the dead Marat. Whatever was ugly was effaced, and only the beatified soul remained to fill the spectator with reverence and move him to compassion. In the case of Poe, Baudelaire expunged or altered anything his sources mentioned as discreditable to his hero.[13] This policy extended to quite trivial details. Where Daniel states: 'his hands and feet were moderately large, and strangely shaped, as were all his joints', Baudelaire changes the derogatory description completely, saying that Poe had small hands and feet – this being popularly regarded as betokening aristocratic extraction. He refuses to allow that Poe ever succeeded in making a decent living from his writing; to admit the contrary would have distanced him from his hero. So he suppresses the information that Poe was 'well paid' for his work on *Graham's Magazine*, and in doing so, strangely enough, came nearer to the truth than his American informants; for Poe himself, in a letter to Frederick Thomas explaining why he had resigned his situation on the magazine in question, gave as one of the reasons that the salary 'did not pay me for the labour which I was forced to bestow'.[14] Baudelaire could not entirely gloss over Poe's addiction to liquor (which the earlier biographers exaggerated in any case), but he inserted a lengthy passage – in part *pro domo sua* – explaining why in the nineteenth century the poet, cut off from all opportunity of enjoying himself in mixed company with wine and lively conversation, was obliged to resort to solitary drinking in the hope of evoking 'the calm or terrifying visions that are his companions of old'.[15]

Baudelaire's most significant interpolation, however, occurs right at the very beginning of his essay. Daniel had referred to Poe's 'disastrous battle of life' and his 'untimely fate', and Thompson had quoted Longfellow, who had never actually met Poe, but who apprehended in him 'a sensitive nature, chafed by some indefinite sense of wrong'. But these conventional phrases constituted at best a fragile justification for Baudelaire's striking introductory passage:

> There are such things as ineluctable destinies; in the literature of every country one reads of certain men who bear the word *misfortune* written in mysterious characters in the sinuous lines of their brows. Some time ago, a wretch hauled before the courts was observed to have tattooed on his forehead the strange device: *No luck*. Thus he bore with him everywhere the motto of his life, as a book its title, and the cross-examination proved that his story was in conformity with the sign that advertised it. In literary history there are analogous fates. It is as though the blind Angel of Expiation had seized hold of certain men and was beating them with rods for the edification of the others.

Baudelaire quotes a couple of familiar instances, Hoffmann and

Balzac, and then asks whether 'there is not some diabolical Providence which mixes the ingredients of an unhappy life from the very
cradle. . . . Can it be that there are souls consecrated to the altar, souls
in this sense sacred, who are called on to make a special sacrifice of
themselves on their path to death and glory?'[16]

What Baudelaire calls in this passage *le guignon*, a word we have
rendered as *misfortune* but which could as well have been translated
ill luck, is merely the popular, layman's expression for what he more
usually thought of by the theologian's term *damnation*: the sense of
being delivered up, from birth and inescapably through life until
death should come to release him, to some inscrutable, demonic
power which delighted in stacking the odds against him and making
sure that, whatever game he played, he would infallibly lose.

Poe's earliest *misfortune* might be seen as the loss of both his
parents in infancy, from consumption, according to Daniel, though
Baudelaire corrected this to make the case sound more pathetic:
'both from the same cause: starvation, privation, destitution'.[17] After
that, he had the further misfortune of being disinherited by the
wealthy man, John Allan, who took care of him after he had been left
an orphan. This abrupt plunge into poverty seemed to correspond
closely to Baudelaire's own experience after his family had taken legal
action to deny him control of his private fortune. The parallels, real
or imagined, in their lives, his own admiration for Poe as a writer,
and above all his conviction that they were both like Ishmael, who
had 'every man's hand against him'[18] – all these things combined to
implant in Baudelaire the strange idea that he and Poe were kindred
souls, that there was an affinity between them pointing to some
supernatural link. As the years passed, this belief grew stronger
rather than weaker. In 1860, needing to explain to the critic Armand
Fraisse how he came to devote so many years of his life to what could
pass as hack translation work, he wrote: 'In 1846 or 1847 I came
across a few fragments of Edgar Poe; I experienced a singular mental
shock; since it was not until after his death that his works were issued
in a single collected edition, I took the trouble to scrape an
acquaintance with certain Americans living in Paris in order to
borrow from them files of the journals that Poe had edited. And it was
then that I discovered, believe me or not as you choose, poems and
stories of which the idea had occurred to me earlier but only in a
vague, confused, and chaotic form, but which Poe had been able to
combine and bring to perfection. Such was the origin of my
enthusiasm and the pains I took.'[19]

As we now know, this account of the sequence of events is not
strictly accurate. The implication of his statement to Fraisse is that

he began his enquiries among Americans in Paris before Poe's death and before his collected works were published, whereas in fact this activity started some time afterwards. Moreover, it was not so much Poe's writings that fired Baudelaire with enthusiasm; he knew little more of them in 1852 than he did in 1848, and what he has to say about Poe's works in *Edgar Poe, sa vie et ses ouvrages* is reproduced almost verbatim from Daniel's review-article. It was the account he read of Poe's miserable life that gave him first to feel this mysterious affinity; their destiny was the same, the curse under which they laboured was the same. Their oneness of mind, and in particular the similarities between his poetry and Poe's which he thought he detected,[20] were largely imaginary.

When his 1852 essay appeared in the *Revue de Paris* he wrote to his mother, now in Madrid, to tell her about it: 'I have discovered an American author who has aroused my sympathetic interest to an incredible degree.' Almost exactly a year later, in another letter to her, he asked: 'Do you realize now why, in the frightful solitude in which I live, I acquired such a clear understanding of Poe's genius, and why I made myself the historian of his abominable life?'[21] The reason, as she knew without his having to spell it out, was that his own life had been 'abominable' – there was no other word for it – for the past five years at least. All the tribulations Poe had known, he had known; nor had he been able to keep the knowledge of them from her, since it was only to her that he could turn in the hope of relief and practical assistance.

At the end of 1847 he had sent her a long, desperate letter in which he described himself as penniless, living in a garret without even a washbasin or a table-lamp, sometimes going without food for forty-eight hours and, if he wanted to buy wood and coal for a fire, obliged to tramp over to Neuilly through the mud and driving rain to try and extort from Ancelle an advance on his monthly allowance. He despairs, he says, of ever getting her to understand, surrounded as she is by all the comforts of her home, what it is like to live as he does. It was not simply of material privations that he complained. 'Imagine perpetual idleness punctuated by perpetual discomfort, together with a deep detestation of this idleness and the utter impossibility of escaping from it because of the constant lack of money. ... I have such perfect faith in my ability to put my time to good use and in the power of my will that I *know for sure* that if I could manage to live a regular life for a fortnight or three weeks, *my intellect would be saved*. ... The strange story of the past six years, which might have been disastrous had I not been blessed with a physical and mental constitution such that nothing has been able to undermine it, is very simple: thoughtlessness, postponing to the morrow measures dictated by the most elementary commonsense, and in consequence poverty and more poverty.'

Re-reading what he had written, he picks up the pen again to express amazement at his own vehemence. 'I have never dared complain so loudly. I trust you will put this excitement down to the agony I am undergoing *of which you have no conception*. The totally idle life which, superficially, I am leading, at war with the perpetual ferment of my mind, drives me into unspeakable rages. I blame myself for my lapses, I blame you for refusing to believe in the sincerity of my intentions. The fact is that for some months now I have been living in an abnormal state.' He then refers to an offer he has received of a post as tutor to the children of a family living in Mauritius – an offer which he will accept, he says, 'to punish myself and do penance for my pride, if I fail to keep my final resolutions'.[22]

The neurotic condition arising from this sense of utter helplessness, of unused powers bottled up within him which could find no outlet in the state of debilitating, grey-faced poverty to which he was now reduced, goes a long way to explain the fury with which Baudelaire flung himself into revolutionary activity less than three months after writing this letter. The downfall of the July Monarchy did in fact mark an upturn in his fortunes, for as long as the Second Republic lasted, journalistic employment, however ill-paid, in Paris or in the provinces did at least raise him above the poverty line. But the respite was only temporary. The period during which the press laws were in abeyance, and when it was therefore relatively easy for writers to place their copy, came to an end with the *coup d'état*. As though his money troubles were not enough, he had to cope additionally with a mistress as disappointed in him as he was in himself, and venting her spleen in bad-tempered outbursts and shrill reproaches. He found he had to work at night, 'so as to have peace and quiet and escape the unendurable pestering of the woman I live with. Sometimes, in order to write at all, I go and hide in a public library or reading-room or sit in a wine-bar or a café, as today. The result is that I live in a state of permanent irritation. Certainly this is no way to bring to fruition a sustained piece of writing.'[23] He took what seemed to be the only possible course and sent Jeanne packing – only to be overwhelmed by a fresh disaster. Exasperated by the avarice and noisy recriminations of his new landlady, he walked out one evening without a word to her and without giving proper notice. Demanding to be paid her rent, even though he was not using the room, she refused to allow him to remove his books and manuscripts, without which he had no hope of completing the work that might have enabled him to pay her off.

The discomfort and insecurity of his life, with all its attendant humiliations, continued unaltered through 1853. There were occasions when he had to go into hiding for fear of arrest for debt; his chief worry then was that his creditors would force an entry and, finding him absent, make off with his precious papers. In December he implored his mother to send him any small sum she could spare, to allow him to buy a few logs and pay off part of his score at the neighbouring restaurant, 'so that I shan't be obliged to write in bed with frozen fingers and shall have enough to live on for two or three days'. He was even short of adequate clothing in the winter of 1853–4, though he comments bitterly that this was the least of his troubles. 'I am so accustomed to physical suffering, I am so used to wearing two shirts under a pair of torn trousers and a jacket too threadbare to keep out the wind, I have got so clever at stuffing straw or even paper into my shoes to stop the wet coming through the holes, that I am scarcely conscious of anything but my moral distress.'[24] Much of his wardrobe was at the pawnbroker's, including some articles that had been there so long that he would never be able to reclaim them. His one overcoat had been sent for mending but, again, he doubted whether he would ever retrieve it since he never had the spare cash to pay the repair bill.

1854 brought no improvement. The same urgent begging letters to his mother continued as before. 'If I don't get the money, I have absolutely no idea what will become of me, there will be nothing left for it but to burn all my books, stop caring about anything and shut my eyes to the consequences.' – 'Oh God, what humiliations have you heaped on me, what kind of cruel satisfaction can there be in inflicting such miseries on a man like me? ... I am suffering a thousand tortures; I await proofs as believers await the coming of the Messiah!'[25] In 1855 the complaints are above all of his homelessness. Lacking the money needed to buy a few sticks of furniture and take the lease on a flat, he is forced to move from one furnished room to another in slum tenements, with plaster on the floor and fleas in his bed, with no fixed address so that even business letters fail to reach him. 'I am sick to death of living in doss-houses and eating in cheap restaurants; it's poisoning me, killing me. I don't know how I haven't succumbed. I am tired of catching cold, suffering from migraine and fevers, and above all of being forced to go out twice a day, in the snow, the mud, the rain,' for a bite of food. The great advantage he foresaw in having a settled establishment was that he could then work steadily, without interruptions. 'Above all, no more wasting time. That is the great wound I bleed from; for if there is something worse than physical sufferings, it is the fear of seeing that admirable poetic faculty, that clarity of ideas, and that fund of hope which constitute my real capital, waste away to nothing in the jolts and jars of this horrible existence.'[26]

It was in this mood that he wrote the sonnet entitled *The Enemy*.

> Like a black thunderstorm my youth has fled,
> Traversed by brilliant sunshine; the wild rain
> And wind have ravaged every garden bed,
> So that few red or golden fruits remain.
>
> The mind's chill autumn now draws on apace;
> So must I dig and fork the sodden soil,
> With spade and rake the rich earth to replace,
> Filling the holes, sweating in day-long toil.
>
> How can this stony and infertile ground
> To these new flowers, with mystic blossoms crowned,
> Of which I dream, their nourishment impart?
>
> – Time round our necks draws tighter still the noose,
> And the dark Enemy that gnaws our heart
> Feeds and grows fatter on the blood we lose.[27]

Baudelaire's critics, with more faith in their own intuitions than in the biographical data available to them, have proposed a variety of unsatisfactory answers to the question: Who or what is the Enemy the poet refers to here, both in his title and in his penultimate line? Time? death? the Devil? remorse? ennui? None of these, obviously, but rather the malign Providence which he saw presiding over his own life as it had presided over Poe's.

The very considerable success of his essay on Poe's life and work when it was published in 1852 – it was even translated into Russian for a St Petersburg periodical, the first of Baudelaire's writings to appear abroad – encouraged him to resume the task of turning Poe's short stories into French. Four appeared in different magazines in the course of the same year (1852): *Berenice*, the text of which he had found in *The Southern Literary Messenger*; and *The Pit and the Pendulum*, *Philosophy of Furniture*, and *A Tale of the Ragged Mountains*, all based on the unfortunately very defective text of a pirated edition of the stories issued by the London firm of Routledge. However, at the beginning of 1853 he at last acquired a copy of the long-awaited Redfield edition of Poe's complete works, and all his subsequent translations were based on this edition, which was certainly the best and fullest available at the time. Most of them appeared in the newspaper *Le Pays*, under the running title *Histoires extraordinaires*, which was also used as the title of the first volume of Baudelaire's translations, published by Michel Lévy in 1856.

1a The portrait of his father that Baudelaire treasured throughout his life

1b Baudelaire as a boy wearing school uniform

2a Baudelaire in his early twenties as depicted by his friend Emile Deroy

2b One of several sketches made by Baudelaire of Jeanne Duval. The Latin inscription at the base translates as: 'Seeking whom she may devour'

3a Narcisse-Désiré Ancelle, the notary who was charged with administering Baudelaire's private fortune from 1844 onwards

3b Courbet's portrait of Baudelaire executed in 1847, showing him with his hair close cropped

4a Apollonie Sabatier, as painted by Meissonier in 1853

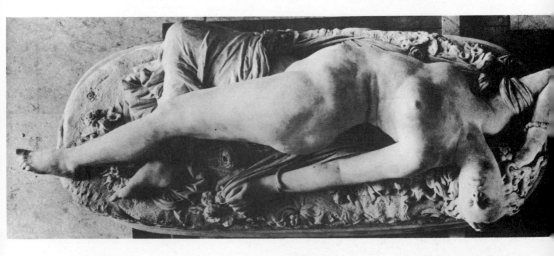

4b Mme Sabatier was the model for Clésinger's statue entitled 'Woman stung by a snake'

5a Marie Daubrun as she appeared in 1854

5b A proof of the dedicatory page of
Les Fleurs du Mal, showing Baudelaire's meticulous corrections

5c A self-portrait, supposedly executed
by Baudelaire while under the influence of
hashish

6 Photograph of Baudelaire taken by Carjat around 1860 when the poet was contemplating suicide

7a General Aupick, Baudelaire's stepfather, as he appeared at the time he was French ambassador to Turkey.

7b The house at Honfleur built by Gen. Aupick on his retirement. The seated figure at the top of the steps is Baudelaire's mother

8a Baudelaire as he appeared when living in Brussels: a portrait by the Belgian photographer Charles Neyt

8b The gravestone with inscriptions commemorating Aupick, Baudelaire, and his mother

He approached the task of translating Poe with the same zealous striving after perfection as he gave to every other literary work he undertook. He found a tutor, a certain Abel Bonjour, who helped him with the more difficult passages. He practised his conversational English on a barman in the Rue de Rivoli whose normal clientèle was drawn from the British grooms and jockeys who found ready employment in Paris at this period; Asselineau paints a pleasant picture of Baudelaire sitting at a table there, surrounded by horsey men in riding-breeches, with a glass of sherry in front of him, leafing through *Punch* while he lent an attentive ear to the Cockney banter around him. Nothing would content him, when he was engaged on translating the *Narrative of A. Gordon Pym*, but to run to earth somehow an English or American sea-captain who could explain to him the exact meaning of the nautical terms he encountered in this work. 'One day,' Asselineau tells us, 'seeing him racking his brains over a detail of orientation, I was so ill advised as to chaff him over the trouble he was taking to get everything exactly right. "Well," he said, raising his head, "and what about those people who are going to read it following the ship's course on the map?"'[28] But the care he took was amply repaid. Even his mother was impressed by the final result though, typically, it was not to her son that she expressed the pleasure she had taken in reading his work, but to his half-brother Alphonse Baudelaire. 'Considered from the point of view of style, [these translations] are something quite remarkable, astonishing in fact, they read like an original work. I had no idea he had so complete a mastery of the English language.'[29] The same tribute essentially was paid by Armand Fraisse, though again Baudelaire had no cognisance of it, since Fraisse's observations appeared in print some time after his death: 'Baudelaire accomplished a *tour de force* that no other translator, as far as I am aware, has ever achieved. He identified so thoroughly with his author that, as one turns the pages, it is just like reading an original work.'[30]

The first two volumes of the collected stories (the *Histoires extraordinaires*, published in March 1856 and the *Nouvelles histoires extraordinaires* in March 1857) were greeted with a unanimous chorus of critical acclaim, though once again Sainte-Beuve, in spite of Baudelaire's earnest solicitations, decided against giving either of them the honour of a review. The clearest proof of their popularity is that during his lifetime they ran through several editions; apart from *Les Fleurs du Mal*, which constitutes a special case, none of his other works were reprinted until after his death. Later on in his life Baudelaire expressed some reservations about this popular success, and declared to one of his correspondents (Mme Paul Meurice): 'I wasted a lot of time translating Edgar Poe, and the only good it has done me is that some worthy folk have maintained that I took my own poems from Poe, when they were written ten years before I had knowledge of his works.'[31] False accusations of plagiarism apart, the time spent translating Poe can only be considered wasted if we were sure it would have been employed in equivalent work of a more original nature; and, given the difficulty Baudelaire always found in drawing material for a book-length piece of writing from his own resources, that possibility can be safely discounted. As it is, he achieved something that he certainly did not set out to achieve, something quite without parallel in the history of literature: he gave a second-rate writer world status. Had it not been for Baudelaire, how would Poe rate today, even in his native country?

IX

HARPOCRATES' FOREFINGER

Over the same period of ten years (1847–56) during which
Baudelaire, homeless, cold, starving, and in rags for much of the
time, was struggling to establish himself in the world of letters, his
stepfather General Aupick was riding high on the tide of official
favour and reaping the ultimate rewards of a career all the more
distinguished in that no one could have accused him of being a
single-minded careerist. Always at his side, Baudelaire's mother
remained torn in her allegiance and affections; convinced that her
husband would at any point have gladly set her son on the path of
success, if only Charles would consent to accept his guidance and
counsel, angry and resentful at what she thought of as her son's
obstinate intractability, wishing she could wash her hands of him and
yet bound in conscience to continue her protective role.

Promoted to the rank of lieutenant-general on April 22nd, 1847,
Aupick was appointed director of the Ecole Polytechnique on
November 28th of the same year, having previously declined the
offer of the headship of the Ecole Saint-Cyr where he had been a
student in his youth. When, less than a year later, Louis-Philippe was
forced to abdicate and go into exile with his family, the new leaders of
France seemed happy to overlook the fact that the general had been,
not just a faithful servant of the Orleans monarchy, but a personal
friend of one of the princes of the blood royal. It was reassuring that
he wasted no time in declaring his support of the provisional
government, and his promptness was duly rewarded by the offer of
the embassy at Constantinople. Lamartine, who was at the head of
affairs at the time, subsequently recorded that his colleagues, when
debating this appointment, were unanimous in judging him to be
politically reliable. 'General Aupick's aptitude alone was considered,
his conscientious honesty of purpose could admit of no doubt.'[1]

Baudelaire's activities during the first few weeks of the revolution,
if they came to the general's ears, can hardly have improved his
already poor opinion of his stepson's good sense. In political matters,
as in all others, Aupick was a steady, earnest, middle-of-the-way
man. His attitude emerges very clearly in a passage of one of his

117

letters to a friend in the diplomatic service. 'We are having to face simultaneously socialism, which would spell the end of civilization and its wonders, and absolutism which would put an end to freedom and the dignity of man. On the one hand Proudhon, performing his notorious function as advanced guard of the scum who, were he to come to power, would soon unmask themselves and push him to one side – and on the other hand, Russia and the rule of the knout. Reason, which lies between the two extremes, is the holy cause we serve.'[2] Fortunately, perhaps, Aupick and Baudelaire were not seeing one another, so there was no risk of confrontation over the political situation, and as far as his mother was concerned, neither he nor she would have imagined it appropriate to raise such matters in conversation. They did meet, a little before she sailed with her husband from Marseilles, and this final interview was a stormy one; not, however, on account of any disagreements about the future of France, but because she used the occasion to take him to task once more for his continuing association with his odious mulatto mistress. He let seven months go by before writing to her at Constantinople, and then referred to the scolding she had given him in terms that make it very clear why he was still attached to Jeanne.

With that neurotic obstinacy, that violence which is peculiar to you, you upbraided me solely on account of a poor woman whom *for long I have cherished only out of a sense of duty*, that's all. How strange that you who have spoken to me so often and so prosily of duty and moral obligations, you do not understand this strange attachment which profits me nothing, and in which the desire to do penance and to reward devotion plays the greatest part. However often a woman may be unfaithful, however hardened her character, when she has shown some sparks of willingness and devotion, that is enough for a disinterested man, especially a poet, to feel obliged to reward her. ... Today, four months from my twenty-eighth birthday, buoyed up by an immense poetic ambition, yet cut off for ever from *respectable society* by my tastes and my principles, what does it matter if, while constructing the edifice of my literary dream-city, I fulfil in addition *a duty*, or what I consider a duty, even though it flies in the face of vulgar prejudices concerning honour, money, and fortune?[3]

At Constantinople, communications between Mme Aupick and her son were all but non-existent. His letters were never more infrequent, and her pride forbade her to write begging for news. There may have been the occasional report from Ancelle, but otherwise it was as if Charles were living on a different planet. That she suffered from this situation, perhaps even more than he did, can scarcely be doubted; it was the one topic she could never broach with her husband and therefore, out of a sense of loyalty, she felt reluctant to question the occasional Parisian visitor whom the general and she entertained at the embassy and who might have had some interesting information to impart.

Two such visitors were Gustave Flaubert and Maxime Du Camp, who in October 1849 had set off on a leisurely tour of what was then known as the Near East. They had taken ship first for Egypt, had sailed up the Nile, and had then travelled by stages through Palestine, Syria, and the Lebanon, countries which were all at that time provinces of the Ottoman Empire. On November 12th, 1850, they had arrived at Constantinople, and received an invitation to dine with the French ambassador and his lady on December 6th.[4] Over coffee, Aupick began asking about the current literary scene in Paris; Du Camp, in reply, spoke of a few personalities of whom mention had been made in a letter just received from Louis de Cormenin. One of them happened to be Baudelaire. No sooner had he pronounced the poet's name than Du Camp realized he had made some sort of gaffe. 'Mme Aupick lowered her head, the General stared at me fixedly as if to take up a challenge, and Colonel Margadel [the general's *aide*] gave me a little kick to warn me I was treading on thin ice. I must have looked a bit sheepish, realizing I had blundered, but at a loss to know how. Ten minutes later, while the General and Flaubert were arguing about one or other of Proudhon's books, Mme Aupick moved over to me and asked in a low voice: "It's true, isn't it, that he shows talent?" – "Who?" – "I mean the young man that M. de Cormenin spoke so highly of to you." I nodded, without adding a word, for I was more and more mystified.' Subsequently, after the party had broken up, Margadel revealed to Du Camp that Baudelaire was Mme Aupick's son by a previous marriage. 'He and the General are at daggers drawn and the General can't stand to hear his name spoken . . .'[5]

The diplomatic crises Aupick was called on to deal with during his tenure of office at Constantinople were not, fortunately, of a desperately acute nature. There was the problem of the Polish and Hungarian freedom fighters who had crossed into Turkish territory after the failure of the nationalist uprisings of 1848–9 and whose extradition, demanded by the Russians and Austrians, was opposed on humanitarian grounds by France and England. Aupick was responsible for arranging political asylum in France for a number of these fighting men who were given the opportunity to join the Foreign Legion. In 1850 there was tension between the French and the British arising out of Palmerston's high-handed treatment of the Greeks over the so-called Don Pacifico affair. Aupick evidently fulfilled all the hopes that Lamartine and his revolutionary council had originally placed in him; the Turks found him a man after their liking and the new President of the French Republic, Louis Napoleon, with whom he maintained a private correspondence, was sufficiently impressed by his capacities to want to transfer him to the Court of St James.

It was not an offer that could be lightly turned down. There was probably no more important diplomatic post at the time than the London embassy; besides, he had in Mme Aupick a helpmate fluent in the language and who was delighted at the prospect of revisiting the scenes of her earliest youth. But, on the voyage back to France, he had second thoughts. Although his allegiance to the new régime needed no demonstration, he was not the man to forget the ties of friendship he had forged with the former royal family, now living in exile in England. He knew that one of the duties of the French ambassador would be to maintain the network of informers that surrounded them, and to report back to Paris any indications of plots to restore the Orleanist monarchy in France. He did not feel he could honourably undertake to spy on a family from which he had received kindnesses in the past, and, in the interview he had with Louis Napoleon on June 4th, 1851, he very honestly voiced his objections, which the President accepted without question. His original posting was cancelled, and on June 18th he was gazetted ambassador to the Court of Spain. He and his wife left within a month and took up residence in Madrid on July 28th.

During the four or five weeks Mme Aupick spent in France she took the opportunity to effect a complete reconciliation with her son, who for his part wanted nothing better. He had moved out to Neuilly in May of the previous year and it was here, in this small suburban town which held such happy memories for both of them, that they met almost daily, making occasional excursions to Saint-Cloud or Versailles. In the last letter he wrote to her before her departure for Madrid he spoke of the 'infinite pleasure' he had had in seeing her again. 'I had been prepared for a cold reception and a chilly inquisition, and had nerved myself for it in advance. You disarmed me entirely and inspired me with complete confidence in the future.' He promised, in the same letter, 'to work unremittingly, not only in order to pay off the debts that make my situation so difficult and so ambiguous, but also in order to foster in myself those habits of a regular life by which I can combat the influence of all the folly and passion which for ever seethe within us.'[6] He also promised to avoid contracting any further debts and to write to her twice a month while she was in Spain.

The restoration of mutual trust and goodwill between mother and son could only have been achieved by a tacit agreement to avoid all mention of the earlier bone of contention, Charles's continuing association with Jeanne. Mme Aupick kept silent out of tact, fastidiousness, and a dread of introducing any subject that might have imperilled the new understanding she and her son had reached. He did the same thing for the same reasons and also, perhaps, because he felt less able to justify the continuance of the liaison than he had in 1848. He preferred not to think of Jeanne during the weeks he was spending with his mother, and once she had left, the shock of the reversion to this joyless, irritating cohabitation was all the more sickening. Jeanne felt the joylessness and the irritation as much as he did and in her case the dissatisfaction was aggravated by the growing realization that the rich young lover she had taken ten years ago, having fallen incomprehensibly on hard times, seemed less likely than ever to be able to establish himself in a position where he could look after her as she had counted on being looked after. The grumbling, the quarrels, the taunts and acrimonious arguments grew more violent week by week, until finally, in bitterness of heart, Baudelaire was driven to the conclusion that they would have to part; if not by mutual consent, then he would have to throw her out quite brutally and remorselessly. He poured out his anguish in a long letter to his mother which she read in the embassy in Madrid with mingled satisfaction and alarm. The passage has to be quoted in full; reading it, as it moves from the dignified tone adopted at the outset to the wild, ignoble, and even trivial complaints at the end, one can see how Baudelaire, even as he was writing, was gradually losing control of himself as his frayed nerves got the better of cool reason.

Jeanne now constitutes an obstacle not just to my happiness – which would matter little; I too know how to sacrifice my pleasures, and I have proved it – but to my spiritual progress as well. The nine months that have just elapsed have made this abundantly clear. Never will I be able to discharge the great duties incumbent on me – the payment of my debts, the recovery of my fortune, the winning of a reputation, the balm to be poured on the wounds I have dealt you – in such conditions as these. *Formerly she had certain qualities*, but she has *lost* them, and I have grown more clear-sighted. TO LIVE WITH A CREATURE who gives you no credit for your efforts, who thwarts them at every turn out of clumsiness or spitefulness, who considers you her servant if she doesn't imagine she owns you, with whom it is impossible to have any kind of discussion about literature or politics, a creature who *refuses to learn anything*, even though you offer to give her lessons yourself, a creature WHO DOES NOT ADMIRE ME, who does not even interest herself in my studies, who would throw my manuscripts on the fire if that brought her more money than letting them be published, who gets rid of my cat, my one and only source of amusement at home, and introduces dogs, *because* the very sight of dogs makes me ill, who won't understand, or doesn't want to understand, that *economizing very carefully, just for ONE month*, would allow me, thanks to this temporary respite, to finish writing a lengthy work – how is it possible, I say, how is it possible to put up with this? I have tears in my eyes, tears of shame and rage, as I write this; and in all honesty I am glad I have no weapon in the house; I have in mind occasions when I find it impossible to follow the dictates of reason, that terrible night when I split open her head against a wall-bracket. That's the sort of life I have instead of the peace and quiet I thought to have ten months ago.[7]

The 'nine months that have just elapsed' mentioned at the beginning of this passage, the 'ten months' referred to at the end, indicate clearly enough how this crisis was precipitated. The letter was written on March 27th, 1852; nine and ten months ago, if we count back, take us to the period he was spending with his mother. Jeanne's jealousy of her; the comparisons Baudelaire made between the dead ashes of his love for his mistress and the sudden eruption of warm affection for his mother once they had agreed to bury the hatchet; these would have been enough to bring about the sudden deterioration in his relations with Jeanne when he found himself alone with her again. Baudelaire goes on to say that he has been wondering, for the past *four* months, how he might end the situation. It was four months previously that the *coup d'état* of December 2nd, 1851, inaugurated a change of régime in France and, given the active interest Baudelaire had taken in the vicissitudes of political life since the February Revolution of 1848, it may not be too fanciful to trace some connection here, the example of new brooms in public life being copied in his own private life. But to break with Jeanne and make a fresh start on his own account was something he had hesitated to do, lacking as he did the funds to pay her off. 'And yet, I must leave. And leave FOR GOOD AND ALL', and the right time to do it would be at the end of the quarter (April 7th); he would terminate the lease on their flat, give her what money he could, 'BUT I WILL NEVER SEE HER AGAIN. She can do what she likes, go to Hell if she wants to. I have wasted ten years of my life in this struggle. All my youthful illusions have fled. Nothing remains but a bitterness that perhaps I shall always feel.'[8]

But the bitterness did not prove eternal, nor was the break a final one, even though they did separate at this time. There were to be other reconciliations, other quarrels, other partings. Jeanne was part of his damnation, he could no more escape her than he could any of the other curses laid on him by a malignant fate, and in the depths of his soul he had a sure premonition of this. It may have been at this time, or it may have been a year or two later, remembering that moment of anguish and helplessness, that he composed the vengeful, doom-laden poem *The Vampire*.[9]

> You who, like a dagger thrust
> Into my aching, plaintive heart;
> You who, mincing, full of lust,
> Strong as the fiend, bedecked with art,
>
> Overcame my weak defences,
> Made of my bed your bad domain,
> Bound me fast by false pretences,
> As the convict by his chain,
>
> As the drunkard to his bowl,
> As the gamester to the dice,
> As carrion-flesh to worms, – ah thrice
> Cursed be you in body and soul!
>
> The swift sharp blade I have implored:
> Render me my liberty!
> And the treacherous poison poured:
> Act for my passivity!
>
> But the poison and the blade
> Mockingly have answered me:
> Are you worthy to be made,
> Simpleton, of this bond free?
>
> Were we to kill her whom you hate,
> This vampire, your dark sovereign,
> A corpse-like vampire once again
> Your kisses would resuscitate!

For a period thereafter, Baudelaire was able to enjoy a kind of emotional convalescence, freed of Jeanne and with his mother far away on the other side of the Pyrenees. A great calm descended on him; he felt purified, almost renewed, filled with vague yearnings for a life dedicated to the spiritual values. A less independently minded man might have experienced a religious conversion at this point and have become reconciled with the Church. What Baudelaire did was to invent for himself a private cult; instead of praying to the Virgin Mary, he singled out a woman of flesh and blood and, by an exercise of the poetic imagination, purged her of all human frailties and endowed her instead with all the qualities he most admired, because he felt himself most devoid of them: gaiety, because he was so often full of anguish and remorse; goodness, because he was eaten up with hatred; healthfulness, because he knew himself sick and disease-ridden; youth and beauty, because the mirror told him he was ageing prematurely and had lost for ever the angelic halo of his early twenties.

The object of his transfiguring devotion was in fact no fresh, innocent girl but a woman of thirty, only a year younger than Baudelaire himself. Christened Aglaé-Joséphine, her surname had originally been that of her putative father, André Savatier. Her real father was a man of aristocratic family, the *préfet* of the department of the Ardennes, at whose establishment in Mézières her mother had worked as a sewing maid; Savatier, a former NCO who had been retired from the army on account of disabling wounds received on active service, was offered a reasonable indemnity for acknowledging paternity of the child when it was born. The name Savatier, having an unfortunately proletarian ring in French (the word *savate* means a worn-out shoe), was changed by the girl to Sabatier when she grew up.

Her mother lived with the crippled sergeant from then on, and had other children by him or more probably by other lovers: a boy, Alexandre, born a year after Aglaé, who went to sea; another who became a house-painter; and, ten years after Aglaé's birth, a second girl, her 'baby sister', always known by the name 'Bébé' in the family circle. Three weeks after the arrival of this last child Savatier died. He had married the mother of this brood in 1825, thereby legitimizing retrospectively the first two children.

By this time the Savatiers were living in Paris, or rather in what was then the outlying suburb of Batignolles. Aglaé was educated at a private boarding-school in the neighbourhood, at reduced fees in consideration of her evident talent as a singer. In her late teens she made her first public appearance at a charity concert, at which her splendid figure, her grace of deportment, and her general air of health and happiness left a deep impression on one of the patrons, a Belgian gentleman called Alfred Mosselman. After making discreet inquiries about her circumstances, he decided she was just the girl he was looking for as *maîtresse en titre*.

Alfred Mosselman, then in his early thirties, came of a rich, old-established Brussels family. His elder sister was married to the Belgian ambassador to France, Charles Le Hon, and for a few years the young Mosselman worked in the legation alongside his brother-in-law. In 1836, however, he resigned from the diplomatic service in order to devote himself fully to the family's banking and mining interests. He was by now a married man, so, not wishing to cause his wife unnecessary distress, he came to an arrangement with Fernand Boissard, a close friend of his, that Mlle Savatier or Sabatier should pass as Boissard's mistress, which explains why it should have been in Boissard's apartment in the Hôtel Pimodan that Baudelaire first met her, some time in the summer of 1845. Gautier, who was also present, gives a lively account of the occasion in his memoirs. Aglaé and another young woman, Joséphine Bloch, better known as Maryx, who worked as a model (she was later to marry a secretary at the Danish legation), had been seen from Boissard's window in the street outside, walking back from the public baths. Invited up, they joined the four men (Gautier, Baudelaire, Boissard, and the sculptor Jean Feuchères) and an animated conversation ensued.

On Baudelaire, not yet the confirmed misogynist he was to become, this intelligent young woman, with her tawny brown hair still wet from her bath and her opulent contours very discernible under the thin muslin dress she was wearing, must have made some impression, however fleeting. But another six years were to pass before he met her again. In the meantime Mosselman had set her up in an apartment of her own in the district known as the Quartier Bréda, a favourite haunt in those days for artists and artists' models; Puvis de Chavannes and Diaz de la Peña both had their studios nearby. Here, under the *nom de guerre* of Apollonie Sabatier, she presided over a kind of literary and artistic *salon* which lasted well into the Second Empire, until, in fact, Mosselman broke with her in 1860.

Apollonie's special charm was experienced not just by men but by women too and even by a little girl like Gautier's daughter Judith who, many years later, drew on her memories to give a very exact description of how she appeared in the days she was setting up her *salon* in the Rue Frochot.

> She was fairly tall, beautifully proportioned, with slender wrists and ankles and charming hands. Her hair, very silky, a golden chestnut in colour, fell naturally in rich, glinting waves. Her complexion was clear and smooth and her features regular, with something witty and saucy in their expression; and she had a merry little mouth. Her triumphant air spread brightness and joy all around her. She dressed tastefully but with great originality, not following the fashion but creating her own. Great artists, who came to her Sunday parties, used to advise her and draw sketches of costumes for her.[10]

One of these artists, the sculptor Jean-Baptiste Clésinger, went much farther than this, and at Mosselman's suggestion and with Apollonie's reluctant consent, took a plaster cast of her naked body writhing in a simulated spasm of sexual pleasure. From this cast Clésinger made a statue which, exhibited at the 1847 *salon*, stole the show. The sculptor had originally thought of calling the work *Rêve d'amour* but, caution prevailing, added a snake biting the woman's foot to give the composition a vaguely mythological character (Persephone had been stung by a snake) and thus make it more acceptable to the viewing committee. The head, fortunately, was not a copy of Apollonie's; her modesty was to that extent spared and it is by no means certain that Baudelaire, when he saw the statue at the exhibition, realized who the shameless model had been.

Mme Sabatier's celebrated Sunday dinner parties were attended, at one time or another, by many of the leading writers and artists in Paris at the time: Gautier, who tended to monopolize the conversation; Flaubert, when he could tear himself away from Croisset and *Madame Bovary*; Flaubert's friends Maxime Du Camp, Louis Bouilhet, Edmond and Jules de Goncourt; and of course Baudelaire who from 1851 onwards was one of the most assiduous, according to Judith Gautier. The painters and sculptors included Meissonier, who did two portraits of her, Henry Monnier, Clésinger and Auguste Préault; and, though not among the 'regulars', Delacroix and Chenavard. The women were always in a minority. There was Apollonie's younger sister Bébé (Irma-Adèle), Gautier's mistress Ernesta Grisi, and the strikingly handsome Italian revolutionary Elisa Neri, for whom Baudelaire wrote an adulatory sonnet, though not until after the publication of *Les Fleurs du Mal*.[11] Apollonie's irregular situation was the reason why no respectable married women were to be seen at her table; but their absence allowed a great freedom of speech, which suited Gautier, an incorrigible teller of bawdy stories. The atmosphere was anything but starchy. The guests came to enjoy themselves, and when the mood took them would organize party games, charades, and even, on one occasion at least, a costume ball, at which Gautier appeared disguised as a Turk, Ernest Reyer, the composer, as a chimpanzee, while Flaubert made his entry as a Red Indian chief, brandishing a kitchen cleaver in lieu of a tomahawk.

It is difficult to imagine Baudelaire participating in vulgar jollifications of this sort, or taking much pleasure in the recitals given by Henry Monnier of the satirical sketches for which he was famous. He was more in his element in quieter moments, putting forward one or other of his outrageous paradoxes when the conversation turned to art, literature, philosophy or politics. Their hostess, though no bluestocking, was perfectly capable of contributing to such discussions; she was a woman of taste and intelligence, admittedly with gaps in her education, but thoroughly versed in the arts, particularly in music. She had a warm and generous nature, knew that men liked her, but did nothing to attract their homage and never tried to make herself the centre of attention; there was not a trace of the coquette in her. Her very presence dispelled gloom. 'She adored brightness, gaiety, sunshine, all these things which were part of her nature,' wrote Meissonier. 'For a tired man, it was a delightful relaxation to find her always the same, always true to herself, helping you forget the worries of day-to-day life with her welcoming smile.'[12] Baudelaire had even more reason than Meissonier to be grateful to her for the haven she provided, a haven of cordiality and good cheer.

But it was a stronger feeling than gratitude that filled him as he plodded back to his dingy, solitary lodgings on a Sunday evening around midnight. The violent contrast between the sullen, thin-bodied, acrimonious mistress with whom he had now broken and this accomplished, even-tempered, smiling society beauty seemed to epitomize the gulf between the sordid struggles of his daily life and the serene paradise of the ideal to which in imagination he always aspired. Jeanne, the black witch, symbolized his damnation; Apollonie, the white angel, his salvation. Far from dreaming of replacing Jeanne by Apollonie, he gave them each a separate and distinct role to play in the private psycho-drama he was for ever acting inside his own mind. Jeanne had been flesh of his flesh; Apollonie was to be for him as the Madonna for the believer: an object of worship rather than desire. The poetry she inspired him to write is soaked in religious sentiment; one was entitled simply *Hymne*, and in others she is addressed as his guardian angel, saving him from sin and the snares of the Evil One. He speaks often in these poems of her eyes, shining like torches to light him along his dark road, or like tapers in an incense-filled cathedral. The poems he had written for Jeanne were also full of references to her eyes, but in those the comparisons were with shining metal or glittering gems, things that reflect light but give out none of their own.

It would be absurd, on the evidence of the poetry, to conclude that Baudelaire was not sexually attracted to Apollonie Sabatier; but in his mood of lassitude combined with the yearning to renew himself, his strongest impulse was to sublimate such desires, to pretend they were sacrilegious, a temptation he had to fight. In *Tout entière* (*The Woman Entire*)[13] he actually dramatized the process, writing a kind of allegorical narrative of which there are other specimens in *Les Fleurs du Mal*, though the form is much commoner in the prose poetry he was to compose a little later:

This morning, in my lofty room,
In walked the Devil on a visit;
Trying to lure me to my doom,
He asked: 'My friend, tell me, which is it,

Of breast or thigh, of rump or arm,
– The hair that's black, the skin that's pink –
Of all that makes her body's charm
Which has the most appeal, d'you think?'

Get thee behind me! O my soul,
Satan you silenced with a word:
'Since she makes up one lovely whole,
Nothing in her can be preferred.

When one is all and all is one,
No one thing gives me chief delight.
She dazzles like the rising sun
And she consoles me like the night.

Her lovely form is governed by
Too exquisite a harmony
For analytic minds to try
And order any hierarchy.

O mystical polyphony
As one sense into the other flows!
Her fragrance plays a symphony,
Her voice is scented like the rose.'

None of the members of Mme Sabatier's circle had the least inkling
of Baudelaire's exalted platonic attachment to the mistress of the
house. In general, he never spoke even to his closest intimates of his
love affairs, which is one reason why several of them, including
Nadar, were convinced he was incapable of ordinary sexual relations
with any woman. Théophile Gautier who, unlike Nadar, was a poet,
or had at least enough of the poet in him to understand the necessary
process of interiorization which has to precede literary creation, was
not deceived by this discretion on the part of his friend. Baudelaire,
he noted, was not what was commonly thought of as shy or retiring.
In company he was a great talker; but his talk always ran along
certain lines; Gautier called it a 'metaphysical conversation'. 'Baudelaire had much to say about his ideas, less about his feelings, and
never spoke about his activities. As for his loves, a cameo incised with
the figure of Harpocrates sealed his sensitive, disdainful lips.'[4]
Harpocrates, the Greek version of the Egyptian deity Horus, was
conventionally represented in painting as a dimpling, naked child

holding his forefinger to his lips and signified, of course, the veil of discretion customarily dropped over the marriage bed.

But however reserved a lover may be with his friends, it would be strange indeed if he did not feel the need to speak of his passion to the woman who has inspired it. Yet even here Baudelaire hesitated; not out of timidity, for Apollonie was anything but awe-inspiring, but because if she were to fill the role of madonna, she must remain intact and inviolate, an object of prayer and worship, essentially transcendental. Once speak to her of his love, as a man to a woman, and whether she responded or rebuffed him, their relations would descend to the purely human plane. Yet mere solitary imaginings would not do; he needed to commune, hence to communicate. So Baudelaire was driven to a curious, and ultimately transparent subterfuge. He wrote her a series of unsigned letters, disguising his handwriting, with each of which he enclosed one or two of the poems he had written in her honour.

Despite his precautions, Apollonie may well have guessed almost from the start who the writer of this delicate, exalted poetry was, if only by a simple process of elimination; no one else, among the men who frequented her, was capable of this kind of bejewelled rhetoric. But she also understood, being a person of considerable understanding, that what Baudelaire wanted above all was that these tributes to her influence over him, written 'for her eyes only', should remain private. He had said in the very first of the letters (dated December 9th, 1852): 'Deep emotions are characterized by a reticence which may not be breached. Is not anonymity the sign of this invincible reticence? He who wrote these lines, lost in one of those reveries into which the image of her who is their object often plunges him, has loved her deeply, without ever speaking to her of his feelings, and will *always* conserve for her the most tender affection.'[15]

The letters, and the poems, continued to arrive at irregular intervals over the next eighteen months. The second of the enclosures was accompanied by a single sentence in English: 'After a night of pleasure and desolation, all my soul belongs to you.' The fact that it was written in English would have allowed Apollonie to penetrate his secret if she had not already done so, for she could not have been unaware that Baudelaire was actively engaged at this time in translating Poe's short stories. She may not have understood what he meant by 'a night of pleasure and desolation'; the explanation lies in an obscure episode of the poet's life in May 1853. He and Philoxène Boyer had taken the train to Versailles for a short stay but found, when it came to settling the hotel bill, that they had not brought enough money with them. The manager insisted on impounding their belongings until they paid what they owed, and they found the only establishment in Versailles which would take them in without luggage was the local brothel. Naturally they availed themselves of all the facilities there. Baudelaire wrote three poems for Apollonie Sabatier in these incongruous surroundings, among them the sonnet entitled *L'Aube spirituelle* (*Spiritual Dawn*) which takes as its starting-point the debauchees' awakening after 'a night of pleasure and desolation' and proceeds to draw an exalted simile between the dawning of a new day and the purifying effect on the poet of the returning memory of his angelic Muse:

These drunken revellers, when pale pink Dawn
Allies itself to the sharp-toothed Ideal,
A mystic, vengeful transformation feel,
As in the snoring brute an angel's born.

Skies beyond reach, azure infinity,
Dreamed of by suffering man stretched there in sleep,
Open before him, lure him to the deep.
Even so, clear Spirit, dear Divinity,

Among the sordid relics of the night,
Bright, rosy, charming, thy sweet memory
Hovers before my eyes incessantly.

The rising sun has dimmed the candlelight;
Likewise, all-conquering phantom, thou art one,
Resplendent Soul, with the immortal sun.[16]

The series of letters ended on May 8th, 1854, when he sent her the poem entitled *Hymne* which, in the whole cycle, shows most strikingly the use of religious imagery in an erotic context. The accompanying letter includes a reference to Mosselman and to the satisfaction Baudelaire takes in her union with so 'amiable' a gentleman. 'Finally, in order that you may understand my periods of silence followed by bursts of enthusiasm, almost religious enthusiasm, I should explain that when my spirit is steeped in the darkness of its native folly and wickedness, it dreams of you profoundly. Out of such exalting and purifying daydreams there commonly issues some happy accident' (by which Baudelaire must mean the particular poem the daydream suggests to him). 'You are for me not only the most attractive of women – of all women – but in addition you are the dearest and most precious of my superstitions.'[17]

To understand Baudelaire's state of mind when he wrote the last of these anonymous letters, one has to know that his mother was now back in France, Aupick having been made a member of the Senate and needing, in consequence, to reside in Paris. Between mother and son, all the old quarrels had flared up again, provoked by the same grievances: on her part, that he had still not completely broken with Jeanne and had still not achieved 'respectability'; on his, that she persisted not merely in refusing to come to his assistance, but in reproaching him even for asking her to do so. The pressing need for ready cash arose when on November 15th, 1853, Jeanne's mother died. Baudelaire felt it was up to him to assume the funeral expenses, since Jeanne was in no position to do so and the alternative would have been a pauper's burial. Of the 140 francs he needed, he had only 80 at his disposal. His mother sent him the balance, but not without reading him a lecture on his improvidence. But he wanted to do more: to purchase a plot in a cemetery so that the old woman's remains could lie undisturbed until the Day of Judgement. 'If I had a substantial sum of money – say 100 francs – I wouldn't spend it on shoes or shirts, I wouldn't visit a tailor or use it to redeem articles at the pawnshop. Yesterday was the last day for the accomplishment of an act which I regard as an *essential duty*, that is the exhumation and reburial of a woman who gave me her last savings, without grumbling or sighing, and *above all without giving me advice*.'[18] The last, underlined words were clearly a shaft directed against his mother, but she must have read the letter with a pang deriving from quite other reflections. Here was her son regretting that he had not the means to render a last service of piety to the mother of his mistress, one which she had omitted to accomplish in respect of his own father, her first husband, out of negligence or stinginess and not because she had been unable to afford it. Touched, it may be, by a twinge of remorse, she wrote him a letter couched in much softer tones than she had used before, and he teased her gently for this in his reply. 'You wrote me a very melancholy, very charming letter, but still marked by your incurable habits of exaggeration. As for the dead woman, what I felt for her was almost hatred. But I let her die in the direst poverty. And besides, did I invent the prejudice that bids us show respect for the dead? I am really doing no more than obeying the conventions . . .'[19]

Estranged from his mother, separated from Jeanne, and no longer finding the same satisfaction in the ethereal cult he had devoted to Mme Sabatier, Baudelaire found himself by the summer of 1854 as forlorn as he had ever been. There remained one woman who might fill the void in his heart: the actress Marie Daubrun. In his correspondence, her name occurs for the first time in a letter to his mother on August 14th; the previous month he had spoken in another letter of going along to the Théâtre de la Gaîté (where Mlle Daubrun had a part in the play currently billed) at eleven in the evening, which could only have been because he had arranged to meet the young woman at the stage door and accompany her home.

He had known her, by sight if not more intimately, for several years, possibly since before the 1848 Revolution. One of the poems she inspired, entitled *L'Irréparable* in *Les Fleurs du Mal*, was originally published[20] as *La Belle aux cheveux d'or* (*The Girl with the Golden Hair*), which was the actual title of a dramatic spectacle running at the Théâtre de la Porte-Saint-Martin between August 1847 and February 1848. Marie Daubrun had a major part in *La Belle aux cheveux d'or*, that of the princess delivered at the end from the persecution of the villain by the intervention of a fairy in a transformation scene to which the last two stanzas of Baudelaire's poem refer directly.

Like most actresses at this period, when no girl from a 'good home' would think of going on to the stage, Marie Daubrun came of poor parents. The surname under which she was registered at birth was that of her mother, described on the certificate simply as a 'working woman';[21] her father, Aimé Brunod, was a stonemason. She began her acting career in the autumn of 1845, when at the age of eighteen she joined the company of the Théâtre Montmartre (the present Théâtre de l'Atelier), taking lead parts in various melodramas and historical plays by Frédéric Soulié, Alexandre Dumas père, and other less well remembered dramatists. The Théâtre Montmartre was regarded as a sort of nursery for the big Paris theatres, and Mlle Daubrun graduated after a few months to the Théâtre de la Porte-Saint-Martin.

She owed this fairly rapid rise more to her looks than to her talent, which was unremarkable. In reporting her move to the Porte-Saint-Martin, the *Mercure des Théâtres* called her 'a charming person who speaks her lines very well when she is favourably disposed, which unfortunately does not always happen'.[22] Baudelaire, who never had any illusions about her ability as an actress, voiced the same reservations about her in later communications with the theatre critic Paul de Saint-Victor: 'Mlle Daubrun is one of those persons who are good or bad according to which quarter the wind is blowing from, according to the state of her nerves, according to whether she is getting good or bad notices ...'; '... Mlle Daubrun, whom I recommended to you rather timidly, for she gives me the impression of someone who occasionally, but quite fortuitously, shows talent.'[23] Even love could not blind Baudelaire to the fragility of this talent, and whatever advantage he might have hoped to reap by promoting her career, he was too honest to do so at the cost of hoodwinking those in a position to secure her advancement.

She had, of course, received hardly any professional training. Taken in hand by an expert director, she might have become the same kind of star in the mid-nineteenth century as Brigitte Bardot in the mid-twentieth. Her special attraction lay in the combination of a magnificent figure with an air of childlike grace; this is a feature referred to not just by Baudelaire but by her other poet-lover too, Théodore de Banville.[24] She had a versatile speaking voice which could range from the crystalline to the harshly sonorous. Her hair was a true 'crowning glory': a thick yellow mane with reddish tints. Though a natural blonde, she had dark eyebrows, and her eyes were of an indeterminate colour, greenish, as Baudelaire called them in *Chant d'automne*, or shifting through various shades and tonalities:

> You gaze at me as though through a light cloud;
> Your eyes (blue, grey, or green, what shall I say?)
> Now gentle, dreamy, yet now cruel and proud,
> Mysteriously reflect the pallid day.[25]

Whether Baudelaire fell in love with her at first sight, watching her from his stall in the Théâtre de la Porte-Saint-Martin in 1847, or whether his passion developed some years later, we shall probably never know; Harpocrates keeps his forefinger on his lips. Unlike Mme Sabatier, Marie Daubrun preserved none of the letters he must have written to her, except one, and even that is problematic; the latest editor of Baudelaire's correspondence calls it 'the most enigmatic' of all his letters. Directed simply to 'Madame Marie', it is undated, and the superscription is found on none of his other letters, so it is impossible to use the address to fix the year in which Baudelaire wrote it. The main reason for supposing the recipient to have been Marie Daubrun is the two sentences: 'How can I express to you how much I love your eyes and how deeply I treasure your beauty? It contains two contradictory graces, which in you are not in contradiction: the grace of a child and that of a woman.'[26] Surely there could not have been two women in whom girlhood and maturity united to cast a spell over Baudelaire?

The truly enigmatic feature of this letter is that Baudelaire, having been at first, it seems, rebuffed by the lady when he declared his love, now asks her to accept his platonic adoration, and in doing so uses phrases which repeat or anticipate the language used – not in his letters to Mme Sabatier – but even more strangely, in the poetry he sent her, and to such an extent that the resemblances amount at times to textual identity.

> Whether you wish it or not, you will be henceforth my shield and my talisman. I love you, Marie, that I cannot deny, but the love I feel for you is that of the Christian for his God. Therefore never apply the mundane, so often shameful word to this disembodied,

mysterious cult, this sweet and chaste attraction my soul feels for yours, even against your will. It would be sacrilege. . . . Henceforth you are my sole queen, passion and beauty, you are that part of me formed by a spiritual caress. It will be through you, Marie, that I shall grow great and strong. Like Petrarch, I will immortalize my Laura. Be you my guardian angel, my Muse and my Madonna, and conduct me along the path of the Beautiful.[27]

Whether this letter was written to Marie Daubrun or to some other – and opinion among scholars is divided; whether it was written in 1852, as the first editor of Baudelaire's correspondence, Féli Gautier, believed, or earlier, or later – and all three theories have found proponents; whatever the truth of the matter, the existence of the letter does at least prove one thing. The poet's yearning for some disincarnate passion, some focus for purely spiritual adoration, was what chiefly motivated him; in the end it was Apollonie Sabatier who, for one reason or another, appeared most suited to play the role, but it could have been almost any other woman.

Marie Daubrun was too public a figure to fill the part, and besides, to judge from the poetry she inspired, her sexual attraction for Baudelaire was too powerful. The poems in the cycle written for her are distinguished by a certain melancholy lassitude in the writer's mood, occasionally shot through with a vein of sadistic fury. They include the beautiful *Invitation au voyage*, with its languorous harmonies, but also *A une Madone*, which ends with the poet imagining himself planting daggers in her heart, and *Le Beau Navire*, as sensual in its way as *Les Bijoux*, though Marie Daubrun is pictured fully dressed while Jeanne, in *Les Bijoux*, was described as totally naked. But none of the component poems of this cycle suggests the reverential, sublimated passion he tried to cultivate for Mme Sabatier.

The dangers of falling in love with an actress had been foreseen long since by Baudelaire, the main one being that 'she is not a woman in the full sense of the word – for her, the public comes first. Suppose a poet compelled to watch his beloved take a boy's part – I would imagine he would want to set fire to the theatre! Or what if he was obliged to write a part for his wife, knowing she was untalented?'[28] Baudelaire, when he wrote these lines, may have had in mind the domestic quarrels involving Hugo, Mme Hugo, and Juliette Drouet over the casting of *Ruy Blas*, or the disastrous acting of Alexandre Dumas's mistress and future wife Ida Ferrier in his tragedy *Caligula*; these scandals were common property and should have served him as a warning. Marie Daubrun was no better an actress than these other two; but she had ambitions, and there was a brief period, around

1853-4, when it seemed possible Baudelaire might get a play accepted at one of the boulevard theatres; if so, it would have been on the understanding that she would be given the principal feminine role.

This play was to be entitled *L'Ivrogne* (*The Drunkard*); the suggestion he should write it had been made by one of the most popular actors at the Odéon, Jean-Hippolyte Tisserant, after hearing Baudelaire give an after-supper recitation of his 'black poem', *Le Vin de l'assassin*. Although written in the form of a monologue, *Le Vin de l'assassin* does in fact present a rudimentary story: the workman, tired of his wife's complaints that his wages go all on drink, decoys her to a lonely spot where they used to meet during their courtship days, kills her and throws her body down a well. He expresses neither regret nor remorse for what he has done, merely satisfaction at being free at last to drink himself into oblivion.

Acting on Tisserant's hint, Baudelaire took the trouble to write out the synopsis of a five-act melodrama, which he sent to the actor on January 28th, 1854. Apart from the possibility of some pecuniary profit if his play was accepted by the administration of the Odéon, Baudelaire saw here a chance to draw closer to Marie Daubrun, who was a member of the company and whom he clearly visualized in the pathetic part of the murderer's wife and victim.[29] But then Marie abruptly switched from the Odéon to the Théâtre de la Gaîté, where the leading male actor was Philibert Rouvière; Tisserant accordingly drops out of the picture and in Baudelaire's mind it is Rouvière who will now incarnate his drunkard while Marie Daubrun, of course, keeps the part originally destined for her. Baudelaire had an interview with the director of the Gaîté, Hippolyte Hostein, which passed off extremely well. All that remained was for Baudelaire, having sold his bearskin, to shoot his bear – in other words to write his play.

This he never did; it was left to Zola, a generation later, to produce, in the dramatized version of *L'Assommoir*, the first successful popular melodrama on the subject of the ravages of drink among the working classes. If Baudelaire did not pursue his original idea, the fault was for once due less to a 'writer's block' than to Marie Daubrun's erratic behaviour; in consequence of some backstage quarrel, she broke her contract and walked out on Hostein at the height of the season. Furious at being left in the lurch, he threatened legal action against any theatre director who gave her a job. With no chance of employment in Paris, the headstrong actress was constrained to join a touring company and left for Italy.

At the end of this engagement she wrote to Baudelaire from Nice in August 1855, asking him to try and get her a part in George Sand's

Maître Favilla which was due to open at the Odéon. Baudelaire had no personal acquaintance with the famous woman writer and no very high opinion of her, but he did his best for his absent mistress and wrote a polite letter pressing her claims. George Sand may well have been disposed to let Marie Daubrun be cast, quite independently of Baudelaire's urging, but the decision did not lie entirely with her; the director of the Odéon, Gustave Vaëz, quailing at the thought of further dealings with this troublesome actress, pretended he wanted someone slimmer for the part, and hastily awarded it to the rising star Marie Laurent.[30]

The failure of these negotiations probably explains why, when she returned to Paris in the autumn of 1855, Marie Daubrun, concluding that Baudelaire was decidedly a broken reed, went and lived with Banville instead. This betrayal made no difference to the close friendship between the two poets, but it completely upset Baudelaire's plans. In anticipation of her return, he had pleaded with his mother and with Ancelle to allow him an advance of 500 francs so as to furnish suitable lodgings in the Rue d'Angoulême. Rather than waive the option he had taken on these rooms, Baudelaire, now desperate to escape from his chronic homelessness and solitude, moved in notwithstanding – but with Jeanne, in default of Marie.

In spite of the rupture of 1852, his relations with his old mistress had never been totally severed. When Jeanne was hard up, she would call on him to beg for help; and whenever he could, he would slip her a 20-franc piece, not, as he insisted, out of pity or for charity's sake, but because of his accursed pride. 'I do not wish that anyone should see a woman of mine going about poor, ill-dressed, and ailing, who was once beautiful, elegant, and blooming with health.'[31] Nevertheless he had convinced himself that any resumption of intimate relations with her was out of the question, and in April 1855 he was badly upset to discover that his old friend Courbet, in his recently completed picture *The Painter in his Studio*, had had the effrontery to include a full-length portrait of Jeanne standing beside him on the right-hand side of the canvas, as though it was impossible to show Baudelaire in a group without his mulatto mistress. Courbet, who had been living for the last few years not in Paris but in Ornans, was unaware that the poet's long-standing liaison had been terminated. But Baudelaire was disturbed to think that at this stage, when all he wanted to do was to put the memory of it behind him, his affair was to receive, so to speak, its official consecration in paint. Supposing Marie Daubrun were to see it on her return to Paris! So he persuaded Courbet to paint out the figure before the picture was exhibited.[32] Ironically, in executing her portrait – she had been shown standing in a provocative attitude in front of a mirror – the artist, to prompt his memory, had used one of the sketches Baudelaire himself had made of his mistress in happier days.

However, by December 1855 he had set up house with her again, more out of desperation at his loneliness and the ruin of brighter hopes than because he felt he could not live without her; and, predictably, the experiment failed. After less than a year they parted again, though this time it was she who broke with him. On September 11th, 1856, he wrote to his mother to tell her that

my fourteen-year-old liaison with Jeanne is over. I did everything a human being could do to prevent this break. The heart-rending struggle has lasted a fortnight. Jeanne kept answering me imperturbably that I was impossible to live with, and that in any case I would thank her myself one day for this decision; exactly the kind of vulgar, bourgeois wisdom one expects from one of her sex. But I know that, whatever good comes my way, whatever pleasure or financial windfall, whatever happens to minister to my vanity, I shall always miss this woman. In case my distress, which I can't expect you to understand properly, strikes you as too childish, I will confess to you that I had staked on her all my hopes, like a gambler; this woman was my sole distraction, my sole pleasure, my sole companion, and in spite of all the inner upheavals of a stormy liaison, the idea of a final separation had never really occurred to me. Even now, although I have calmed down completely, I find myself thinking, whenever I see some pretty object, a fine piece of landscape painting, anything attractive – why isn't she with me, so that we can buy it together? You see I am making no secret of my sufferings. It was not until a long while afterwards, I assure you, so violent was the wrench, that I came round to thinking that perhaps I should find some pleasure in work, and that after all I had some duties to discharge. I kept saying to myself all the time: What's the point of anything? – not to mention a sort of dark veil before my eyes and an endless buzzing in my ears. That went on some time, and then finished. When it became clear to me that the *irreparable* had truly come to pass, then I fell into a nameless rage. I couldn't sleep for ten days, I kept on being sick, I had to hide myself away because I was in tears all the time. The idea that obsessed me was a purely egoistic one. I saw stretching before me an endless succession of years with no family life, no friends, no mistress, years in which I would live alone, buffeted by fate, with no balm for my broken heart. I could not even call on my pride to console me. For it has been my own fault that this has happened. I used her and misused her. I tortured her for my amusement, and now I am tortured in my turn.[33]

One has always to make allowances, in Baudelaire's letters to his mother, for some exaggeration of his feelings; she was the only person to whom he could truly open his heart, but he needed her sympathy and for that reason he may sometimes have yielded to the temptation to over-dramatize. But there is no doubt that he thought – wrongly, as it emerged – that he had lost Jeanne for good; this meant the end of an era; fourteen years is a long time in a man's life. In this letter he is more concerned with the bleak future; but when, in a calmer mood, he looked back over the past, he forgot all the irritations, the quarrels, the way she had betrayed him, the way he had humiliated her, and remembered only the close companionship that had knit them together over this long period and which was what he most keenly regretted. As a kind of farewell present, a keepsake, he wrote her a poem entitled *The Balcony*,[34] in which sensuality, tenderness, and the magic of memory are woven together into an inexpressibly lovely verbal tapestry. These six stanzas are not merely the gentlest and most evocative of all he ever composed for Jeanne or any other woman, but also as touching a piece of writing as can be found anywhere in the whole literature of love.

     Mother of memories, mistress of my dreams,
     To whom I am in love and duty bound,
     You will recall, as red the firelight gleams,
     What fond embraces, what content we found,
     Mother of memories, mistress of my dreams!

     Those twilit evenings, while the embers glowed,
     And rosy mists entwined our balcony,
     How softly swelled your breast, how kind you showed
     Yourself! what words we spoke in harmony!
     Those twilit evenings, while the embers glowed.

     The beauty of the sun at eventide!
     How deep the blue of heaven! Closely held,
     Bent over you, my queen, stretched by your side,
     It was as if your warm heart's blood I smelled.
     The beauty of the sun at eventide!

As darkness fell, as died the flickering taper,
My eyes would seek your eyes, nights without number,
And I would breathe your breath, sweet deadly vapour!
And, cradled in my hands, your feet would slumber,
As darkness fell, as died the flickering taper.

Those happy moments live on in my mind
Whene'er I lay my head upon your knees.
Why should I look elsewhere, or seek to find
Some other ecstasy to rival these?
Those happy moments live on in my mind.

That lingering kiss, those vows, that fragrance rare,
Will they from unplumbed depths once more emerge,
As the sun rises in the morning air,
Cleansed by the ocean's endless ebb and surge?
O lingering kiss! O vows! O fragrance rare!

X

MISUNDERSTANDINGS

'There are two ways of becoming famous,' Baudelaire observed in his *Salon de 1845*: 'by piling up successes year after year, or by bursting on the world in a clap of thunder. The second way is assuredly the more original.'[1]

He was, of course, thinking of painters when he wrote these words; but up to a point they were applicable to writers too, and particularly to poets like himself. The first category was best illustrated by Victor Hugo who at the age of thirty-six, the age Baudelaire had reached when he published his first and only volume of poetry, had already produced seven verse collections – which even so represented less than half his total poetic output during his lifetime. Though few poets were quite as prolific as Hugo, most of them, including his own friends Gautier, Banville, and Leconte de Lisle, brought out new volumes periodically, as each harvest ripened. Baudelaire, without ever formulating the difference, knew that his concept of creative writing was quite another. It was not, for him, a question of milking a cow-like Muse whenever her udders were full. His book would constitute the distilled essence of his life and thought, the thought evolving through the life but remaining all the time peculiar to him, *sui generis*, to use one of his favourite tags. There could therefore be only one book; it was important to ensure that it did not appear before its time and that when it did appear it should give the impression of a 'clap of thunder'.

No doubt a slimmer volume could have been published earlier, had Baudelaire so chosen; if we are to believe Asselineau, by 1844 'the majority of the pieces printed in the volume *Les Fleurs du Mal* were already composed'.[2] At the end of 1849 he engaged a calligrapher to copy out all the poems he had written, and had them bound up in two cased quarto volumes with gilt lettering. This may have been intended to constitute a fair copy for an eventual publisher but, if so, would have been of little use; Baudelaire was bitterly indignant about the ludicrous errors of transcription made by the copyist. The first real step in the direction of ultimate integral publication was taken in 1851, when *Le Messager de l'Assemblée* agreed to print eleven poems he had submitted. Although a few isolated samples of Baudelaire's poetry had appeared here and there in various journals prior to this, it was the first time he had brought out a group of poems under a general title; not, however, *Les Fleurs du Mal* as yet, but *Les Limbes*.

This strange title first appears, applied to the poems, in 1848, at which time it would have had vaguely revolutionary implications, the word 'limbo' having been used by Fourier to designate the historical period preceding the establishment of the socialist utopia. But to readers of Dante, and to Catholic theologians generally, the word conveyed quite a different meaning, one which Baudelaire also intended, if not in 1848, certainly by April 1851 when his eleven poems were published under this title in *Le Messager de l'Assemblée*. The souls consigned to limbo are those of good men who, having lived their lives on earth before Christ's coming, missed being baptized and consequently could not be issued with a passport to paradise.[3] Limbo was supposedly situated in a kind of no-man's-land on the outskirts of hell. Dante visited it at the beginning of his conducted tour of the infernal regions, and learned from Virgil the reason why so many departed spirits were penned in this spot; it was solely for want of being sprinkled with baptismal water before they died.

> For such defects, and for no guilt entire
> We are lost, afflicted only in this sense,
> That without hope we linger in desire.[4]

In limbo there was 'no sound ... Of wailing, only sighs and sighs again, That made the eternal air all tremulous', for the spirits that dwelt here were not suffering torment, as were those imprisoned in the circles of Hell proper; nor were they in Purgatory, suffering, but with the expectation of eventually being transported to Paradise. They were without hope, but still capable of *desire*.

This may have been the main reason for Baudelaire's provisional choice of *Les Limbes* for the title of his book of verse, for the state of hopeless longing described here, of nostalgia mingled with desperation, is closely akin to the mood which a number of his poems translate, and for which the fashionable name in France at the time was *le spleen*; indeed, the connection between *limbo* and *spleen* had been made quite explicitly by one of the members of the Jeunes-France school, Philothée O'Neddy, in a poem published in 1841 which Baudelaire may well have seen.[5] At this date the word *spleen* had been current in the vocabulary of the romantics for at least ten years. Sir Ralph Brown, one of the characters in George Sand's first novel *Indiana* (1832), had been subject since the age of fifteen, we are told, 'to attacks of spleen, a purely physiological disorder in the foggy climate of England, a purely psychological one in the bracing climate of Mauritius'. Vigny's *Stello*, published in book form in the same year as *Indiana*, begins with a consultation between the poet-hero and his doctor, in the course of which Stello complains: 'All this morning I have been suffering an attack of spleen, and such spleen that everything I look at, when I am here on my own, fills me with the deepest loathing. I hate the sun, and the rain gives me the horrors. To an invalid's tired eyes, the sun shines so boastfully, with all the insolence of a *parvenu*; and as for the rain, ah! of all the plagues Heaven visits us with, I think the rain must be the worst of all.'[6]

Since the word was borrowed directly from English, it is not surprising that George Sand mentions spleen in a specifically English context, as indeed Baudelaire himself was to do in an essay on the comic spirit which he published in 1855: 'If one is looking for savage, really savage humour, one needs to cross the Channel and visit the foggy realms of spleen.'[7] But the connection Vigny establishes between spleen and rain is of more help in tracing the ramifying connections of the word for Baudelaire. Of the four poems in *Les Fleurs du Mal* that bear the same title, *Spleen*, three refer directly to the depressing effects of rainy weather on the poet's spirit. One begins with the line:

'I'm like the monarch of a rainy country';

another starts by evoking Pluviose, the god of rain; while the third will have to be quoted in full to show the bitter virtuosity with which Baudelaire plotted a complex network of associations between wet weather, claustrophobia, and despair.

When like a coffin-lid the lowering skies
Weigh on the spirit groaning in its plight,
Grey overhead, where'er one turns one's eyes,
Greyer than grey and gloomier than the night;

When, shut on every side by these damp walls,
The world's an oubliette in which Hope seems
A frightened bat that flutters, swoops and falls,
Beating its head against the mouldering beams;

When, streaming down the filthy window-panes,
The rain of prison bars puts us in mind,
And, spinning sticky webs within our brains,
Foul spiders scuttle silently behind;

Sudden, a clangour and a furious din,
As the church bells ring out discordantly,
Like spirits punished for some unknown sin,
Who wander, lost, and howl incessantly.

– And, with no sound of drums, in silent grief,
Through my soul pass processions for the dead;
Hope weeps, and Anguish, like a pirate chief,
Plants his black banner on my lowered head.[8]

Spleen provided Baudelaire with much more than the theme for a few black poems. Taking this cliché of romanticism, he used it as a twig round which could cluster all the cruel crystals of his self-loathing. He saw spleen as akin to the *accidie* that monks of the Middle Ages were said to be subject to, something that ate deeply into the soul and was not to be compared with mere boredom or *ennui*, a passing affliction of the spirit. Spleen had to do also with the sense of the irretrievable passage of time, and with the terrifying premonition that he would never achieve what was in him to achieve, what he had been sent into the world to achieve. It fed on knowledge that none of the errors and beastlinesses of the past could ever be wiped out: the knowledge of the *irreparable*. It was a self-tormenting, sterile, sado-masochistic mood, in which the most solemn sounding of his conscience led to no absolution, and only confirmed him in his conviction that he belonged to the hopelessly damned.

Spleen was, in fact, evil as he knew it, and evil in both senses: as one says an evil smell (affecting one disagreeably), and an evil thought (leading one to sin). The title which eventually replaced *Les Limbes*, *Les Fleurs du Mal*, pointed to both these meanings. The flowers or poems[9] demonstrated how the magic of poetry could turn evil (that is, sin, ugliness, cruelty, decrepitude) into a thing of beauty; but the title also implied that the poetry was a kind of blossoming of evil. It was not a title of Baudelaire's own invention, having been suggested by an obscure critic, Hippolyte Babou, one evening when the poet and his cronies were sitting round a café table debating various possibilities; but no title could have been found more perfectly suited to the contents of the book.

Baudelaire first used it as the heading for the batch of eighteen poems he sent to the *Revue des Deux Mondes* in 1855, and which were published in that periodical on June 1st. Three of them had appeared previously in *Le Messager de l'Assemblée*, but otherwise they were quite unknown even to Baudelaire's closest friends. Many of them were love-poems, though of a kind that had scarcely ever been seen before; he seems to have chosen deliberately the most sombre for the novelty of the impact. The selection included a few from the cycle written for Jeanne Duval (*Remords posthume* and *Le Vampire*);[10] others were taken from among those written for Mme Sabatier (*Réversibilité*, *L'Aube spirituelle*, and *Confession*), and finally there were a couple (*L'Irréparable* and *L'Invitation au voyage*) inspired by Marie Daubrun. In addition there were three not classifiable strictly as love-poetry, since they were not addressed to any particular woman, but which none the less dealt with aspects of the erotic passion. In these the tone was not just disillusioned – it was tragic; one cannot help thinking that Baudelaire had, at the back or in the forefront of his mind when he composed them, the remorseless advances made year by year by the syphilitic infection he had contracted in his teens. The longest of the three, *Voyage à Cythère*,[11] was based on a story he had read in Gérard de Nerval's account of his travels in the eastern Mediterranean in 1843. The ship that carried Nerval took him past the shores of Cerigo, one of the Ionian Islands which at that period formed a British protectorate. In antiquity this island, under its name of Cythera, had been covered with flowering groves and was dedicated to the worship of the goddess of Love. As Nerval saw it from the deck of his ship, it was nothing but a barren rock on which he could make out distinctly only one man-made feature: a gibbet, with a hanged man dangling from it. Baudelaire, in adopting this story, changed very little, but described in horrific detail the naked corpse at which birds of prey had been busy; the eyes had been plucked out, the entrails were spilling over the thighs, even the wretch's genitals had been torn away by those savage beaks. All this material was added to give point to the allegory, for Baudelaire saw, in this disgusting spectacle, a vision of his own fate; it was he hanging from the gallows in the isle consecrated to Venus, it was his flesh that served as food for the vultures, while the dogs prowled below in expectation of snatching some gobbet.

If one excepts the two nostalgic rhapsodies placed centrally in the sequence (*L'Invitation au voyage* and *Moesta et errabunda*), where the poet imagines himself travelling with his beloved to far-off lands or back in time to a golden, innocent past, all the poems Baudelaire offered to the *Revue des Deux Mondes* have the same character; all are steeped in the same savage bitterness, self-reproach or sadistic recriminations. The sample was not wholly characteristic of the later volume, for in *Les Fleurs du Mal* there are luminous poems balancing the sombre ones, or to use the terms Baudelaire adopted, the *ideal* is present alongside *spleen*. It is hardly surprising that the editor, François Buloz, should have felt some concern about the reaction of his readership, and to fend off possible objections, should have decided to insert a prefatory note in which, after smugly congratulating himself on his broad-mindedness, he went on to explain: 'What appears to us to deserve attention is the vivid expression, curious even in its violence, of certain lapses, certain forms of moral suffering of which, however little the reader may participate in them or wish to discuss them, he needs to take cognisance as a sign of the times.' One can almost see the Pharisee pulling his robe around him. To take this line, however – that the evil Baudelaire wrote about was special to himself and to a small coterie of aberrants like him – meant ignoring the message implicit in the very first of the eighteen poems, retained as the prologue for the book when it was published: the dedicatory ode *Au Lecteur*. The last line of this poem – that last line which T. S. Eliot incorporated into *The Waste Land*:

> *Hypocrite lecteur, mon semblable, mon frère!*

asserts complicity, if not identity, between poet and reader, and in all the preceding stanzas the pronouns are plural, 'we, us, our', never singular, 'I, me, mine':

> Error and folly, sin and avarice,
> Have breached the walls and ta'en our souls by force,
> And lovingly we nourish our remorse,
> As beggars sit and flaunt their crawling lice . . .
>
> The Devil holds the strings that make us twitch!
> We take delight in all that's foul; each day
> And step by step, toward Hell we wend our way
> Blithely, through stinking vapours black as pitch.

It was not the poet alone who was accursed, as the romantics of the previous generation had believed; the whole human race was consigned to damnation along with him, and it was only by the exercise of hypocrisy that the readers of the *Revue des Deux Mondes*, beginning with its editor-in-chief, could blink the fact.

This 'bizarre and paternalistic little note', as Baudelaire called it in a polite letter of protest to Buloz,[12] might have served the poet as warning; the public was not going to appreciate his 'flowers of evil', and was certainly not going to accept his impertinent assimilation of the whole human race with his own remorseful self-condemnation. All the optimistic expansionism of the early Second Empire was against him; the nineteenth-century devotees of the myth of progress were not prepared to have their brave new world called into question by this thunderous prophet of doom and damnation.

Nevertheless the die was cast; Baudelaire could not much longer delay the publication of the book, and the time had clearly come to make the necessary arrangements. He was in close contact, in the mid-1850s, with Michel Lévy who was bringing out his translations of Poe's short stories; but for *Les Fleurs du Mal* he had his eye on a publisher less well known and also less commercially orientated, but with whose aims and outlook he felt much greater sympathy. Auguste Poulet-Malassis, whose acquaintance he had first made in 1850, was four years younger than Baudelaire and was at this time 'a tall fellow, with a very pale complexion which gave him some resemblance to Henry III, and with two wisps of blonde moustache on his upper lip'.[13] His family had been printers at Alençon for more than one generation and in 1852, on his father's death, he succeeded to the business. But before this happened he had led a life full of excitement and danger. A student at the Ecole des Chartes when the 1848 Revolution broke out, he had, like Baudelaire, thrown himself into the struggle but, less fortunate than Baudelaire, had been arrested during the June insurrection and sentenced to a spell in the hulks at Brest. After his release in December 1848 he returned to Paris where he spent much of his time hobnobbing with members of the literary bohemia to which Baudelaire and Banville belonged. Poulet-Malassis remained throughout his life a rebel, refractory to authority, and in this respect rather unlike Baudelaire; but he was, in his own line, a man of taste and erudition, and at a time when the art of typography had fallen into complete decadence in France, he was one of the few who tried to restore standards. When he returned to Alençon it was with the intention of expanding the family business, which traditionally had relied for its revenues on a standing contract to print the local newspaper. Using the connections he had made in Paris, he first of all brought out a handsome edition of Banville's *Odes funambulesques*, after which he got in touch with Baudelaire and offered to publish *Les Fleurs du Mal*.

The contract was signed on December 30th, 1856, along lines which Baudelaire himself appears to have suggested and with which he declared himself very content though, if so, his expectations were certainly modest: the print run was to be 1000 and the royalties were fixed at 25 centimes per copy sold. The maximum return to the author on this first edition would therefore be 250 francs. In the event, since the book was banned before more than a few copies were sold, and since in addition he was faced with a fine of 300 francs imposed by sentence of the court for publishing it, Baudelaire found himself, as so often, considerably out of pocket; it is true that the fine was reduced, on appeal, to 50 francs.

The precise contents of the book had not been determined at the time the contract was signed, but it is clear that there was no shortage of material; since the intention was to limit the number of poems to a hundred, the only difficulty lay in deciding what to omit. His letters to Poulet-Malassis in February 1857 indicate that the poet was quite content to accept his publisher's advice on this important matter; all he asked was that the manuscript copies of the poems Poulet-Malassis had marked down for exclusion (Baudelaire calls them the *pièces sacrifiées*) should be returned to him. But there is no telling what poems had been 'sacrificed' nor on what principles, though to judge by a reference he made in a letter to his mother after the publication of the book, it was less because they were aesthetically inferior than because Poulet-Malassis and he felt them to be too audacious that he agreed they should be left out.[14] They amounted to one-third of the poems he had written, and unfortunately he did not keep them; he told Alphonse de Calonne much later that he had destroyed 'masses of verse' at the time *Les Fleurs du Mal* was first published, and that these poems, some of which dated back to 1837, had passed completely out of his memory.[15]

Poulet-Malassis was also called on to help decide the sequence of poems in the volume, a fact to which not enough weight is always given by the numerous critics who are still speculating on the intentions Baudelaire may have had in choosing to arrange the component 'flowers' of his evil garland in the order he did arrange them. It was his friend Jules Barbey d'Aurevilly, in a review article intended for publication in *Le Pays*, who coined the famous phrase 'a secret architecture' over which so much ink has been spilt since.

> Those artists who can trace the lines behind the luxuriant efflorescence of colour will have no difficulty in recognizing here the presence of a *secret architecture*, a plan drawn up by the poet with forethought and deliberation. *Les Fleurs du Mal* are not strung together haphazardly, like so many lyric pieces scattered hither and thither by the winds of inspiration and collected together for no other reason than to have them all between two covers. They constitute not so much single poems as one poetic work *of the most marked homogeneity*.[16]

Reading these words, Baudelaire may well have been as surprised as he was delighted; perhaps privately he thought Barbey went a little too far with his 'secret architecture', but he took care not to undeceive him or to make any public disavowal. On the contrary, when the time came to issue the second, enlarged edition, which is the one that invariably forms the basis of modern reprints, he claimed that he had written all the new poems to accord with the original scheme. 'The one thing I would like to have recognized,' he wrote, 'is that this book is not a pure anthology, that it has a beginning and an ending. All the new poems have been fashioned in order to fit in to the special framework I had chosen.'[17]

But how premeditated was this design, this 'special framework'? No one supposes that the poems assembled for the 1857 edition, some of which were first put on paper fourteen or fifteen years earlier, were all originally written as parts of a unified whole of which Baudelaire had a clear vision from the start. *Les Fleurs du Mal* was not composed according to a preconceived plan in the way Tennyson may have composed his *Idylls of the King* or Browning *The Ring and the Book*. Faced, at the end of 1856, with an untidy heap of undated manuscripts which he wanted to include in his book, he sorted them into groups as best he could. Since the opening stanzas of *Benediction* deal with the poet's birth,[18] it seemed logical to place that poem at the beginning; and here was another, *The Artists' Death*, which could with equal appositeness come right at the end. (This is probably all Baudelaire meant when he told Vigny 'it has a beginning and an ending'.) Two other poems about death and the afterlife were conveniently to hand to back it up, and so they too were placed at the end. Baudelaire sorted out no fewer than five poems about wine and its effects, including the famous *Vin de l'assassin* which had been the starting-point for the melodrama that Tisserant had suggested he should write; obviously they would have to be grouped together. Over one-third of the total number was made up of love poems; Baudelaire picked out those he had written for Jeanne, lumped them together – though in no particular order, as far as one can see – then those inspired by Apollonie Sabatier, and finally those composed during his erratic affair with Marie Daubrun. After these three important cycles he placed a few which could hardly be called love poems, but which may be described as poetic tributes to different women whose beauty had aroused his admiration at various times; one of them was the sonnet written in Mauritius for Mme Autard de Bragard.[19] But he forgot to include here another poem celebrating the charms of a little auburn-haired street-singer whose portrait had been painted by Deroy; although it is of exactly the same kind as *A une Dame créole* it was inserted, under the title *A une mendiante rousse*, among a number of miscellaneous, presumably unclassifiable poems and – in the first edition, though not in the second – comes immediately before a poem describing a gambling den.

Thus, the 'secret architecture' of *Les Fleurs du Mal* amounted to little more, it seems, than the kind of thematic grouping of disparate pieces that one might expect any writer to undertake when faced with the need to put them into some kind of an order before the book went to press. The pre-existing 'plan' was a product of Barbey d'Aurevilly's imagination and has been responsible for more misunderstandings than almost anything else that has been said about *Les Fleurs du Mal*. The clearest proof of this lies in the very considerable differences that emerge when one undertakes a comparison between the ordering of the contents in the first and second edition, both of which were due to Baudelaire working in concert with his publisher. The positioning not just of individual poems but of whole cycles was altered, apparently quite arbitrarily, although modern critics have amused themselves inventing plausible reasons for these changes.[20] But if there had been a fixed plan, there would have been no changes.

Again, if there really was a 'secret architecture', why did the architect show himself so casual about it and so ready to delegate his functions to his friend and publisher? Of the two, it was Poulet-Malassis rather than Baudelaire who appeared more concerned with the proper sequence of the poems in the second edition. 'This business of deciding on the order, which bothers you so,' Baudelaire wrote to him reassuringly, 'can be settled in *an hour*'; on July 14th, 1860, he wrote again: 'I hope we shall settle the arrangement of the *Fleurs* together, during the last two days of this month, unless I begin my journey by paying you a visit.'[21] There is no question that if Baudelaire had felt the arrangement of the contents to be of vital significance he would have worked it out himself, taking all the time he needed, and would not have regarded it as something that could be polished off in an hour or two by Poulet-Malassis and himself sitting side by side at a desk.

The kind of detail to which Baudelaire paid much greater attention was the typographical presentation of each poem. He insisted on absolute fidelity to his punctuation which, he reminded Poulet-Malassis, 'serves not just as a guide to meaning but to the way the lines are to be spoken'. There was disagreement between the two of them over the use of inverted commas, and Baudelaire's criticisms of the first proof of the title page must have driven Poulet-Malassis to despair. 'I believe it would be a good idea to put *Fleurs* in italics – in sloping capitals, since it is a punning title. Further, although all the lines and letters are well proportioned, each in respect of the others, I find they are all too thick; I think the total effect would be more elegant if you could choose a slightly smaller face for each line while keeping the proportions . . .' Poulet-Malassis, in his reply, could not help betraying irritation at these niggling observations. 'You call me mad,' Baudelaire replied, 'but I would like to see you venture a work of your own in conditions that were not entirely satisfactory.' (These 'conditions' included the awkwardness of having to send proofs to and fro through the post, with risks of loss or delay, for *Les Fleurs du Mal* was being printed down at Alençon.) 'I realize how irritating I must seem to you, but I also know that you are too intelligent not to profit from your irritation . . . and you yourself have acknowledged in my hearing, more than once, that no matter what the product, nothing short of perfection is admissible.'²²

The expensive and time-wasting proof corrections do not seem to have upset the production schedule unduly, and the first edition of *Les Fleurs du Mal* was ready for distribution on June 25th, 1857. To Baudelaire's renewed annoyance, neither Poulet-Malassis nor his partner and brother-in-law Eugène de Broise were proposing to come to Paris to launch the book, and he complained tartly about this in a letter to De Broise on June 13th: 'You don't publish a book in a cupboard!' But at this time the firm had no Paris office. Distribution of *Les Fleurs du Mal* in the capital was therefore entrusted to an agent; a singularly inappropriate one, since his normal stock-in-trade consisted of devotional works. Still, it was only a matter of time, Baudelaire thought, before the news about his book got around. He anticipated some hostile reviews, 'a fine slating from all quarters which will stimulate curiosity',²³ after which he reckoned the edition would sell rapidly.

He got his 'slating', but the results were quite different from what he had expected. A short article entitled 'This and That', signed by Gustave Bourdin, the son-in-law of the editor of *Le Figaro*, appeared in that paper on July 5th; Bourdin, while not positively hostile to *Les Fleurs du Mal*, singled out the three 'lesbian' poems and also *Le Reniement de Saint-Pierre*²⁴ as being so outrageous as to warrant the intervention of the Minister of Justice. The authorities took the hint; within two days, a civil servant in the Ministry of the Interior submitted a confidential report to his superiors in which he advised that 'several pieces in this collection', of which he named five in particular, 'appeared to me to constitute a contravention of the laws protecting public morality'.²⁵ The same day (July 7th) the minister referred the matter to the Public Prosecutor and Lanier, the bookseller with whom Poulet-Malassis had made arrangements to stock copies of *Les Fleurs du Mal*, wrote him an agitated letter saying he could no longer offer him this service for any of his future publications.

Baudelaire, meanwhile, remained serenely unaware of these developments. Writing to his mother on July 9th to promise her a copy of his book as soon as he could get one tastefully bound, he discounted the rumours of prosecution that were flying around. 'A government which has on its hands this dreadful election campaign in Paris has no time to put a madman like me on trial.'²⁶ Two days later he was forced to change his tune, and sent an urgent letter to Poulet-Malassis advising him to find a secure hiding-place for all the unbound sheets. He told him further that he had personally removed that day fifty out of the hundred copies deposited with Lanier, who had, however, refused Baudelaire's request to distribute the remainder over various points of sale in Paris. On July 17th he received word that the previous day 270 copies of *Les Fleurs du Mal* had been impounded by the authorities at Alençon. Seeing him in the streets wearing deep mourning, a journalist asked him whether this suit of solemn black was worn as a token of respect for Béranger, whose funeral was taking place that day. Baudelaire, whose contempt for the author of *Le Dieu des Bonnes Gens* not even death could soften, answered flippantly: 'I am in mourning for *Les Fleurs du Mal*; it was seized yesterday evening at five o'clock.'[27] Seizure was a normal preliminary to a state trial.

The legislation in virtue of which proceedings were taken against Baudelaire dated back to 1819. The so-called 'lois de Serre', promulgated that year, laid down penalties ranging from fines up to 500 francs and imprisonment of not more than a year for uttering any book or pamphlet that in the opinion of the court constituted 'an outrage to public and religious morality, or to good morals'. Provision was also made for the 'suppression or destruction' of the offending writings. Like all legislation that tries to draw the line between what is decent and indecent in the public eye, the 'lois de Serre', though quite often invoked, were applied with varying degrees of rigour depending on the repressiveness of the current régime. Earlier in 1857 Flaubert had faced prosecution for the alleged immorality of *Madame Bovary*, but Gautier's novel *Mademoiselle de Maupin*, which most readers today would judge far more titillating than *Madame Bovary*, escaped unscathed when it was published in 1835. Flaubert had, it is true, been acquitted, but grudgingly, and the rumour was that the minister, Adolphe Billault, had ordered proceedings against *Les Fleurs du Mal* largely in the hope that this time the government would win and so wipe out the humiliation of its earlier defeat.

In the weeks before the case came on, Baudelaire busied himself, just as Flaubert had done, in enlisting support among well-placed colleagues. Mérimée, who was in the best position to help, having the ear of the Empress Eugénie, unfortunately thought the volume 'very mediocre' though 'in no way dangerous'.[28] The timorous Sainte-Beuve claimed he would suffer disgrace were he to praise *Les Fleurs du Mal* in *Le Moniteur*, the quasi-official newspaper for which he wrote; nevertheless, to Baudelaire's surprise and delight, an extraordinarily favourable review did appear in *Le Moniteur*, over the signature of Edouard Thierry, in which he was spoken of as the equal of Dante. Other reviews were written – for *Le Pays* by Barbey d'Aurevilly, as already mentioned, and for *La Revue Française* by

Asselineau – but were not allowed to appear; the editors, on referring to the Ministry of the Interior, were told it would be inadvisable to make any reference to *Les Fleurs du Mal* while the prosecution was impending. But it was obvious that the authorities were not of one mind over the question; that the one complimentary review of the book should have appeared in the government-sponsored *Moniteur*, while other papers were being warned against printing a word for or against it, argues at the very least some uncertainty in high places.

It was widely thought that Flaubert owed his acquittal to the intervention of the Princess Mathilde, a member of the Imperial family with whom the novelist was on the best of terms, as were Gautier and Sainte-Beuve. But Baudelaire was never sufficiently a society figure to have been invited to her literary *soirées*. Nevertheless, as he told his mother on July 27th: '*What I lack is a woman*; there might be some way of involving Princess Mathilde in this affair; but I rack my brains in vain to discover how.'[29] He hesitated for another three weeks and then, only two days before the hearing, in desperation, he wrote to Mme Sabatier, imploring her to pull whatever strings she could.

The letter was a long one, and accompanied a presentation copy of *Les Fleurs du Mal* bound in pale green morocco. Unlike the previous letters, this was written in his normal handwriting and with his proper signature at the bottom. The book he was sending her contained all the poems he had posted to her earlier, anonymously and in disguised handwriting; so his secret was out, but he admits he had long realized she had penetrated it – there had been the embarrassing moment when Bébé had asked him, laughingly: 'Are you still in love with my sister, and are you still writing her such superb letters?' But now that the mask was, so to speak, officially removed, and the period of childish pretence was over, he was anxious there should be no misunderstandings; his feelings for her remained the same as they had always been. 'One has heard of poets who have lived their whole lives with their eyes fixed on a cherished image. I truly believe (but I have too great an interest in so believing) that *fidelity is one of the signs of genius*. You are more than a dear image I dream of, you are my *superstition*. When I commit some enormous stupidity, I say to myself: *My God, what if she knew!* When I perform some good deed, I think: *This is something that draws me closer to her . . . in spirit.*'[30]

He was saying no more, in these lines, than he had been saying for the past four and a half years, in prose and verse; what he overlooked was the difference it made that he was no longer hiding under a cloak – however threadbare – of anonymity. Had he been the wiliest of seducers, and Apollonie the chastest of matrons, he could hardly have chosen a more beguiling tactic for protracted seduction, and the result was what it was bound to be, however innocent his intentions. Apollonie had had four and a half years to get used to the idea that he was in love with her, that he idolized her, that he had chosen her to be the Laura to his Petrarch; she had accepted what she must have regarded as a charade of courtly love, since her lover wanted to play it that way and since she had a long training in lending herself uncomplainingly to men's whims. But now the pretence was dropped, he was speaking to her openly, their relations were at last to move on to a normal plane, unless she much misunderstood him . . . which she did.

She wrote him an immediate reply, which has not come down to us except for the few phrases in it that Baudelaire quoted back to her in a later letter. Using *tutoiement*, the form of address permissible in those days only between lovers and close relations, she told him that she had felt she was his 'from the very first day I set eyes on you' (which, if one takes the statement literally, must mean the afternoon in the Hôtel Pimodan when she had been walking back from the public baths with Maryx, a full twelve years ago). 'You'll do what you like about it, but I am yours in body, mind and heart.' Short of playing the ridiculous part of Joseph with Potiphar's wife, there was only one thing Baudelaire could do, and, nature coming to his aid, he made her, as she said in the second of her letters, 'the happiest of women. . . . You may preen yourself if that flatters you, but don't look at yourself in the mirror; for whatever you do, you will never succeed in giving yourself the look you had for one second. Now, come what may, I shall always see you like that, that is the Charles I love; you may tighten your lips as you will and frown, I shan't mind, I'll shut my eyes and see the other . . .'[31]

This phase of delirium and ecstasy was of the briefest. There was no second meeting but instead a letter which amounted to an embarrassed but none the less insulting withdrawal. Their affair, he wrote, could not last; sooner or later she would forget him, betray him, or lose interest in him. 'You see, my sweet darling, I have *odious* prejudices where women are concerned. – In a word, I lack faith. You have a lovely soul but when all is said and done, a feminine soul. Consider how in just a few days our situation has been thrown into confusion. To begin with, we are both haunted by the dread of hurting an honest man [Mosselman] who has the good fortune to be still in love. Then we go in fear of the very tempest we have conjured up, for we know – I do, particularly – that such ties as these are hard to loosen. And lastly, lastly you were, a few days ago, a divinity, which is so convenient, so splendid, so inviolable. And now, you are a woman.'[32] This was the crux of the matter. What Apollonie had not

153

understood, and could never understand, was that his idealization of her was genuine. He was no Pygmalion praying that the statue he had carved in chilly marble should turn into a woman of flesh and blood – on the contrary. And eventually he provided the clue to his conduct in the form of an allegorical story, which it is to be hoped she failed to understand, if indeed she ever read it.[33] In this prose poem, variously entitled *The Ideal and the Real* or *Which is the true one?*, Baudelaire relates how he had come to know a certain Benedicta, 'who filled the circumambient air with the breath of the ideal, and whose eyes communicated a desire for all that is noble and fine and glorious, all that inspires belief in immortality'. But Benedicta, 'too beautiful to live long', died a few days later. He buried her himself, but as he stood there, his eyes fixed sorrowfully on the spot, 'up danced a little woman who bore a strange resemblance to the departed and who, trampling on the freshly turned earth in a fit of bizarre, hysterical violence, exclaimed with a burst of laughter: "It's me the real Benedicta, it's me, a notorious whore! And to punish you for your blindness and folly, you will love me just as I am!" Enraged, I shouted back: "No, no, no!" And to give greater force to my refusal, I stamped on the earth so violently that my leg sank up to the knee in the recently dug pit and, like a wolf caught in a trap, I have remained, and always shall remain perhaps, stuck with one foot in the grave . . . of the ideal.'[34]

This version of what happened – if that is what it is – reflects very unfairly on Apollonie, who behaved with more dignity than many women might have in the circumstances. In sending an immediate reply to the letter in which he declared himself to 'lack faith', she commented that it was 'so explicit that it freezes the blood in my veins' and could only mean that he did not love her. 'What more can be said? Isn't it crystal clear? Oh God, how the idea tortures me, how I would like to weep on your breast!'[35] She would, however, obey his wishes and do her best, when they next met, to behave as though they had never been more than friends.

However, it is clear from the short notes he sent her over the next fortnight that he was making sure they should not meet. In the last of them, dated September 13th, he apologized in advance for missing her dinner-party the following Sunday; he would do his best to drop in later in the evening for a few minutes . . . This stung Apollonie to send him, at last, a long letter full of plaintive reproaches. 'Your behaviour has been so strange over the past few days that I don't understand anything any more. It's all too subtle for a dull-witted lump like me. Enlighten me, my dear friend, all I ask is to be helped to understand. What deadly blast has blown on this fine flame? Is it simply the result of calm reflection? It's a little late for that . . .' In her simplicity and straightforwardness, only the idea that she might have a rival seemed to explain his second thoughts. 'What must I think when I see you avoiding my caresses, if not that you are thinking of that other woman, whose black face and black soul have come between us? in a word, I feel humiliated and humbled. Were it not for my self-respect, I would heap insults on you. I would like to see you suffer. I am burned up with jealousy, and no one can reason coolly at such moments. Ah! my dear friend, I hope such suffering is spared you. What a night I have spent, cursing this cruel love over and over again!'[36] The letter ends, however, with the luckless woman agreeing to resign herself to losing him. She had had, after all, a lot of practice in bowing to the inevitable.

By this time the court case, which had been the occasion for the violent alteration in their relationship, had long been decided. Only sparse records survive of the proceedings, the official transcript having been consumed in the flames that destroyed the Palais de Justice in 1871. However, it is known that of the thirteen poems originally incriminated (four for offences against religion, nine for offending public morality), the court rejected all counts in the first category and three in the second category. There remained six poems judged to be indecent; an order was made that they should be deleted from any copies of Les Fleurs du Mal offered for sale in the future. Baudelaire was fined 300 francs. Although not as fortunate as Flaubert, he can be reckoned to have got off lightly. When, a little later the same year, Eugène Sue's novel Les Mystères du Peuple was arraigned before the same court, the judges ordered the destruction of the entire edition together with the plates from which they had been printed. In default of the author, who had died before the case was brought, publisher and printer were given stiff prison sentences and the fines totalled 9000 francs. The difference was that Les Mystères du Peuple was a socially subversive work in the eyes of the imperial régime, whereas the worst that could be said of Les Fleurs du Mal was that it included half a dozen poems the eroticism of which was a little too explicit.

Baudelaire pretended to be outraged at the verdict. As he left the court, Asselineau asked him whether he had expected to be acquitted. 'Acquitted!' the other replied. 'I expected a full apology!'[37] As part of his defence, he had composed a justificatory brochure destined for distribution to members of the court in advance of the trial. For the most part it simply reprinted the favourable reviews the book had received, but Baudelaire added a brief prefatory note in which he made the revealingly naïve remark: 'No one, including myself, could suppose that a book imbued with such an evident and ardent spirituality as Les Fleurs du Mal could be made the object of a prosecution, or rather could have given rise to misunderstanding.'[38] And long after the event, Baudelaire persisted in his conviction that the trial had gone the way it did because of a 'misunderstanding'.[39] It is easy to see how the misunderstanding arose: from the inability or unwillingness of the judges to take into account the total effect of the book on the reader. They concentrated myopically on certain lines in certain poems, like Thomas Bowdler hunting down the dirty bits in Shakespeare. But lawyers and magistrates have always proceeded in this way and always will, so long as they are asked to rule on questions of obscenity in literature.

XI

'O JUST, SUBTLE, AND MIGHTY OPIUM!'

One of the more engaging, if rather disconcerting qualities of Baudelaire as a judge of literature was his readiness to give rather more than their due to writers of minor talent whose works, for one reason or another, happened to fire his enthusiasm. It was not that, like Hugo, he blandly distributed fulsome praise to every scribbler prepared to reciprocate, secure in the knowledge that his own Olympian superiority was such that he ran no risk of encouraging awkward rivals. But – to take a peculiarly blatant example – how is one to explain Baudelaire's boosting of Théophile Gautier, both in the dedication of *Les Fleurs du Mal* 'to the impeccable poet and consummate magician in the French language' and in his 1859 monograph with its astounding assertion (astounding as much for its uncharacteristic chauvinism as for the confusion of standards it implies): 'Our neighbours say: Shakespeare and Goethe! We can reply: Victor Hugo and Théophile Gautier!'?[1] Had his critical faculties deserted him on this occasion, or was he, for once, playing the sycophant? When one turns to Edgar Allan Poe, however, the second of these questions cannot arise; there is no point in paying court to a dead man. A third instance of eccentric overvaluation was Thomas De Quincey, the Manchester journalist whose enormous output contains, among much flatulent and pretentiously overwritten stuff, just a few essays thanks to which he deserves his small niche in the gallery of the minor English romantics, along with Thomas Love Peacock and Walter Savage Landor. When he first came across De Quincey, Baudelaire thought he had made a sensational discovery; here was 'a magnificent author, unknown in Paris'[2] whose *Confessions of an English Opium-Eater* he was eager to begin translating. It looked as though De Quincey might turn into a second Poe, yet another Anglo-Saxon duck that Baudelaire would present to the guileless continental public as a gorgeously plumaged bird of paradise.

De Quincey's *Confessions* had in fact been turned into French once already, by Alfred de Musset who produced a very loose and unsatisfactory version as early as 1828, and it is possible Baudelaire had a copy in his hands around 1845. The subject of the book – the effects of hallucinogenic drugs on an educated man of letters – could not have failed to interest him. In 1851 he published a long essay devoted to a comparison between the mental states induced by wine and hashish,[3] which came down heavily in favour of the first of these two intoxicants as being less dangerous and less debilitating.

> Wine heightens the power of the will, hashish annihilates it. Wine increases bodily vigour, hashish is a suicide weapon. Wine encourages kindliness and good fellowship, hashish isolates you. The one is industrious, so to speak, the other essentially indolent; for what is the sense of working, tilling the soil, writing a book, fashioning anything whatsoever, when one has immediate access to paradise? Lastly, wine is for the working man who has earned the right to drink it; hashish, which belongs to the category of solitary pleasures, is meant for idle wastrels.[4]

The moral issues involved in the use and abuse of stimulants were, to judge from this extract, central to Baudelaire's concerns from the moment he started writing on the subject. Both in this essay and in certain poems later included in the 'wine cycle' of *Les Fleurs du Mal* but all written around 1850 (*L'Ame du Vin*, *Le Vin des Chiffonniers*, and *Le Vin du Solitaire*), one notices that wine-drinking is generally absolved from the censure incurred by other forms of artificial stimulation. Dionysus, for Baudelaire, was always a kindly god.

In 1858 he returned to the topic of hashish and published a new essay in *La Revue Contemporaine* entitled: 'De l'idéal artificiel – le Haschisch'. Two years later this text was coupled to his version of De Quincey's work on opium eating to give a book-length study, published by Poulet-Malassis under the title *Les Paradis artificiels: Opium et Haschisch*. The title had not been arrived at without lengthy cogitation. The editor of *La Revue contemporaine*, Alphonse de Calonne, offered a number of suggestions, all of which Baudelaire rejected quite rudely as being altogether too banal. He himself hesitated between *Perilous Paradises*, *The Paradise of the Damned* (a most suggestive and arresting title), *The Lotus-Eaters* (which would have been a tribute more to Tennyson than to De Quincey), before finally settling on *Artificial Paradises*, 'a good selling title', as he said to Poulet-Malassis.[5]

The social disapproval that attaches today to the use of hallucinogens scarcely existed in the middle of the nineteenth century. Neither mescaline nor LSD were known then, but simple preparations based on the juices of the poppy-head or the flowering tops of the hemp plant could be freely bought at any pharmacist's; it was not until 1908 that the sale of opium was brought under control, and not until 1916 that hashish was listed as one of the officially proscribed toxic substances. The gradual change in attitude towards these exotic stimulants, if it was due to any one writer, must be attributed principally to Baudelaire, the first in France at least to insist that there was a moral dimension to the drug habit. More characteristic of his contemporaries' point of view is the account Dumas gave of Franz d'Epinay's introduction to the delights of hashish eating by the Count of Monte-Cristo in his subterranean retreat on the island whose name the Count had assumed. Dumas describes the delicacy as being served in the form of a greenish paste and eaten with a spoon; Franz finds it far from succulent when he tastes it, but the erotic dream into which he subsequently drifts fully confirms his host's claim that it can be identified as the very ambrosia served at the table of the gods on Olympus. There is nothing sinister in this scene; the offering of hashish gives the finishing touch to the Count's magnificent display of hospitality.

It was not until the beginning of the nineteenth century that hashish and its effects became widely known in France; the original initiates were supposed to have been soldiers returning from Napoleon's Egyptian campaign. In a study published in 1818 on the origin of the sect of the Assassins, the orientalist Silvestre de Sacy related the story of the Old Man of the Mountains and the use he had made of hashish to secure the allegiance of a devoted band of Moslem kamikazes – a story retold by Dumas in his novel and referred to by many other writers of the time, Nerval, Gautier, and Baudelaire himself. The peculiar properties of hashish were investigated by the medical profession, and a certain Dr Joseph Moreau de Tours began experiments to determine whether it could be used as a medicine in the treatment of certain forms of mental disorder. Needing reliable accounts of the kind of hallucinations hashish could produce, he recruited a few artists and literary men who agreed to take the drug under controlled conditions and to report their experiences to him subsequently. This was the origin of the so-called 'Club des Haschischins'. There was nothing particularly clandestine about their meetings; Gautier, one of the participants, reported on them for the press, and Moreau de Tours eventually published his findings in a volume intended as much for the general public as for his scientific colleagues.[6]

The club met regularly in Boissard's rooms in the Hôtel Pimodan, and started its sessions at a time when Baudelaire was still living there. But he had been introduced to the drug earlier, either immediately before or immediately after his voyage to the east, by Louis Ménard who used to invite his friends to sample his supply of 'damawesc'. Damawesc was the jam or paste in which hashish was commonly absorbed at that time as an alternative to being smoked. The resin was extracted from the hemp plant by boiling up the flowers with water and a small quantity of butter, the resultant mixture being then strained through a cloth; honey, sugar, or spices were customarily added to disguise the somewhat unpleasant, rancid taste of the preparation. One curious relic has come down to us of Baudelaire's participation in Ménard's hash-parties: a water-colour he painted, supposedly under the influence of the drug, in which he represented himself as a gigantic figure, standing top-hatted, cigar in mouth, next to the Colonne Vendôme which appears only half his size.

We have Gautier's word for it that Baudelaire used occasionally – but only occasionally – to attend the meetings of the Club des Haschischins, the regular members of which included several painters who belonged to Gautier's circle of friends and who, at a later date, were guests at Mme Sabatier's receptions in the Rue Frochot: Delacroix, Meissonier, Chenavard. Gérard de Nerval was also to be seen at these hash-parties, and so too was Balzac, who on one occasion (December 22nd, 1845) ventured to taste the mixture, as we know from the report he gave the following day in a letter to his future wife. 'I heard celestial voices and saw divine pictures. It took me twenty years to descend Lauzun's staircase. I saw the gilding and the paintings in the drawing-room bathed in an indescribable splendour. But this morning, ever since waking, I am half asleep still and without the strength of will to do anything.'[7] Many of the more characteristic symptoms of intoxication by hashish are summarized here: the magical enhancement of sounds and colours, the apparent distension of time and space, the abulia or loss of will-power experienced in the stage of disintoxication.

Curiously, Baudelaire specifically relates in the pages of *Les Paradis artificiels* how on this occasion he saw Balzac in the company of the other hashish eaters, listening to their accounts of their visions, questioning, sniffing the spoonful of damawesc but refusing to taste it. 'Balzac probably thought there was no greater shame and no worse suffering for man than to abdicate the power of the will ... It is difficult to imagine the theoretician of the *Will*, the spiritual twin of Louis Lambert, consenting to yield up a single particle of this precious *substance*.'[8] No doubt Baudelaire preferred to think of his hero Balzac resisting temptation. The power of hashish to deprive its addicts of the exercise of their free will was his main reason for condemning the drug in his 1851 essay. The rulers of Egypt, he asserts here, had expressly forebade its manufacture and sale, and rightly so: 'No man who, with a spoonful of jam, can gain instant access to all the delights of heaven and earth, will ever exert himself to acquire the thousandth part of them by dint of hard work.'⁹

Was this the reason why Baudelaire rarely experimented with hashish at the Hôtel Pimodan, preferring to listen to what the others told him about their own dreams? Or was it simply because he knew he was constitutionally unable to experience the full effects? Gautier admits that it is 'possible and even probable' that Baudelaire tried hashish once or twice, to see what would happen, but 'he never made regular use of it. In any case the idea that one could purchase happiness at a chemist's and carry it round in one's waistcoat pocket repelled him, and he compared the ecstasies it procured to a crank's preference for having painted canvases and crude stage sets in place of real furniture and gardens full of the scent of real flowers.'¹⁰ This sounds very like an actual quotation of what Baudelaire may have said; it was the *artificiality* of these 'paradises' that he objected to. But there is a paradox here, if not a contradiction in his system of thought. In other contexts, Baudelaire made no bones about extolling the virtues of artificiality. The man who claimed he preferred a woman to wear a wig rather than her natural hair was not so different from the 'crank' who would rather contemplate a *trompe-l'oeil* painted garden than walk about in a real one.

For whatever reason, Baudelaire always fought shy of hashish, and for his information on its effects relied partly on friends who had no scruples in indulging in it, partly on written sources, including quite technical ones such as a well-known encyclopedia of pharmaceutical preparations.¹¹ But with opium the case was entirely different; his personal experience of this drug was intimate, protracted, and painful.

It is more than likely that he started taking it, just as did De Quincey originally, as a pain-killer; in De Quincey's case, to relieve a facial neuralgia brought on by toothache, in Baudelaire's, to combat the discomforts of advancing syphilis and also, it may be, to relieve the pangs of hunger; the very first mention of laudanum in a letter to his mother immediately precedes a reference to the fact that he had recently gone for forty-eight hours without food. Although the custom of smoking opium (in a special form called *chandoo*) was quite widespread in the nineteenth century, Baudelaire never seems to have tried that method, probably because it was commonly practised by groups of addicts who passed the lighted pipe from hand to hand. Laudanum, a mixture of opium, honey, and alcohol, was taken in a glass of hot water. It was not without its unpleasant side-effects. Baudelaire found that it produced violent cramps in his stomach and bowels which he tried to combat by the use of ether; but after a few years there was no question, for him, of doing without the drug. The phrase in *Les Paradis artificiels* about 'the solitary, concentrated intoxication of the writer who, obliged to have recourse to opium to relieve physical suffering, and having in this way discovered a source of morbid pleasures, has gradually made of it his sole diet and as it were the sun round which his spiritual life revolves'[12] – this phrase, in its context, might be read as referring to De Quincey, but there can be little doubt Baudelaire was thinking of himself when he wrote it.

By the 1860s he was absorbing quite large amounts of opium and was totally dependent on it; one of the drawbacks of living away from Paris was that the local chemists demurred about letting him buy it in sufficient quantities.[13] A little before the onset of his last illness, referring to the various remedies he is taking, he told his mother by way of reassuring her: 'as for opium, you know that for several years I have been used to taking up to 150 drops without the slightest danger'.[14] This is, of course, very little compared to the 8000 drops De Quincey says he absorbed on occasion; but even so, it was twice as much as would have constituted a 'safe dose' for a non-addict, and far from improving his physical condition, almost certainly contributed to the gradual ruin of his health. The process appears to have been that the spirits he started drinking to alleviate the discomfort of the secondary syphilis brought on a painful gastritis which he treated by swallowing massive doses of laudanum. From 1856 onwards, the venereal infection, alcoholic excess and opium addiction were working in an unholy alliance to push Baudelaire down to an early grave.[15]

The extent to which his experiences of drugs were reflected in his creative work and particularly in the poetry is a question to which every kind of answer has been given; there are critics who detect opium dreams behind almost all the poems he wrote, while others doubt whether any of them demonstrably originated in the memory of such visions.[16] The one poem in *Les Fleurs du Mal* which is most likely to translate an opium-induced hallucination is *Rêve parisien*; it falls into two parts, the dream of a Piranesi-like city, followed by the anticlimax when the sleeper awakes in his horrible hovel. The same schema was adopted later, though perhaps not much later, for a prose poem entitled *La Chambre double* (*Two Rooms in One*), where the vision, however, is mildly erotic, not architectural, and the 'rude awakening' is described far less concisely than in the poem. Of the two rooms, the first is

a truly *spiritual* room, where the still air is faintly rose-coloured, azure tinted.

The soul bathes indolently in waters perfumed with desire and regret. – It is dusky, bluish, pinkish, a dream of delight in the sun's eclipse.

There are ottomans of elongated shape, prostrate, languid. They too seem to be dreaming, endowed with a sleepwalker's consciousness, as plants and minerals. The draperies speak the silent language of flowers, of skies, of sunsets.

The walls are bare of all artistic outrage. Relative to the pure dream state, to the unanalysed impression, art which posits and defines is blasphemy. Everything here has the adequate brightness and delightful obscurity of music.

A barely perceptible fragrance, compounded of the finest perfumes, permeates this slightly humid atmosphere in which the drowsy spirit, as in a hothouse, slumbers.

Then Baudelaire describes the apparition.

Torrents of white muslin stream down the windows and spread in snowy cascades over the couch where lies the queen of my idolatry. How came she here, who brought her, what witchcraft set her on this throne of meditation and delight? Idle questions! It is she indeed, and hers those eyes of flame that burn in the dusk, those subtle orbs of fearful potency that mockingly attract, subdue, absorb the gaze of any man who risks a glance at them. Often enough have I lost myself in contemplation of those two black stars, pondering the miracle of their compulsive fascination.

To what benignant genie must I render thanks for thus surrounding me with mystery, silence, peace and sweet aromas? O paradise! Even in its moments of most joyous exaltation, what is commonly called life has nothing to compare with this supreme mode of being which is now revealed to me and which I am savouring minute after minute, second by second.

No, there are no more minutes, no seconds, for time has been dethroned, Eternity holds sway instead, an eternity of bliss . . .

Then comes the awakening.

The door is struck a loud and terrifying blow. As in some hellish nightmare, it is as though a pickaxe were swung at the pit of my stomach.

In comes a Spectre. It is some bailiff's man come to torment me in the name of the law; that infamous concubine of mine with a string of complaints who comes to smother the sorrows of my life under the vulgar worries of her own; or else some editor's errand-boy to dun me for an overdue article.

The chamber of paradise, the dream-queen, the Sylph as the

poet calls her, – all gone; the spell that conjured them was broken the instant the Spectre started hammering on the door.

Finally, there is the description of the real room which has replaced the chamber of delights:

... this den, this haunt of everlasting boredom, this is where I live. These are the stupid chairs and table, dusty and notched, the hearth stained with spittle where no fire burns, no cinders glow; the dreary windows where the rain has driven furrows in the dirt; the scored out or unfinished manuscripts, the calendar with the dates ringed in pencil when the bills fall due. And that perfume from another world that so transported my enraptured senses, alas, it is replaced by a fetid stench of pipe smoke, a sickening smell of must. Here the lungs breathe the rancid vapours of decrepitude.

This world, so narrow, is yet crowded with disgusting objects, on only one of which I look with cheerfulness: the phial of laudanum. Our love-affair together has been long and stormy, full of caresses and betrayals as are all love-affairs.

Ah yes, and Time has taken charge again; this hideous ancient has resumed his reign, bringing in his train familiar demons, Memories, Regrets, spasmodic Terrors, anguished Nightmares and neurotic Rages.

The seconds now, believe me, tick away solemnly and loudly, each as it flies from the clock proclaiming: 'I am Life, Life the intolerable, Life the implacable!'

There is but one Second of all we live that comes bearing good tidings, those good tidings that fill us all with unaccountable dread.

Yes, Time's reign has been restored. The brutal tyrant drives me forward with his two-pronged goad as though I were a beast of burden. 'Up, jade! On, you sweaty slave! Live, you prisoner of Hell!'[17]

This text bears the authentic stamp of autobiography, and it is conceivable that Baudelaire, had he been so minded, might without too much difficulty have written out of his own experiences that part of *Les Paradis artificiels* planned to deal with opium addiction. If he preferred to summarize, with extracts, De Quincey's *Confessions*, the reason can only have been that he found the book so fascinating that he could not resist the temptation of presenting it in this way to his readers. Nevertheless, the undertaking proved more difficult and time-consuming than he had anticipated, as is clear from the excuses he felt obliged to make to the editor of *La Revue contemporaine*, where the work was to be serialized, for his slowness in preparing his copy. 'I assure you it's no easy matter to condense into a small space the description of a highly complex book, without omitting any nuance. . . . The biographical details take up a lot of space; but, apart from their intrinsic interest, they were necessary as providing the key to the very individual fantasmagoria of *Opium*. Let's hope Mr De Quincey will address a fine letter of thanks to your journal.'[18] In the event, since the 'English Opium-Eater' died on December 8th, 1859, and Baudelaire's digest of his book did not appear in *La Revue contemporaine* until January 1860, the pious hope expressed here remained of necessity unrealized.

This letter to Alphonse de Calonne is couched in more cheerful tones than Baudelaire used elsewhere when speaking about the book. He confided to his mother that the work was giving him endless trouble and that he was full of misgivings about whether it was worth the effort. 'I feel deep down that what I've done is no good. What's the sense of learning how poisons work if one can't put the knowledge to better use?'[19] His principal difficulty lay in the task of compression; De Quincey had written a long, discursive work and Calonne wanted something short and snappy. By mercilessly cutting the numerous and often charming digressions in the English text, he managed to reduce it to half its original length. In so doing he shifted the emphasis away from the weird and sometimes poetic dream-sequences the book contains, and brought into greater prominence those passages which deal with the effect of the opium habit on the character of the addict; and it is in respect of these changes that the moralistic overtones in Baudelaire's adaptation are most apparent.[20] Where De Quincey, by and large, shows himself grateful to the drug for the extraordinary stimulus it gave to his poetic faculties, Baudelaire is inclined to dwell on the more disturbing aspects, in particular on the writer's cowardly capitulation to an outside agent with dangerous powers to which he eventually succumbs. Here he was thinking primarily of his own case, and he seems to have realized that his point of view was radically different from De Quincey's. The risk, as he saw it, was that its dual origins might destroy the artistic unity of the work, turning it into something hybrid and unfocussed. De Quincey, as he complained to Poulet-Malassis, was 'a frightfully informal and digressive writer, and it was no small task to give a dramatic shape to this résumé and to reduce it to some sort of order. In addition, I had to try and fuse my personal feelings with the opinions of the original author and to make an amalgam in which the separate parts would be indistinguishable.'[21]

Baudelaire retained, in his own version, De Quincey's preliminary invocation: 'O just, subtle, and mighty Opium!', and none of his rare interpolations are designed to qualify the English writer's indulgent attitude to drug-taking. The passages in which the habit is criticized are all to be found in that part of *Les Paradis artificiels* which was not based on the *Confessions of an English Opium-Eater*, in other words, in the sections dealing with hashish, which might give the reader the curious and quite erroneous impression that Baudelaire condemned more strongly the drug to which he was not addicted, hashish, than the other, opium, to which he was hopelessly enslaved. It is in the chapter entitled 'Le Poème du Haschisch' that he speaks of 'the immorality . . . implied in this pursuit of a false ideal', and argues that 'it is forbidden to man, on penalty of degenerating or dying an intellectual death, to interfere with the basic conditions of his existence and to upset the balance between his faculties and the environment in which they are meant to operate. . . . Truly, any man who will not accept the conditions of life, sells his soul' – just as Faust did, and risks damnation. Baudelaire even goes so far as to condemn the use of narcotics such as chloroform or ether on patients requiring surgery. For drugs are a species of witchcraft. 'If the Church condemns magic and sorcery, this is because such practices frustrate the intentions of the Creator; they short-circuit the slow processes of time and aim to make superfluous the dictates of morality and purity; while the Church considers lawful and genuine only such treasures as one may acquire by the practice of virtue and constant effort. The card-player who has invented the trick of winning every time, we call a cheat; what shall we call a man who tries to buy happiness and genius on the cheap? It is the very infallibility of the method that constitutes its immorality, just as the supposed infallibility of magic spells constitutes the proof of their diabolical origin.'[22]

It was no doubt passages such as these that Flaubert had in mind when, after reading *Les Paradis artificiels*, he took Baudelaire gently to task for having forsaken scientific objectivity and 'insisted too much (?) on the Spirit of Evil. Here and there one detects the old leaven of Catholicism, if I may so put it. It would have been better, I think, if you hadn't *blamed* hashish, opium, excesses. How do you know what will come of it all later?'[23] Baudelaire's answer to this objection must have taken his correspondent by surprise. The Spirit of Evil did exist, he was convinced of it. 'As far back as I can remember, I have been obsessed by the impossibility of accounting for certain sudden acts or thoughts in man save on the hypothesis that there is an evil power external to him. – That's a candid confession for which not all the serried ranks of the nineteenth century combined will make me blush.'[24] Then, in a post-script to the same letter, Baudelaire quite slyly, and seemingly out of the blue, tells Flaubert that he has often wanted to read in full the latter's *Temptation of Saint Antony*, of which at this date only fragments had appeared in the review *L'Artiste*. The implication is clear: if Flaubert is so dismissive about the 'Spirit of Evil', why has he gone to such pains to dramatize the story of a saint wrestling precisely with this 'evil power external to him' – with the Devil, not to put too fine a point on it?

There remains one final consideration which could weigh with the poet tempted to have recourse to hallucinogens. Where would he find a more effective way of stimulating his powers of invention and imagination? – for these drugs, as is well known, unlock the inner worlds in which swarm all the visions, fancies, and buried memories which are the raw material of the creative act. Granted; but visions, says Baudelaire, are of little value if one is robbed, by the very drug that summons them to consciousness, of the power to clothe them in vivid language. The poet's work depends quite as much on the labour of realization as on the stimulation of his imaginative faculties. Thus, if he turns to drugs, he is caught in a vicious circle, 'for it is a property of hashish that it diminishes the will, and that it grants with one hand what it takes away with the other; it heightens the imagination but does not allow you to profit thereby.'[25]

Better, then, in the long run, to rely on one's own powers and, recognizing that the Muse visits one unbidden, to await her coming patiently, not to try and use the witchcraft of opium or hashish to drag her down from Mount Helicon. For Baudelaire was well aware that certain of the most curious and, from the poet's point of view, most valuable phenomena induced by these drugs – the distortion and distension of time, for instance, or the assumption by surrounding objects, however banal, of a preternatural significance – can occur in one's waking moments when one has done nothing to provoke them. 'There are occasions in life when time and space increase in profundity, and the sense of existence is immeasurably augmented. ... In certain almost transcendental states of the soul, the vastness of life is revealed all entire in the scene that one has before one's eyes, however ordinary it may be.'[26] At the end of his monograph on the 1855 Exhibition, Baudelaire recalled how the hero of one of Poe's stories, who took opium in the form of morphine, had described the 'customary effect of the drug' as being 'that of enduing all the external world with an intensity of interest', so that 'in the quivering of a leaf – in the hue of a blade of grass – in the shape of a trefoil – in the humming of a bee – in the gleaming of a dewdrop', the addict experiences 'a whole universe of suggestion – a gay and motley train of rhapsodical and immethodical thought'.[27] Having quoted or rather summarized this passage, Baudelaire continues: 'Without resorting to opium, which of us has not known those splendid hours, truly festive occasions for the mind, when the senses, unusually acute, receive more vivid impressions, when the sky, more transparently blue, opens up like an immeasurable abyss, when sounds ring out musically, when colours speak and perfumes convey a world of ideas?'[28] It was with the memory of such privileged moments in mind that Delacroix painted his more mysteriously evocative canvases and also, we may add, that Baudelaire wrote some of his most luminous and suggestive verses, which are far too consciously fashioned to have been a product of the 'immethodical thought' that Poe admitted was all that opium could provide.

XII

THE WIDOW AND HER SON

General Aupick's tenancy of the Madrid embassy lasted for less than two years, which passed uneventfully. Relations between France and Spain were cordial. This was the time when negotiations (in which, however, the ambassador had no part) were being conducted in view of the forthcoming marriage of the Emperor of France to the Spanish Countess Eugénia de Montijo. The wedding took place at the Tuileries on January 29th, 1853, and it was on April 21st that the Aupicks left Madrid to return to France. Reasons of health were what lay behind the ambassador's request to be relieved of his post; by the time the couple were back in Paris he had indeed less than four years to live. They spent this time partly in Paris, where Aupick devoted a few hours each day to work alongside Mérimée on an official edition of the Correspondence of Napoleon I, and partly in the village of Honfleur, on the coast near Le Havre, where he occupied himself superintending work on a small seaside villa where he and his wife could spend their declining years. The old soldier was feeling the need to return to his roots; having spent his childhood in a port further up the Channel coast, he liked the idea of watching the same tidal sea from the windows of this modest residence perched on the cliff. It was what the General called a 'toy house', exiguous in comparison with the spacious palaces they had been used to living in abroad; its most attractive feature was a handsome double flight of steps leading to a veranda from which a splendid view could be had of the sailing-ships passing up and down the estuary of the Seine.

He had little enough time to enjoy his semi-retirement in this chosen retreat. His old wound, which had never properly healed, was crippling him more and more; the end came on April 27th, 1857. At least he was spared, said his old army friends, the final blow of learning of the disgrace his stepson incurred in being prosecuted as a pornographer by the very government he had served so faithfully.

Baudelaire attended the funeral out of a sense of duty. Among the small band of mourners, only the old solicitor Antoine Jaquotot, who had been one of the witnesses at Caroline's second wedding, had a kind word to say to him: 'You will now, I trust, be living with your mother.' She, however, had quite different ideas, and even before he broached the subject with her, declared outright that she would never agree to his living under her roof. Though hurt by this open hostility, he realized he should make allowances for the distress of the bereavement, and accordingly let a few weeks go by before writing to remind her that from now on he would be in the world's eyes her natural support. 'I have sometimes been very unkind and very brusque with you, my dear mother; but remember that at that time I always knew there was someone beside you who had responsibility for your happiness. On learning of his death, my first reaction was to remind myself that henceforth this responsibility would fall on me. Unconcern, selfishness, outbursts of rudeness – all these things of which I have been guilty and which were the inevitable result of the disordered and isolated life I live, were now forbidden me. Everything humanly possible to create a new and special happiness for you in the autumn of your life, *will be done*.'[1]

The olive branch was not grasped. Mme Aupick expressed something like terror at the thought he might move in with her at Honfleur, even though he had not openly proposed doing so. She had visions of the little house overrun by his disreputable companions and, even worse, of the embarrassment of visits from insolent debt-collectors. Besides, could she rely on him to behave properly with the friends she had in the neighbourhood? The influence of Aupick lived on, kept alive by his old comrade and former aide Louis Emon, who had joined him in his retirement at Honfleur. Emon, whose earlier career had been similar to Aupick's (both had fought in the same campaigns during the closing years of the First Empire), took it on himself after the death of his fellow officer to step into his shoes, to the extent at least of advising the widow on her investments and pension rights, while his wife, a cheerful, bustling body, gave her the companionship which she badly needed at the time and for which she was deeply grateful. But both the Emons were violently prejudiced against her son, whom they regarded as more likely to drag her down with him into poverty than to provide the staff she needed in her old age. When *Les Fleurs du Mal* was published, and even more when the prosecution was set on foot, she reacted as they reacted, siding, said Baudelaire, with his persecutors. In time she revised her opinion on the book but, following the practice she had pursued ever since his boyhood, instead of praising him directly, put her feelings in writing to the one person least likely to pass on to him her expressions of pleasure and delight – her stepson Alphonse.

Do you realize that your brother is in process of acquiring a great and shining celebrity? His *Fleurs du Mal*, a book which has caused

170

so great a stir in literary circles, has some very fine things in it besides the repulsive and shocking descriptions it unfortunately includes here and there. There are admirable stanzas, of such purity of language and simplicity of form that the poetic effect is altogether magnificent. He possesses to the highest degree the art of literary composition. Charles, in spite of his eccentricities, has *undeniable talent.* If *Les Fleurs du Mal* had been a mediocre work it would have passed unnoticed, like so many others, you can be sure. Isn't it better to have too much fire and fury than to suffer from intellectual sterility and banality of thought?[2]

In the latter part of 1857 Mme Aupick began making timid approaches, but so clumsily that her son could not but take umbrage and rebuff her. 'The day after my stepfather's death, you told me that I dishonoured you, and you forbade me – even before it occurred to me to ask you – ever to think of living with you. Then, you required me to make humiliating overtures to M. Emon. Give me credit, my dear mother, for having endured all this with the gentleness and humbleness that your melancholy situation demanded. But later, after writing me letters containing nothing but bitter reproofs, after taking me to task for that accursed book, which after all is no more than a very defensible work of art, you invited me to come and see you, giving me to understand that the absence of M. Emon made it possible for me to stay at Honfleur, *as if M. Emon had the privilege of barring or unbarring my mother's door to me* ...'[3] Baudelaire's irritation was probably exactly what was needed to make his mother adopt a more conciliatory tone. She realized she had wounded his pride and was at fault and so, at the end of January 1858 she wrote again, sending him what he called, in his reply, 'a very charming letter – the first of that kind for many a year', which gave him to think 'that I am still loved, more than I thought, and that many things could be put right and that we might yet contrive to be very happy'.[4] Even so, he went on, there were all kinds of difficulties in the way of his paying her even a short visit; principally, of course, the need to reach some accommodation with his creditors before he left Paris.

However, by the end of the following month, having had another pressing letter from her with a promise of financial help, he began to make his preparations, packing all his belongings in three cases. 'Within ten days of the money being remitted, I'll be with you in Honfleur.'[5] But the remittance of the money proved the great stumbling-block. He needed 3000 francs in cash. This large sum could be raised only by mortgaging his monthly allowance for the rest of the year and for 1859 as well, or by making inroads on his capital, neither of which courses could be taken without Ancelle's agreement

– and what Baudelaire dreaded above all was to have to negotiate with Ancelle. He may have hoped his mother would advance him the sum or would simply send Ancelle the necessary instructions; but when it became apparent that she would not or could not do either of these things, he decided reluctantly he would have to stay where he was. The bare thought of bringing Ancelle into the business made him feel sick.

Unfortunately Mme Aupick had already got in touch with Ancelle to suggest he might make her son a private loan; Charles would be more likely to reimburse him in time than to replace the sum if it were taken out of the estate. Ancelle, wanting to check up on the situation, secretly interviewed the manager of the hotel where Baudelaire was staying and asked him all kinds of indiscreet questions about his lodger's private life. This, at least, was what the man told Baudelaire subsequently, whereupon the poet flew into a towering rage and threatened to go that very day to Neuilly, confront Ancelle and strike him across the face in the presence of his wife and family. At the very least he wanted an apology before witnesses. 'I have tears of rage in my eyes and bile rising in my throat that is making me vomit. There must be an end made to this. . . . Do I have to go on suffering insults all my life?'[6] In the end he did nothing, his anger being vented entirely in long, furious letters to his mother, of which he wrote and sent off no fewer than five in the course of a single day. A week or so later he and Ancelle were more or less reconciled. The notary denied having asked improper questions of the hotel-keeper, and Baudelaire accepted Ancelle's version of what had passed between them.

For him to lose control of himself in this way was totally out of character; no other instances are on record of his having given way to ungovernable rages except when driven beyond endurance by Jeanne's taunting or else, at the very end of his life, when loss of the power of speech caused him such frustration that he would on occasion fling objects across the room. Generally, he had the reputation of possessing a remarkably phlegmatic disposition. When gathering material for his biography of the poet, Eugène Crepet asked Prarond, who had known him longer than most, whether he could recall any occasions when Baudelaire had given way to rage and indignation; and Prarond's reply was that he could remember no such instances, his friend's behaviour being invariably pacific and the expression on his face, though sometimes ironical, always calm and reflective. The dandy, after all, would think it shame to be other than impassive at all times. But Baudelaire knew what hysteria was, even if its causes, as he noted sardonically in his review of *Madame Bovary*, still defeated the experts in the Academy of Medicine, and he knew that men of a neurotic temperament, as well as women, were

172

subject to it. 'I have cultivated my hysteria,' he wrote elsewhere, 'in terror and delight.'[7] The explosion of fury when he discovered the backstage manoeuvres concerted between his mother and the notary was probably less uncontrolled than it appeared, and may not have been directed against Ancelle personally so much as against the endless irritations of the financial tutelage in which he was kept.

The immediate result of the fracas was that Baudelaire abandoned all plans to settle permanently in Honfleur, at any rate for the moment, though he continued to ponder the possibility. There would be so many advantages in getting away. Far too much of his time in Paris was wasted in visits to editors and publishers, in meeting friends in cafés and restaurants, or looking for casual lodgings for the night when his creditors were hot on his trail. At Honfleur, his expenses would be halved – he might even save enough money, in time, to pay off his debts. He would have leisure to read. How he envied Flaubert, living a hermit-like existence at Croisset in a house that he shared with his mother and young niece, and writing his masterpieces in that tranquil retreat! All this he confided to Jaquotot, and to the objection he imagined his new friend making: are you sure you would not miss Paris? he answered in advance: 'I detest Paris and the cruel life I have led there for over sixteen years, which has been the one obstacle standing in the way of the fulfilment of all my projects.'[8] And he added that even if his debts were cleared, even if the Paris literary world were lionizing him, he would not return, he would be happier hidden away in Honfleur. Finally, the change might work wonders from the point of view of his state of health. He had been suffering from colic and difficulties in breathing, which the sea air might help to overcome, and if he could find a good fencing-master at Honfleur or Le Havre he was sure the exercise would do him good.

But the plan remained a pipe-dream. He paid his mother a brief overnight visit on October 20th, 1858, and at the end of January 1859 arrived for a longer stay; after that, he came down only for short visits, widely spaced out. Baudelaire found the spectral presence of the dead general a little oppressive; his widow had kept his bedroom and its furnishings unchanged, and she always had a place laid for him at table, even when Charles was staying with her. As compensation, there was always the view of the sea and the ships beating up the Channel in windy weather which, even in mid-winter, filled him with enthusiasm. The spectacle, monotonous and yet oddly exciting, seemed peculiarly designed, as he said in one of his prose-poems, 'for one whose soul is worn out in life's struggles. The wide vault of the sky, the mobile architecture of the clouds, the shifting shades of colour in the water, the glittering rays from the lighthouses, are a prism marvellously apt to distract the eyes of the beholder without ever tiring them. The tall ships with their complicated rigging, swaying harmoniously in the swell, minister to the soul's sense of rhythm and beauty. And above all, there is a kind of mysterious, aristocratic pleasure for one who has shed all curiosity and all ambition, to contemplate, lying in the watch-tower or leaning over the breakwater, all the activity of those who are setting forth and those who are returning home, of those who have still the strength to form wishes, the desire to travel or to amass riches.'[9]

The last few words of this prose-poem, which he entitled simply *Le Port*, may have given him the starting-point of the long poem *Le Voyage*, the central part of which consists in a dialogue between those who have yet to travel and those who are returning from their voyages. The first group press the second to hear what stories they have to relate, and the seafarers answer. They have seen, of course, many an exotic marvel in the mysterious east, idols with elephants' trunks, thrones studded with gems, snake charmers and painted dancing-girls. What else, what else? ask the stay-at-homes, and the reply comes in leaden accents:

> Let's not forget the one thing above all.
> In every land and sea we voyaged in,
> We saw the fatal fruit of Adam's fall:
> The tedious pageant of immortal sin.
>
> Woman, vile slave, mindless and self-adoring,
> Unsmiling, proud, cold-hearted and impure;
> Man, brutal tyrant, greedy, ever whoring,
> Slave of that slave, a gutter in the sewer.
>
> The torturer's chuckle and his victim's scream;
> The smell of blood at every celebration;
> The despot, lost in power's corrupting dream,
> Applauded by a masochistic nation.
>
> Several religions, none in any doubt
> They hold the keys of Heaven. Many a monk
> On bed of nails in ecstasy stretched out,
> Like dainty creatures deep in slumber sunk.
>
> Blinded by science, chattering Humanity,
> Deeming itself lord of the universe,
> Shouting to God, in its death-agony:
> 'Made in my image, Thee I hate and curse!'

While the wise few, fleeing their fellow men
Herded like kine by unrelenting Fate
Seek solace in great opium's regimen.
– Such is, and always was, the earthly state.[10]

In these stanzas Baudelaire passed devastating judgement on every aspect of human society as he saw it, taking in turn the individual man and woman, the state, the Church, and the new religion of science. Having completed the poem, he decided to dedicate it to Maxime Du Camp, partly because Du Camp was one of the great travellers of his generation, partly in a spirit of irony, for ever since the publication of his *Chants modernes* in 1855 Du Camp had been recognized as the outstanding exponent of the doctrine that social progress would be achieved by scientific advances. *Chants modernes* had appeared very opportunely to coincide with the opening of the first World Exhibition to be held in Paris; these exhibitions, of which the prototype was the Hyde Park 'Great Exhibition' of 1851, were primarily devoted to displaying the latest applications of technology to industry. Baudelaire, too, had written about the 1855 Exhibition, but in very different terms; his essay includes a strongly worded attack on 'a very fashionable sophistry . . . the idea of progress. . . . Ask any good Frenchman who reads his paper every day in his favourite bar, what he understands by progress. He will tell you it's steam, electricity, gas-lighting, miracles the Romans knew nothing of and which amply demonstrate our superiority over the ancients – so darkened is his wretched mind, so strangely muddled are his ideas of the difference between the material order and the spiritual order!'[11]

Scepticism regarding this basic tenet of nineteenth-century optimism coloured the whole of Baudelaire's thought in the last ten or twelve years of his life, and was normally associated with a call for a return to the old values of traditional Christianity. There is the famous statement in *My Heart Laid Bare*: 'Theory of true civilization: it lies neither in gas nor electricity nor in table turning, but in diminishing the traces of original sin.'[12] Only the individual could rid himself of the traces of original sin; thus social progress could come about only through individual effort, and to suppose that it would happen automatically, thanks to scientific advances and the creation of new wealth, was an idea implanted and propagated by the Devil for the perdition of mankind. And as for the 'tedious pageant of immortal sin', there was really no need to go on distant voyages to discover it; one had only to open the daily paper to see it displayed in all its dreadfulness. 'Every newspaper, from the first line to the last, is nothing but a tissue of horrors. Wars, crimes, theft, rape, torture;

outrages committed by princes, by nations, by individuals, a frenzy of universal atrocity.'[13] Were Baudelaire to return, a century and a quarter later, the only difference he would notice would be the supplementation of the printed sheet by spoken commentary and visual newscasts; but the 'tedious pageant' remains unchanged.

Le Voyage was only one – though the longest, and if not the most accomplished, possibly the most important – of the new poems Baudelaire wrote between 1858 and 1860 to replace those that had to be excised from the first edition of *Les Fleurs du Mal*. In pronouncing sentence on August 20th, 1857, the court had ordered the deletion of six poems in the original edition, but since these six were scattered through the book, and were printed on pages which included other poems or parts of poems judged to be inoffensive, it was not practical simply to rip out certain pages and offer the mutilated copies for sale. Unwilling to destroy the whole edition and so lose his investment, Poulet-Malassis set his workpeople to cut out the leaves on which the offending poems had been printed and to stick in, by means of binding-strips, new leaves on which were printed the beginnings or endings of the 'acceptable' poems. Baudelaire was not consulted over this device and when he got to hear about it he was furious. He was not going to have his masterpiece presented to the public as a thing of shreds and patches. His own solution was to pulp the entire first edition and bring out a second one, with six new poems replacing those that had been banned. The first mention of this project occurs in a letter to his mother written on Christmas Day 1857; his determination was reiterated in a letter to Poulet-Malassis on December 30th: 'You know that in any case I have resolved to submit myself completely to the sentence and to compose six new poems much finer than those that were suppressed. But when will the poetic mood descend on me again?' This was the difficulty; inspiration depended on chance illumination, on unpredictable stimulus, on some happy conjuncture that he had no power to bring about, and he complained bitterly to his mother of the need to 'become a great poet again, artificially, by an exercise of the will . . . simply in order to comply with the requirements of three inane magistrates'.[14]

There had always been, in Baudelaire's experience, a yawning gap between project and realization – the Shadow that T. S. Eliot spoke of as falling

> Between the idea
> And the reality,
> Between the motion
> And the act

176

– but at no time was it so marked as in the months immediately following the publication of *Les Fleurs du Mal* and the ensuing prosecution. The trough of depression into which any author is liable to slide when a book which has cost him years of labour is finally released to the world was deepened by the scandal of the trial, the verdict and the sentence which amounted to an embargo on sales until the book could be reissued in an altered form. Over these weeks he spoke to his usual confidant, his mother, of the 'languor' he had fallen into, which prevented him from settling to anything, even to so mechanical and undemanding a task as correcting proofs. 'An immense despondency – that is what I feel, together with an unbearable sense of isolation, perpetual apprehensions of some vague disaster, a complete loss of confidence in my powers, a total lack of motivation, an inability to find any distraction whatsoever. . . . I am for ever asking myself: What's the point of it all?' It was, he concluded, the 'authentic mood of spleen'. Once more he had relapsed into his old vice, for which she had so often chidden him at school – procrastination. 'When a man's nervous system is badly undermined by a succession of anxieties and troubles, the Devil, in spite of all good resolutions, steals into his mind every morning to whisper the thought: "Why not take a rest today and forget about everything? There will be time this evening to polish off all the urgent jobs in one go." – And then night comes, and one feels terrified at the thought of all the accumulated arrears of work; a crushing melancholy reduces one to impotence and the next day the same comedy is enacted, all in good faith, with the same confidence and the same seriousness.'[15]

It may have been his pride, in the end, that came to his rescue, in the form of the thought that he could not allow this work, which alone could promise him immortality, to remain in the shadows, branded as impure. The log jam was broken, a flood of new ideas burst through, irrigating what he himself called his 'new flowers', and in the end it was not just the six poems to make up the tally of a hundred, but a whole late harvest that sprang up in the ravaged garden. On November 10th, 1858, he told Calonne that 'the new Flowers of Evil have been started'. Moreover, 'the court decision required no more than that six pieces should be replaced. I shall perhaps compose as many as *twenty*.' (In reality, of course, the court had made no order that these six poems should be replaced; Baudelaire was attributing to his judges his own determination.) In the same letter he makes two further statements about the nature and probable impact of the new poems: firstly, that they will make it apparent that he is an 'incorrigible Catholic'; and secondly, that even the most prejudiced of his critics will have to acknowledge 'the deliberate impersonality of my poetry'.[16]

In referring to the Catholic inspiration of his poetry, Baudelaire may have been thinking of what Barbey d'Aurevilly had said at the end of his review of the first edition of *Les Fleurs du Mal*: 'After *Les Fleurs du Mal*, the poet who caused them to blossom has only two alternatives to choose from: to blow out his brains ... or to become a Christian!'[17] But in fact, apart from occasional expressions of pity for the disinherited of this world which might be construed as springing from Christian charity, there is little in the additional material that would strike the reader as being of specifically religious inspiration. This is not to say that Baudelaire did not write at this time a number of poems which could be regarded as the work of an 'incorrigible Catholic'; but they were all published in periodicals (*La Revue européenne* and *Le Boulevard*) between 1861 and 1863 and none of them formed part of the second edition of *Les Fleurs du Mal*. They include *Le Rebelle* (a translation of which we gave in the introduction to this book); *L'Avertisseur* (*The Warning Voice*) and *L'Examen de minuit* (*Midnight Self-Examination*), both of which deal with the troublesome importunity of conscience; and *L'Imprévu*, which provides perhaps the clearest testimony one can find in all Baudelaire's poetry of his belief in the Devil, lying in wait for the damned and bearing them off, at the appointed time, to hell. The title, *The Unexpected*, refers to Satan himself, whose existence is constantly denied by the hard-hearted, the insincere, the procrastinators, and whose appearance at the hour of death takes them all by surprise.

Of these poems we know only that they must have been written in the early 1860s,[18] possibly too late for inclusion in the second edition of *Les Fleurs du Mal* which was published in February 1861; or it may be that Poulet-Malassis, a determined Voltairian and anti-Catholic, objected to their presence in the book. However, the other feature of the 'new flowers' that Baudelaire stresses in his letter to Calonne, the 'deliberate impersonality', is readily detectable. For whatever reason, he seems to have discovered at this ultimate phase of his poetic evolution an altogether new source of inspiration, one that was external to himself, though the observer is never totally excluded from the picture and the argument, by one detour or another, always leads back to himself. The difference between these poems and the earlier ones is that the poet now leaves his garret room where he had been wont to sit alone in morose self-communion or exalted reverie, and describes what he sees as he walks about the streets and parks of Paris.

In this way he succeeded in inaugurating a new kind of urban poetry hardly represented at all in the 1857 collection; this vein proved so rich that he was able to group these 'impersonal' poems in a new cycle with a new heading, *Tableaux parisiens*, *Pictures of Paris*.[19] So he writes of the blind men who could be seen tramping the pavements like sleepwalkers, turning their sightless orbs up to an empty sky; of a passing woman he glimpsed, whom he might have loved, who knew he might have loved her, but whom he was never to see again; of a foggy morning, when hideously decrepit beggars, all seemingly identical, approach him menacingly at every street corner. There are references to the changes made in the appearance of the city by Haussmann's demolishment of so many old landmarks to clear the ground for his new boulevards; and the longest poem in this cycle treats of the decayed old ladies who could be observed sitting on benches or hobbling past the shops on errands he could only guess at. Baudelaire expresses movingly, after speculating on the pleasures and passions that filled their youth and the sorrows that came on them later, the quasi-paternal sympathy with which he follows with his gaze their tottering footsteps.

This new stream of inspiration did not immediately dry up, but broadened out later in the series of prose poems he composed in the 1860s and for which he invented the title *Paris Spleen*. But of all the verses he wrote concerning this much loved, much hated city, the most enchanting of all occur in a sonnet, written perhaps a little too late for inclusion in the *Tableaux parisiens* where it would have been in its proper place, and first published in the *Revue européenne* for November 1861. Entitled simply *Recueillement*, a word that can be translated *Meditation* provided this is understood at least partly in a devotional sense, it takes the form of a dialogue between the poet and his 'Sorrow', regarded as an inseparable companion as in the lines in Keats's *Endymion*:

> To Sorrow
> I bade good-morrow,
> And thought to leave her far away behind;
> But cheerly, cheerly,
> She loves me dearly.
> She is so constant to me, and so kind.

Sorrow, in Baudelaire's sonnet, has been waiting impatiently for the fall of evening; taking her by the hand, the poet leads her away from the streets thronged with the 'vile multitude' in search of pleasure and amusement and guides her down to the Seine, on to one of the bridges:

Leave them,
And stand you here. Behold the Past lean down
Over heaven's balcony in antique gown;
While from the river's depths Nostalgia smiles;
Beneath an arch the dead sun sinks from sight,
And in the east, trailing her shroud long miles,
Hark, my love, hark! the gentle tread of Night![20]

Once he had broken through the barrier and started writing poetry again, all Baudelaire's depression lifted. He reckoned, delightedly, that the new poems were just as likely to scandalize the critics as the old ones. 'Have written some new Flowers of Evil', he notified Poulet-Malassis on April 29th, 1859. 'They'll smash everything, like a gas explosion in a glassware shop'; and, on May 16th, in a letter enclosing some pieces that had appeared recently in the press, he told Nadar that 'along with some others that have not been published anywhere, they will I hope rejuvenate my blighted book. You'll observe that I'm ignoring my critics, and am obstinately digging myself in, more incorrigible than ever.'[21] Long before the book was ready, remembering how the partners, Poulet-Malassis and De Broise, had tried to publish the first edition 'in a cupboard', he started pestering them to launch it properly this time. He wanted advertisements, posters, choice bits leaked to the papers in advance, and if the firm felt the expenditure unjustified, declared himself ready to find the money – though how, one wonders. With proper publicity, he was convinced the book would sell. It was all very well for Poulet-Malassis to load him with compliments on the 'aristocratic character' of his works, 'but I want the plebeians to pay; it matters little to me whether they understand.'[22] In all this, Baudelaire showed himself to have a better grasp of the commercial realities of his time than his publishers, who were more concerned with the appearance of their products than with their saleability.

Thus, it was decided to enhance the look of the book by giving it a frontispiece. This was a fashion that had fallen into desuetude but that Poulet-Malassis wanted to revive; he had an illustrator, Félix Bracquemond, who had designed frontispieces for some of the earlier products of his press and whom he proposed to employ to embellish in this way the new edition of Baudelaire's work. The motif was chosen by the poet, and explained to the artist by the publisher; the design was to consist of a tree vaguely resembling a human skeleton and surrounded by the seven deadly sins, in the form of poisonous plants, each labelled with the appropriate Latin name: Avaritia, Luxuria, Invidia, etc.[23] But when Baudelaire was shown Bracquemond's sketch he was horrified and refused to allow it to be used.

When the book finally appeared, the authorities, as was to be expected, examined it carefully to make sure Baudelaire had not overstepped the bounds of decency this time; but the Public Prosecutor, making his confidential report, certified that the newly added pieces, 'although they give proof of an imagination eccentric to the point of incoherence and extravagance, did not appear to me to constitute a clear offence . . .'[24] There were no hostile reviews such as the first edition had provoked. The 1857 trial had turned Baudelaire into a minor literary martyr, and won him the support even of those who would normally have had little to say in his favour. Now, in his fortieth year, he could enjoy the sense of having at last arrived. 'Those who saw him at this moment of his life, smiling, relaxed, still looking youthful under his long hair turning white, recognized the salutary, calming effect on him of time and an established position. His old enemies were laying down their arms and new approaches were being made him by younger men. When, the day's work done, he left his room to walk down the boulevard, he found hands stretched out to grasp his, and he shook them all, varying his exquisite politeness to the proper degree of familiarity and acquaintanceship.'[25] One of the 'younger men' who had occasion to call on him at the Hôtel de Dieppe where he lodged at this time has left a rare description of Baudelaire at work,

with his sleeves rolled up, according to his custom, exactly like a labourer in the fields or on the public highway. A soft silk cravat, red with black stripes, tied negligently, encircled the thick, strong neck of which this refined man was so proud. Clean-shaven, with scrubbed cheeks, he sat hunched in his loose, snow-white cloth jacket of a very old-fashioned cut. On seeing me, he smiled, tossed back his long, grey, slightly curling locks which gave him a kind of priestly appearance, and his large fine eyes, 'as deep and dark as night', turned towards me; then, without a word, he pushed away the page, heavily scored and crossed out, on which he had been working for several days probably, and carefully stacked a number of printed sheets scattered over his worktable; then he motioned me with a glance to a high-backed Empire chair, shaped like a Roman magistrate's seat, a twin of the one he was sitting on himself, and turned to contemplate admiringly his aristocratic hands and his pink finger-nails no less transparent and carefully manicured than an infanta's . . .[26]

But in all the gratifying chorus of appreciation and esteem with which the enlarged edition of *Les Fleurs du Mal* was greeted in 1861 there was one discordant voice: his mother's, whose praise he thirsted after more than anyone else's, not because he had a specially high opinion of her critical judgement, but because the need to win her approval had been implanted in him as a child, and in this one respect that child lived on in him. What criticisms she made we do not know, but they drove him into such a fury that he could hardly spell the words that spilled from his pen. 'Always you join with the mob in stoning me,' he raged. 'All that goes right the way back to my childhood, as you know. How is it that you always contrive, except in money matters, to be for your son the reverse of a friend? . . . A book that I have worked at for twenty years, and which in any case *I had no choice but to have reprinted!*'[27] The last phrase, heavily underlined, suggests very strongly that among the reproaches his mother had uttered, the most hurtful was that he should have reissued the book at all; much better, in her opinion, if he had withdrawn it completely in view of its condemnation in open court.

She must also have told him that her confessor, who had specially asked to be sent a copy, had thrown it in the fire. People don't burn books these days, he said angrily, apart from lunatics who derive an insane satisfaction from seeing paper go up in flames. He had only a limited number of complimentary copies, and several of his friends would have been glad of one! This outrage too he laid at his mother's door; she lacked pride, she always had to be on her knees before some man or other; it used to be Emon, now it was this ignorant priest — and before that, he would have added had he dared, Aupick.

The outburst was the more remarkable because, over the preceding two years (the letter in which he made these violent expostulations was written on April 1st, 1861), he appears to have drawn closer to his mother than ever before. The visit to Honfleur, though curtailed, had lasted long enough for feelings of mutual sympathy, understanding and affection to spring up afresh; it was only when they were living apart from one another that misunderstandings arose and reproaches and recriminations were exchanged. Mme Aupick was now in her late sixties; approaching old age was beginning to blunt her disappointment that her son had, as she thought, gratuitously thrown away his chances of an honourable career; she was growing more indulgent and less quarrelsome because peace and quiet were now what she chiefly looked for. Charles was quick to respond to this new kindness, to the softer and more generous attitude he detected in the letters she wrote after he left Honfleur, and the replies he sent are full of expressions of gratitude and affection. The one thing that troubled him above all else was that he could not hope to conserve her for ever. 'Sometimes I quake with dread at the thought of the solitude I shall be plunged into one day. Even supposing I become famous, nothing will compensate for the loss of this life of regular domestic affection which I have desired so much and never known.'[28]

For he knew now that he would never find a woman with whom he might share his life. Marie Daubrun had abandoned him, he had broken irretrievably with Mme Sabatier. There remained only Jeanne Duval, from whom he had parted but over whom he continued to watch from afar. On April 5th, 1859, she had a paralytic seizure which necessitated hospitalization; Baudelaire, although as usual penniless, undertook to meet the nursing and medical expenses and sent Poulet-Malassis a note-of-hand from Honfleur asking him to try and get it discounted, using the proceeds to pay the nursing-home its charges. His friend followed his instructions and remitted 150 francs to the invalid who, however, kept it for her own uses instead of paying it over to the almoner. On receiving a sharp letter from the hospital authorities protesting against the delay in payment, Baudelaire jumped to the conclusion that Poulet-Malassis was finding difficulty in raising the money, and, at his wit's end, applied to his mother for the sum required. Learning the purpose for which he wanted it, she refused to help him, and a violent quarrel ensued. In the end the matter was cleared up and he forgave Jeanne in consideration of the probable weakening of her mental faculties.

He continued to keep an eye on her after her discharge from hospital; as he put it wryly to his mother, 'after being for so many years an idler and a profligate, I am obliged now (which would be funny if it were not so sad) to play the part of fatherly guardian'.[29] But in consideration of the past he felt he had a continuing responsibility for her welfare and in the autumn of 1860, when his own health took a turn for the worse and he feared he might not have much longer to live, he begged his mother, if she survived him, to ensure that the remainder of his private fortune, after the settlement of his debts, should go to Jeanne.

Then there was a quite extraordinary development. Baudelaire had moved to Neuilly, to be nearer the convalescent, and discovered she was seeing a great deal of a brother, of whom he had never heard before, and who was spending most of the day with her. The man was in employment, but when Baudelaire suggested he ought to contribute to support his sister, he refused point-blank, arguing that Baudelaire had contracted a common-law marriage with her and had therefore all the obligations of a husband. Further investigation showed that the fellow was, to some extent, living off Jeanne, borrowing from her the money that Baudelaire gave her out of his slender resources for food and medicine.

He remained at Neuilly for three or four weeks, spending his time, as he told Poulet-Malassis, 'between a rascal and an unfortunate woman whose mental faculties are impaired'.[30] Finally he fled, sick with indignation and disgust, and returned to Paris. Ten weeks later Jeanne came round to see him, in the utmost distress; she had had to go into hospital again, and when she came out, it was to find that her brother had absconded after selling part of her furniture.

No doubt Baudelaire would have stood by her in this extremity, had it not been for another discovery he made over which a certain mystery hangs, since he refused to speak about it to anybody, not even to his mother, saying that it would 'scald his tongue' were he to do so; it was something 'monstrous, that made me ill'.[31] The interpretation most often put forward of these guarded words is that he had found out that this so-called brother of Jeanne's was in reality one of her lovers and no relation at all. But it may not have been as simple as that; Baudelaire had been accustomed to her infidelities of old, and the discovery of one more could hardly have upset him so violently. What is more likely to have sickened him is that, knowing they were brother and sister (some facial resemblance, or the darkness of the man's complexion, would have been proof enough that they had the same mother at least), he found that they were sleeping together. To speak of incest might have 'scalded his tongue' where ordinary promiscuity would have been accepted with resignation.

This was not quite the end of the affair. Baudelaire continued even after this to send Jeanne financial help, though always anonymously. In May 1864, having heard she was going blind, he wrote to Ancelle giving her address and asking him to remit her 50 francs. Then he died, and there was no one. For a few years longer she continued to drag out a miserable existence; Nadar claimed to have seen her in 1870, hobbling down the boulevard on crutches. Mme Aupick, who had always regarded her as a bloodsucker of the worst type, chose to ignore her son's earlier instructions that the remnants of his fortune should be devoted to providing for her, and one can only surmise that, reduced to abject poverty, she eventually died of starvation in some cupboard-like room like Gervaise Macquart in *L'Assommoir*, or perhaps in the ward of a public hospital. But we cannot be sure how or when she met her end any more than we can be certain when or where she was born or what her legal surname was. There remains an aura of dusky unreality surrounding Jeanne, making it easier to think of her as a phantasmal symbol than as a real woman with a certain life-span who was once beautiful and then became old and sick. Posterity sees her and her lover frozen in an unvarying attitude, locked together in the same close but distant contact as the sculptured group that Rodin called *The Eternal Idol*; he with his hands clasped behind him as if to avoid embracing her, she straining back and looking down at him with an air of faint disdain. Or again one can fancy her to have been some devouring lamia, some demonic avatar of the *Ewig-Weiblich*, clothed for a time in bronzed and comely flesh to delight, distract, and drive almost to madness the poet whom she inspired with some of the most superb and the most sinister love-lyrics in the French language.

XIII

PARIS SPLEEN

Over the last six years of Baudelaire's life, between 1861 and 1867, the Second Empire reached a zenith of prosperity and self-confidence. The Treaty of Villafranca (1859) had marked the conclusion of Napoleon III's successful campaign against Austria, in which France reasserted herself as the dominant military power in Europe, for the time being at any rate. There followed a period of peace on the Continent and of economic expansion inside France, powerfully assisted by a free trade treaty with Great Britain and by the completion of the internal railway network. The new era was symbolized by a surprising transformation of the external appearance of the capital, achieved within the space of a very few years thanks to the vision and energy of Baron Haussmann and the exertions of his hundreds of demolition and construction crews, working with pick, shovel, and wheelbarrow. Old slums disappeared, new squares and boulevards were laid out, and on all sides arose glittering restaurants, cafés, department stores and apartment houses, while below ground miles of sewers were tunnelled, helping to make the fearsome cholera outbreaks of earlier times nothing but a bad memory. All these extensive public works provided something like full employment in building and allied trades, which in that age were far more labour-intensive than today. The amusement industry – show-business – flourished too as never before; the old theatres of the Boulevard du Crime were pulled down and huge new ones, the Châtelet, the Vaudeville, the Gaîté, were erected in their place but in more convenient locations. This was the period when Offenbach popularized the *opéra-bouffe* and when the *café-concert* came into its own; while horse-racing, a sport imported from England, attracted crowds of onlookers and punters to Longchamp, the Paris equivalent of Epsom Downs, on the edge of the Bois de Boulogne. Everywhere there was bustle, noise, activity and gaiety, as the well-sprung carriages swept down the streets and the gold napoleons chinked on marble counters.

Although the term had not yet been invented, it was already a consumer society ruled by the values appropriate to such a society.

Baudelaire stood aloof from it, partly because he remained as poor as a church-mouse, partly because he judged these values to be immoral in any case or, as he would have put it, satanic; did they not depend on the exploitation of instincts rooted in at least four of the seven deadly sins: avarice, envy, lust and greed? If an eighth were to be added, it would be insensitivity, that amalgam of egoism and callousness which he saw as peculiar to his age and native country and which he denounced in a fable short enough to be quoted here in full.

The New Year had exploded in a chaos of snow and slush, everyone's carriage on the street, toys and confectionery glittering in the shops, greed and despair rampant everywhere; the licensed delirium to which the city had succumbed was of a kind to turn the brain of the most strong-minded solitary.

In the midst of this hubbub and hurly-burly, a donkey was trotting along briskly, harassed by a great brute armed with a whip.

As the donkey was rounding a corner near the footpath, a fine gentleman wearing gloves and patent leather shoes, his throat cruelly constricted in a tightly knotted cravat and his body squeezed into a suit of clothes straight from the tailor, swept off his hat and executed a courtly bow in front of the lowly animal, exclaiming as he did so: 'A happy and prosperous New Year to you!' Then he turned round to the rest of the party accompanying him, grinning fatuously as if to invite them to add their applause to his self-satisfaction.

The donkey, not seeing this elegant humorist, continued to trot zealously to where his duty called him.

As for me, I was left grinding my teeth in a towering rage against this witless exquisite, who seemed to me to embody the very quintessence of our sense of humour in France.[1]

This text is one out of twenty similar pieces published in *La Presse*, at that time edited by Arsène Houssaye, between August 26th and September 24th, 1862, under the general heading *Petits Poèmes en Prose*. The words designated the form rather than the content of this new kind of literature; at a later stage Baudelaire tried out an alternative title, *Le Spleen de Paris*, using it for a collection of six prose poems published in *Le Figaro* on February 7th, 1864. In the same issue of this newspaper Gustave Bourdin – the very man who had written the unfortunate review of *Les Fleurs du Mal* which had precipitated the prosecution of the book[2] – offered an explanation of the title, an explanation almost certainly furnished by the author himself. '*Le Spleen de Paris* is the title adopted by M. Charles Baudelaire for a book he is engaged on writing and which he hopes will prove a worthy complement to *Les Fleurs du Mal*. All the specificities of ordinary life which by their nature are impossible, or at least difficult, to express in verse have their place in a prose work in which the ideal and the trivial are fused in an inseparable amalgam.' As for the significance of the title, Bourdin goes on, 'there are those who believe that Londoners alone enjoy the aristocratic privilege of suffering from spleen and that Paris, gay Paris, has never been subject to that grievous affliction. But it may be that, as the author claims, there exists a special kind of Parisian spleen, known, as he argues, to many people who will recognize what he is talking about.'[3]

The prose poem was to all intents and purposes a literary form of Baudelaire's own invention. He himself suggested he had a forerunner in the minor romantic Aloysius Bertrand, whose *Gaspard de la Nuit* (published posthumously in 1842) can, however, at most have provided him with a starting-point. Bertrand's pseudo-medieval fantasies are poles apart from Baudelaire's rigorously modern and realistic street scenes; and his archaic vocabulary and contorted syntax have nothing in common with Baudelaire's limpid, contemporary style. He appreciated Bertrand's book, which is not without its special charm to which Debussy in his turn proved susceptible, but soon dismissed the idea of imitating him, if that idea ever really crossed his mind. At the most, *Gaspard de la Nuit* may have suggested the title *Poèmes nocturnes* under which the first specimens of his prose poetry appeared in the press in 1857.

This was only two months after the publication of the original edition of *Les Fleurs du Mal* and long before the appearance of the second edition with its numerous new poems. There was in fact a period of five years or so during which Baudelaire appeared to be hesitating between prose and poetry as his proper medium for creative writing in the future. Among the first prose poems to be published are several which are simply prose versions of what had previously been written as verse. Such doublets are sometimes even given identical titles; thus, we have two versions, the earlier in verse, the later in prose, of *L'Invitation au voyage* and of *La Chevelure*.[4] It sometimes happens, however, that the same title was used for two compositions, one in verse and one in prose, of which the actual contents bear little resemblance to one another. Thus, *Crépuscule du soir* was the title used for an ode written towards the end of 1851 and included in the first edition of *Les Fleurs du Mal*; it was also the title given to a prose poem which exists in various versions, though the oldest certainly postdates the ode. In spite of the identical title, suggesting an identity of themes, the two works are very dissimilar in mood and content. The poem stresses the sinister aspects of the coming of dusk; under its cover the criminal will go about his business and the prostitute will steal forth to hunt for clients. The prose poem begins, it is true, in a similarly sombre tone by discussing how nightfall tends to darken still further the minds of those unfortunates who are subject to attacks of mania; but it finishes with a couple of paragraphs describing how very differently the crepuscular hour can affect a man of poetic disposition.

Twilight, soft and gentle hour! The pale red streaks that glimmer still above the horizon like the day's death-wound delivered by night's victorious scimitar – the glow of street-lamps crimsoning dully against the ultimate incandescent glory of the sunset – the heavy hangings drawn from the abyssal east by an unseen hand – what are all these but a visible projection of the warring emotions in man's heart at the gravest hours of his life?

Yet again the beholder will be put in mind of certain fantastic dresses worn by ballet-girls, whereon through a dark, transparent gauze shine the dimmed splendours of a skirt of brilliant colours, even as past joys shimmer through the sombre veil of the present; and the gold and silver spangles with which it is stitched, and which dance as the dancer moves, figure those lights of fantasy which never glint so brightly as under the funereal canopy of Night.[5]

In the first section of this prose poem, to illustrate his contention that those whose minds are unhinged grow more frenzied as the night approaches, Baudelaire relates two brief but striking anecdotes. In *Les Fleurs du Mal*, narrative passages are rarely found, whereas in the prose poems they are a fairly constant feature, and it is indeed likely that Baudelaire, in switching to prose poetry, was at least partly impelled by the desire to appear in a new guise, as story-teller. Sometimes the story encapsulated in the prose poem is manifestly of his own invention, at other times it can be shown to have been borrowed from some earlier author, and occasionally it derives from an incident he witnessed or heard about. In this last category falls *La Corde* (*The Rope*), one of the few prose poems which bears a dedication: 'To Edouard Manet'. In Antonin Proust's reminiscences of Manet one may read how 'while living in the Rue de la Victoire, he completed *The Child with the Cherries*, using as his model a little boy employed to wash his brushes and clean his palette. This poor lad, temperamentally very unstable, hanged himself; Manet was greatly upset by the tragic end of the little fellow to whom he was deeply attached.'[6] The story, which Baudelaire must have had from Manet's own lips, is related in very much greater detail in *La Corde*. We are told how the painter came to take the urchin under his roof, how his presence in the studio enlivened Manet's lonely and laborious life, and how he used him as the model for several pictures. We also learn how Manet gave him a severe scolding after discovering he had been raiding the larder – his great weakness being 'an unreasonable craving for sweetmeats and liqueurs' – and how, returning later in the day to the house, he found the boy had hanged himself from a nail driven into the same cupboard where Manet kept his provisions.

Up to this point the story sounds exactly as Manet might have told it to Baudelaire; but the sequel may as easily have been the poet's invention, though it gives point to what would otherwise be no more than a horrifying news-item. We are told how Manet had to cut down the corpse, face an embarrassing police inquiry, and finally break the news to the dead child's parents, who were poor, uneducated folk living in the neighbourhood. The mother appeared quite stunned and lost in thought; she asked only one thing of Manet, to be allowed into the studio, ostensibly to view the corpse; once admitted, she begged him with a kind of morbid insistence to let her carry away the rope with which her little son had hanged himself. The reason why she was so intent on gaining possession of this grisly relic became apparent the following day, when the bemused painter received a stack of letters from his neighbours on other floors of the house, all requesting a snippet of the fatal rope. It was only then that it dawned on him why the mother had been so intent on making off with it; he remembered the old superstition that a piece of the rope that has served a suicide brings good luck. She had lost her son, but had gained something she perhaps valued more: a highly marketable piece of merchandise.

As it stands, this gruesome little episode might have furnished Maupassant with the subject for one of his *contes*; it has everything that master of the short story required, even down to the 'whiplash ending'. But Maupassant would have been content to let the story stand for itself; not so Baudelaire, for whom the whole point of an anecdote was that it should serve as peg for some moral reflection, which sometimes frames it, sometimes concludes it, or else, as in *La Corde*, precedes it. However, since Baudelaire's moral outlook was original to the point of perversity, the lessons he draws from the stories he tells in his prose poems are invariably unexpected and usually disconcerting. A more commonplace moralist might have used the tale of the rope as pretext for denouncing the prevalence of idle superstition among the lower classes. Baudelaire has something much more profound in mind. This is how he introduces his idea, in the first paragraph of *La Corde*.

'It may well be,' my friend said to me, 'that illusion is present in all the dealings men have with one another or with the world of natural objects; and when the illusion ceases, that is, when we see the other person or fact as it exists objectively, we experience a strange feeling, compounded in equal measure of regret for the phantom that is no more, and pleasurable astonishment at the novelty, the reality. If there is one universal, unmistakable, and unchanging phenomenon, of a nature that can mislead no one, it is surely maternal love. It is as hard to imagine a mother without maternal love, as it is to imagine a source of light that is not also a source of heat; is it not therefore very understandable that we should attribute to maternal love everything a mother does, everything she says, where her child is concerned?'[7]

After which the story is related, its unexpected purpose being to demonstrate how unwise we are to make any assumptions whatsoever about human nature, or perhaps to illustrate how events continually upset our preconceived view of reality.

(Of course, with the knowledge we now possess, but which was not available to his first readers, of Baudelaire's warped relations with his own mother, it would be perfectly possible to interpret *La Corde* in terms of a private allegory in which he is obliquely denouncing Mme Aupick's scale of values where maternal affection took second place, in his judgement at least, to money and possessions.)

Dearly as Baudelaire would have liked to follow in Poe's footsteps and adopt the lucrative profession of short-story writer,[8] he was never able to convince himself that an intelligent reader's interest could be sustained by nothing more than the dramatic tension generated by the narrative itself; the fiction had to point to some specific, if ambiguous, philosophical conclusion predetermined by the story-teller. This was never Poe's practice in the best of his works. What morals are implicit in *The Black Cat* or *The Pit and the Pendulum*? In the absence of any direction by the author, the reader could only reach some such banal conclusion as that 'murder must out' or that the instinct for self-preservation will survive everything. It is certainly not for such bits of humdrum wisdom that one reads the *Tales of Mystery and Imagination*.

Anecdotes play a part in perhaps thirty of the fifty prose poems that make up *Le Spleen de Paris* as we have it. Not all of them are 'realistic' in the way *The Rope* is; a few are pure fables, like *Which is the True One?*; others, like *The Port*, are non-narrative descriptive pieces, but still mingled with moralistic reflections.[9] But a sufficient number are infused with the authentic flavour of contemporary life to demonstrate that, having by the 1860s reached some kind of resigned accommodation with his private predicaments, Baudelaire was ready to turn his vision outwards and interest himself in the humble dramas of ordinary life and in the sad, unassuming, sometimes pitiable lives of lowly folk. In *Les Fenêtres* he describes himself looking out at night from his balcony into the uncurtained windows of other houses in the crowded, working-class district where he had his lodgings.

> Beyond a tossing sea of roofs I descry a woman advanced in years, her face already lined, poor, always bent over something, never leaving the room. Guided by what I can see of her face and her garb, by the movements of her hands, by the slightest hint or nothing at all, I have reconstructed this woman's history, or rather her legend, and now and again I weep to retell it to myself.
> Had it been a poor old man, I should have reconstructed his with as little trouble.
> And so I retire to bed, proud to have lived and suffered in others beside myself.
> You may ask: 'Are you sure this legend is the truth?' But what do I care for the facts, if this reality which is outside me has helped me to live, to know I exist, to understand the kind of man I am? [10]

The subjective imagination still counts for more than fact-finding inquiry, and Baudelaire is still as much concerned with his own self as he always was and always would be; but the poetic gift is now allowed a wider sphere of operation.

Possibly De Quincey helped to point the way here, in those passages of his *Confessions* where he describes himself wandering, homeless and short of food, through the modern Babylon of broad streets and narrow passage-ways, splendid palaces and rat-infested hovels that made up the London of his youth. In his analysis of the book Baudelaire comments, concerning these chapters: 'Even if he had not naturally been, as the reader must have noticed, gentle, sensitive, and affectionate, one might readily suppose him to have learned, in the course of those long days spent wandering hither and thither and of the even longer nights passed in anguish of spirit, to love and pity the poor. The erstwhile scholar now desires to make fresh acquaintance with the lives of the humble; he wishes to plunge into the midst of the throng of the disinherited and, as the swimmer opens his arms to the sea and so embraces nature directly, so he too longs to bathe, as it were, in the multitudinous sea of men.' [11] This last phrase (in the original, *prendre un bain de multitude*), is found textually repeated at the beginning of another of the pieces in *Le Spleen de Paris*, entitled simply *Les Foules* (*Crowds*). Baudelaire here speaks of the poet as a man peculiarly adapted to participate in the lives of others and thus, while retaining his singularity, to embrace thanks to his imaginative gift and powers of empathy, a plurality of existences.

The poet enjoys an incomparable privilege: he has the right, when he so desires, to be himself or someone other. Like those spirits that drift through the world seeking to be made flesh, he can enter into what soul he will. For him alone, there are no bolts nor bars; and if certain habitations seem closed to him, it is simply that in his eyes they are not worth his while to visit.

The solitary, pensive wanderer will derive a singular delight from this universal communion. He who finds no impediment in wedding the crowd makes himself familiar with such heady ecstasies as are for ever denied to the egoist padlocked like a strong-box, to the indolent loafer shut up like a shellfish. He adopts as his own all professions, and has his part in every joy and every sorrow that circumstance reveals to him.

What men call love is a pitifully mean, pinched, anaemic thing compared with this ineffable orgy, this temple prostitution of the soul which in poetic charity embraces whole-heartedly every unexpected appearance, every unknown passer-by.[12]

Les Foules, published first in Catulle Mendès's Revue fantaisiste in November 1861, was composed at a time when Baudelaire had already begun work on his long and important essay on Constantin Guys, which was not to appear in print until 1863. The same train of thought as one finds in Les Foules underlies this monograph which he entitled Le Peintre de la vie moderne; the curious expression 'wedding the crowd' occurs in both, applied in the first instance to the poet, Baudelaire himself no doubt, and in the second to the artist, Guys.

He is in his element in the crowd, as the bird in the air and the fish in the water. His passion and his profession is to wed the crowd. For the professional stroller, the passionate observer, the keenest of pleasures is to take up his abode in what is multifarious, diversified, agitated, fleeting, and unbounded. To be abroad, and yet to feel oneself at home everywhere; to observe the world, to be in the world and to be hidden from the world, these are the least of the delights enjoyed by those independently minded, passionately involved and yet aloof spirits whom our language can denote but awkwardly. The observer is a prince who is free to wander everywhere incognito. The lover of life looks on all humanity as his family, just as the lover of the fair sex finds his family in all the beautiful women he has met or might meet or will never meet; just as the art lover lives in an enchanted world of dreams painted on canvas.[13]

Constantin Guys was already in his mid-fifties when Baudelaire first made his acquaintance, in the autumn of 1859, and started collecting his drawings. He belonged to the last generation of artist-illustrators, before they were replaced by professional photographers; he was widely travelled and had been sent to the Crimea by the *Illustrated London News* to record scenes of camp and battlefield. The last years of his life were spent in Paris, where he busied himself making hundreds of sketches of the passing scene, concentrating particularly on people bent on amusement, and in this way contributed in no small measure to the legend of 'gay Paris' which first took shape under the Second Empire. Baudelaire was not alone in admiring him; Manet, Gautier, Delacroix shared something of his enthusiasm, and Nadar was one of Guys's closest friends. For all this, Baudelaire discovered the graphic artist to be almost pathologically shy, to the point that he insisted on being designated only by the first letter of his name in Baudelaire's monograph. When it was finally published Guys was so embarrassed that it was a long time before he could bring himself to read it.

However one may regret Baudelaire's failure to appreciate at their proper value some of the truly great artists he knew personally, like Courbet and Manet, his fanaticism in defending and eulogizing those to whom he was attracted, even if like Guys they were relatively minor figures, is something one cannot but admire. He always had the courage of his convictions, he never hedged his bets, and the praise he bestowed so unstintingly was utterly disinterested. And it happened from time to time that his judgements, so much at variance with those of the majority of his contemporaries, have been ratified by posterity, as in the case of Delacroix and also of Richard Wagner.

The German composer had already achieved European celebrity at a time when in Paris he was still disregarded and decried, although he had had his defenders even there, chiefly among amateurs rather than professional music critics; Gérard de Nerval and Gautier, both friends of Baudelaire's, had attempted in 1849 and 1850 to publicize his aims and make the French aware of his achievements. But their efforts availed little; ten years later, when Wagner came to Paris, he still faced the same hostility and incomprehension among French critics. Berlioz was lukewarm and Meyerbeer, jealous of his own supremacy as an operatic composer, quite venomous. Baudelaire went along to the concerts Wagner gave in January and February 1860 full, as he subsequently admitted, of 'erroneous prejudices'; but as he listened he underwent a total conversion, and wrote a lyrical letter to Poulet-Malassis about Wagner's 'sublime works'; the occasion had been 'a landmark in my intellectual life ... I have experienced nothing like such rapture for fifteen years at least.'[14] As happened when he 'discovered' Poe, he could not keep his delight and astonishment to himself, and bored his friends who were far from sharing his admiration.

As usual, finding himself in a minority, Baudelaire decided it was up to him to show the majority how wrong they were. He would perform the same service for Wagner as he had for Poe and, to some extent, for Delacroix. And since Wagner was in Paris, the first step was to get in touch with him. He wrote him a long, fulsome letter in which he repeated what he had said to Poulet-Malassis: 'I owe you the *greatest musical delight* I have ever experienced.' He added that 'in the first place it seemed to me that I already knew this music and later, pondering over it, I realized the source of this illusion; it seemed to me this music was *my own*, and I recognized it as every man recognizes those things he is destined to love.'[15] The remark may remind us of the statements Baudelaire made in letters to Fraisse and Thoré, to the effect that he had been drawn to Poe through discovering in the American's writings ideas and even turns of phrase that he had thought of himself earlier.[16] The same almost mystical sense of spiritual affinity was given him by his first encounter with Wagner's music as by his first reading of Poe's stories.

The long essay on Wagner that Baudelaire then settled down to write is unique in being the only piece of music criticism he ever ventured on. He had had no musical education whatsoever and very little contact with composers or instrumentalists (his friendship with Liszt came later). We seldom hear of him attending concerts, operatic performances, or musical soirées. The two composers he most often refers to in his published writings are Beethoven and Weber (he seems to have had little knowledge of Berlioz or his works), and the one pleasure he derived from listening to music – to judge by the sonnet *La Musique* in *Les Fleurs du Mal* and by scattered references elsewhere – was that it could give him a feeling of liberation, of being transported to great heights.[17] He had the same impression while listening to Wagner, but to a greater degree than ever before. 'No musician excels Wagner in *painting* space and depth, in both the material and the spiritual sense. ... One sometimes has the impression, listening to this ardent, despotic music and torn between it and one's dreams, of rediscovering, painted against a sombre background, the heady transports of opium.'[18]

The long essay in which Baudelaire recapitulates all he had been able to discover concerning Wagner's life and musical career and offers analyses of the three operas known to the French at the time (*The Flying Dutchman*, *Tannhäuser*, and *Lohengrin*), is dated March 18th, 1861. It was on that day that *Tannhäuser* was given its second performance at the Paris Opéra. Even the presence of Napoleon III and Eugénie on this occasion failed to keep the unrest of the audience within bounds; while on March 24th the jeers and boos of a noisy and determined cabal turned the third and last performance into total disaster. The curtain had to be rung down before the end; Niemann, the German tenor, was seen shaking his fist at the audience from the stage with tears of rage and frustration in his eyes. It was not until many years after Baudelaire's death, and indeed not really until after Wagner's death, that the revolution he had accomplished in operatic music became generally accepted in France.

Originally published in *La Revue européenne*, Baudelaire's study was reissued as a pamphlet, under the title *Richard Wagner et 'Tannhäuser' à Paris*, in May 1861. Emboldened perhaps by the attention it was given, he told his mother on July 10th that he was seriously thinking of seeking election to the French Academy. She was clearly excited by this possibility, and he felt it necessary to write again warning her that he had by no means made up his mind and that in any case nobody ever got elected at the first try; but the number of votes cast in one's favour gave a useful indication of one's chances for the future. He took soundings over the next five months and then, on December 11th, formally submitted his candidature to the Secretary of the Academy, Abel Villemain.

It was in all sincerity that he told his mother it was chiefly for her sake that he was making the attempt. He knew that whatever his literary standing in Paris, she would never believe he counted for anything until he had received some official mark of approval. 'I realize you attach an immense importance to public honours and if, *miraculously*, that's the right word, I were to succeed, you would be filled with an immense joy.'[19] It would be like winning first prize at school all over again. Moreover, there could be certain material advantages, not just in the form of the emoluments paid to academicians but also because, if he were elected, she would surely agree at last to the annulment of the court order which, back in 1844, declared him unfit to have control of his financial affairs.

About this time, his resentment at the part she had played in placing him under this judicial disability seems suddenly to have intensified. He refers repeatedly to the *conseil judiciaire* in letters to her written in 1861, calling it 'that accursed invention, the invention of a mother with an obsession about money, which has dishonoured me, driven me yet deeper into debt, soured my good nature and even hampered my artistic and literary education which is still incomplete. Blindness causes more damage than malice.' Formulated here in a letter written in April, these complaints and accusations are reiterated even more bitterly the following month. 'My situation is atrocious. . . . Never any peace – insults, affronts, humiliations such as you have no idea of and which poison and paralyse my imagination. I am earning a little money, after all; if I were free of debt, and *if I had no private fortune left*, I WOULD BE RICH, think of it! I would be in a position to let you have money and to exercise my charity towards Jeanne without danger.'[20] This line of thought led him to the strange, but perhaps correct deduction that if no legal steps had been taken seventeen years earlier to stop him squandering the rest of his capital, the consequence would undoubtedly have been that he would have spent it all, but then, with nothing behind him, he would have been forced to rely completely on his own earning capacity. He might still have been poor, yet perhaps not so poor, since he would not have had to waste his energies dealing with grubby debt-collectors and devising ignominious expedients to keep them at bay, for ever robbing Peter to pay Paul.[21] The temptation to borrow, when he knew and when his creditors knew that in the fullness of time – on his death, that is – what was left of the original inheritance, carefully husbanded through the years by Ancelle, would be sufficient to meet their claims, would no longer have been there. Whatever income his writings brought in would have been applied to his own needs, instead of being frittered away on interest payments for unsettled debts.

Apart from these sordid calculations of profit and loss, in making his bid for a seat in the Academy Baudelaire was moved by the consideration that the time had surely come for some official recognition of his contribution to literature. He knew his own value, however the average bourgeois might ignore him or sneer at him. Of course he would never be a popular writer; his ideas and attitudes, his uncompromising frankness went too much against the grain of the times. 'I *know*,' he remarked in a letter to Hugo, 'that henceforth, whatever field of literature I venture into, I shall always be a monster, a bogeyman', and to Sainte-Beuve he quoted – implicitly applying the words to himself – from Shelley's *Stanzas written in dejection near Naples*: 'for I am one Whom men love not, – and yet regret.'[22] 'Original' was what people called him when they wanted to be polite. 'I have never known what it is to be original myself', said the erudite scholar Villemain when Baudelaire called on him to solicit, half-heartedly, his support in the election. 'Why, sir,' answered the postulant with a rare flash of humour, 'if you wish to be original, you could start by voting for me.' But, while fully realizing how slight were his chances, he felt he had to stand, since by doing so he was striking a blow for all the *poètes maudits*, all who suffered neglect and unmerited dispraise because their work was too much in advance of their time to please the pundits and too serious to appeal to the frivolous masses. 'How could you fail to understand,' he remarked reproachfully to Flaubert who had expressed amazement that his friend should so far demean himself as to enter on this undignified competition, 'that Baudelaire stands for Auguste Barbier, Théophile Gautier, Banville, Flaubert, Leconte de Lisle – that is to say, for pure literature?'[23]

This was too subtle, not just for Flaubert but for most of his other well-wishers. His eccentric campaign was widely regarded as a stunt, a piece of tasteless self-advertisement, and the only real satisfaction he gained from it was that it gave him an opportunity to enter into contact with Alfred de Vigny who alone, among the academicians he called on, did not, he observed, judge his candidature to be ridiculous. Though they belonged to different generations, Vigny and Baudelaire had much in common. Vigny's pessimism, his misogyny, his dandified disdain of the crowd, were all features he shared with Baudelaire; even their admiration for the literature of the English-speaking world created a certain bond – Vigny had translated Shakespeare as Baudelaire had translated Poe and Longfellow.[24] After his first visit, Baudelaire was pressed to come again, and on each occasion Vigny kept him talking for several hours. It is clear that their conversation was not confined to literary matters; a note Baudelaire sent him later gives advice on the best brands of English ale and where to buy them (he recommended Allsopp and Bass, to be procured preferably in Gough's store on the Rue de Rivoli near the Place de la Concorde).

Vigny's vote might well have been the only one Baudelaire would have received, if he had not decided, on the earnest advice of Sainte-Beuve among others, to withdraw his candidature. He never submitted it on any subsequent occasion and so his name can be added to the long list of great French writers whose presence never graced this august assembly.

The excitement of these few months – the consultations with friends, the official visits he was obliged to make, the comments on his candidature in the press, even though they were more often wounding than encouraging – did at least serve to distract Baudelaire from the chronic, deep-seated depression he was suffering from over the years 1860 to 1862, the root cause of which may well have been an abrupt deterioration in his physical well-being due to the relentless advance of syphilis. Twenty years after the original contamination, the disease was now starting to affect his nervous system. On January 14th, 1860, he had what he took to be an apoplectic stroke as he was walking down the street; an old woman gave him first aid, but he had a further turn later that day as he was climbing a flight of stairs, and came near to losing consciousness. After a few hours he was able to return home, apparently none the worse apart from a sensation of immense fatigue. These attacks did not recur immediately, but for a while he was subject to fits of vomiting even when he had nothing in his stomach and when nothing had occurred to stir his bile. He was finally obliged to admit to his mother that he was a syphilitic; she reacted by expressing acute alarm, and he was at pains to calm her fears – potassium iodide and steam baths would cure him in three months. And, whether or not he followed this régime, he did enjoy a respite from the unpleasant physical symptoms, though only a temporary one. There was a further warning sign on January 23rd, 1862, of so alarming a nature that he did not dare tell his mother of it, but consigned it instead to a private notebook; he felt, so he wrote, that he had been 'fanned by the wind of the pinions of madness'.[25]

But, luckier than Maupassant, Baudelaire never sank into insanity as a result of venereal disease; it must, however, have contributed to his almost perpetual depression, which once more made him think obsessively of suicide, and more seriously than in 1845 when he actually had made an attempt on his life. It was only the thought that Jeanne might be left completely destitute, and his mother with no one to console her, that made him stay his hand, as he told her in October 1860. Some five or six months later he reverted to the subject in a letter to Poulet-Malassis, to whom he could speak more openly. 'For some time now I have been on the verge of suicide, and the one thing that stops me is a consideration that has nothing to do with cowardice or even regret; it's pride – I don't want to leave my affairs in disarray. *I should leave enough to pay everything off*; but even so I should need to make careful notes for the person appointed to settle everything. As you know, I am neither a whiner nor a liar, but over the past two months particularly I have fallen into an alarming state of lethargy and despair. I feel myself assailed by a sort of sickness *à la Gérard*, that is, the fear of never being able to think again or to write another line.'[26] What may have driven Gérard de Nerval to hang himself in 1855 will probably never be known precisely, but among his friends the story that had gained the most credit was, as Baudelaire indicates here, that Nerval felt his brain had so softened that he had become permanently incapable of literary expression.

Baudelaire had not reached that point, though there were times when, after a series of bad nights, waking up every morning without the will or energy to trace a single word on the paper, not even to address an envelope, he would sit in front of his desk day after day brooding miserably. 'In this horrible state of mind, suffering from impotence and hypochondria, I was revisited by the idea of suicide. I can admit it now that it has passed; at every hour of the day the idea dogged me, promising me absolute deliverance, release from everything. At the same time, *and for a full three months*, by a strange contradiction – though only superficially so – I prayed! all the time (to whom, to what Being exactly, I could never have said) to obtain two things: for myself, the strength to go on living; and for you' (he is writing to his mother) 'many, many long years of life.'[27] The necessity of completing the articles on Wagner saved him from this obsession; in three days of furious work, he improvised them in the printing-shop. After that, he suffered from various psychosomatic symptoms, of which the worst were the peculiar hallucinations that came to him as he was falling asleep, when he would hear very distinctly voices pronouncing complete sentences which bore no relation to his affairs and were in themselves quite remarkably banal. He dreaded falling asleep, since his sleep was disturbed by incessant nightmares; and he could never wake up without a feeling of horror at the thought of the day that lay ahead.

The alteration in his appearance was dramatic. Only four or five years before, regarded by the younger generation as one of their masters, he cut a striking figure in the boulevard cafés, neatly dressed in black, with his cravat invariably wound high under the chin so as to leave the smooth, white skin of his neck visible below it – for which reason he earned the nickname *le guillotiné*. But now his clothes were threadbare, his hair had turned quite white, he walked with rounded shoulders and bent head, and wore a haunted look on his face. Jules Troubat, Sainte-Beuve's secretary, used to come across him sitting in front of a beer in a corner of the Casino de la Rue Cadet, a notorious night-spot, while in the background a tinny piano banged out an Offenbach quadrille and the girls in search of clients moved from table to table, swinging their skirts as they passed. On the whole they gave him a wide berth, frightened by his haggard stare; but he once called one of them over and asked her, without naming himself, whether she had ever read any of his poetry. Timidly, she answered that the only poet she liked was Musset; Baudelaire dismissed her, snarling.

His celebrity, even so, and the faint whiff of brimstone they imagined clung to him, was such that other women, undeterred by his forbidding appearance, were ready to go to great lengths to become intimate with him. His young disciple Léon Cladel related how he used sometimes to meet Baudelaire by appointment in a particular boulevard café; one evening as he sat waiting he was approached by a strikingly handsome blonde who asked him to introduce her to the poet if he should come in that evening. Cladel agreed, performed the introduction, and Baudelaire bought her a drink. The conversation between the three of them lasted for an hour or so, after which the master went off on his own. The following evening the woman joined them again and finally, after several meetings, suggested she should go home with Baudelaire. Cladel walked back with them and upstairs to the hotel room which Baudelaire occupied; here the poet's fair admirer, with eyes only for him and oblivious of Cladel's presence, began slowly to undress. She had a magnificent body and her long yellow hair reached all the way down to her hips as she stood before the two men, posing provocatively, her right hand lightly pressing the back of one of his antique armchairs. Cladel judged he had already stayed too long and bowed himself out; but hardly had he closed the door behind him when he heard Baudelaire say, in his grating, tired, prematurely aged voice: 'Right, now you can get dressed again.'

Whatever the truth of this anecdote (Félicien Champsaur, who related it, claimed to have heard it from Cladel himself), it would be wrong to regard it as in any way corroborating the stories current during his life and long after about Baudelaire's sexual impotence; it should be seen, rather, as a case of principle triumphing over temptation. It was over the years 1861–3 that he kept a number of notebooks with memoranda about people he needed to visit, lists of his creditors with notes of what he owed them, and also addresses; these include the addresses of a number of call-girls. The implication is that from time to time he continued to have recourse to them, as indeed, from time to time, he had all his life. His habits in this respect were not very different from those of most men of that period, but what others tended to regard as permissible debauchery, almost a necessary hygiene, Baudelaire had come to see as a surrender to evil. It was not just promiscuity that he condemned, but any form of sexual indulgence whatsoever. Men and women making love were abjuring their spiritual natures and becoming, for the time being, pure animal, 'making the beast with two backs', as Iago so crudely put it. Proof of this lay in the endearments lovers customarily used: 'My little pussy! My great big wolf!' These 'bestial forms of address', as Baudelaire called them, were evidence of 'a satanic side to love; do not devils assume the shape of animals?'[28] He reasoned that to make love necessarily involved transforming oneself into an animal and hence abandoning oneself to satanism. 'Spirituality, the invocation of God, testifies to the desire to ascend; animality, the invocation of Satan, to the joy taken in abasing oneself. The latter must be seen as including the love of women and cosy conversations with animals, dogs and cats, etc.'[29]

A few years earlier, Baudelaire had tried the experiment of a purely spiritual, platonic love for a woman; it failed – we have seen how his 'madonna', Mme Sabatier, finally refused to play the game. No doubt one of the reasons why *Tannhäuser* moved him so profoundly was that Wagner's opera seemed to dramatize the conflict, for ever present in himself as in every man, between spiritual aspirations and the surrender to Satan in the form of the evil goddess inhabiting the Venusberg. The act of carnal love could never be sanctified; Baudelaire reached the same conclusion as Tolstoy was to later, though he expresses the idea in a formula very different from any used by the author of *The Kreutzer Sonata*: 'As for me, I say: the sole, supreme pleasure of love is the certainty that one is committing *evil*. And men and women know from birth that in evil lies all pleasure.'[30]

A topic one never finds discussed in any of Baudelaire's writings, whether intended for publication or not, is the institution of marriage. This omission can be explained with reference to his reluctance to contemplate the one example of a happily married couple always before his eyes – the Aupicks. But it must be said that the argument most people would use in favour of monogamous union – that it can foster a deeper human relationship than any other form of association – would have carried no conviction with Baudelaire. He never thought of sexual love as a means of establishing any genuine communion. At the most, one had the illusion of intimacy, but in the closest of embraces 'the unbridgeable gulf, preventing communication, remains unbridged'.[31] This idea was beautifully illustrated in one of his prose poems, *Les Yeux des Pauvres*, where he describes how he and his mistress entered a café to refresh themselves after a long day spent together, during which 'we had undertaken to communicate to one another every thought that came into our heads, so that our two souls would henceforth be one – not a very extraordinary project after all, save in so far as it is extraordinary that all couples have tried to realize it and no couple has ever succeeded.' As they sat sipping their drinks Baudelaire became aware of a ragged family standing outside in the street looking in at all the gilt and marble splendour behind the plate-glass window; he could read in 'the eyes of the poor' their admiration, their envy and regrets.

> Not only did I warm towards that bright-eyed family, but I felt a little ashamed of our glasses and carafes, so much bigger than our thirsts. I turned and looked into your eyes, dear love, to read *my* thoughts reflected in them; into your so strangely soft, so lovely eyes, into those green, moon-goddess eyes where dwells Caprice ... whereupon you said: 'Those people get on my nerves with their eyes like saucers. Couldn't you get the manager to move them on?'

It is so hard, my angel, for two people to understand each other, such are the barriers to a free exchange of thoughts, even between lovers![32]

Baudelaire's misogyny, so violently and often repellently expressed, was founded not on a contempt for women, nor on any resentment he might have felt of their demands on him, but on his own splenetic self-hatred and the delight he took in torturing himself. Convinced he was 'committing evil' every time he gave way to his instincts, unable nevertheless to resist giving way to them, he could not but look on women, so long as they were young and fair enough to tempt him, as agents in his own destruction. Only when they had grown old, frail, and sexless was he able to draw near them in sympathy and compassion.

XIV

FLIGHT INTO SILENCE

The bankruptcy of Auguste Poulet-Malassis at the end of 1862 made it imperative for Baudelaire to look round for a new publisher who might be prepared to re-issue *Les Fleurs du Mal* and to bring out his prose works: the treatise on narcotics, *Les Paradis artificiels*, which was out of print, and his collected critical works in two volumes, one to be entitled *Curiosités esthétiques* and the other *Opinions littéraires* (a title later changed to *L'Art romantique*). In addition there were the prose poems, of which a sufficient number had now been written to make up a slim volume. Michel Lévy, to whom he had sold the rights on the most profitable section of his work, the translations of Poe's stories, seemed disinclined to make an offer for the rest, so Baudelaire's thoughts turned to the Belgian firm of Lacroix and Verboeckhoven which appeared to be well capitalized and had a reputation for treating their authors generously; had they not recently paid Hugo the enormous sum of £5000 (something like £250,000 in today's values) for the manuscript of *Les Misérables*? But to sound them out, it would be necessary to make contact with them in Brussels.

One of the few Belgian friends he had was a certain Arthur Stevens, adviser to King Leopold I on the purchase of works of art, whom he had met through Manet. Stevens obligingly offered to arrange for Baudelaire to give a short series of lectures to the Cercle artistique et littéraire, a club which had been founded in Brussels in 1852 by a group of political refugees from France;[1] Lacroix would be invited to the first lecture so that Baudelaire could meet him socially as a preliminary to the serious business talks which it was hoped would follow. After a series of delays, Baudelaire finally arrived in the Belgian capital on April 24th, 1864, and on May 2nd delivered his first lecture, which was on Delacroix.

To judge from the report published the following day in *L'Indépendance belge*,[2] the hall was full and the lecture generally appreciated. On his second appearance, Baudelaire was billed to speak on Théophile Gautier, a figure of much less importance in the eyes of the Belgians than Delacroix. Confidently, he walked across the platform to his lectern and, as the polite applause died away, began with his penetrating, metallic voice: 'I am the more touched by the kind reception you have given me, in that it has helped me to overcome the natural shyness of one who has had no earlier experience of speaking in public, especially before so select and distinguished an audience. However,' he went on imperturbably, 'I find that the virginity of the novice orator is no more difficult to lose than the other virginity, and no more to be regretted.' The mixed gathering could hardly believe their ears and, according to Nadar, a whole row of young ladies from a local boarding-school, on a sign from the horrified teacher in charge of them, vacated their seats and filed out.[3] The other ladies in the audience, after some hesitation, slipped away one by one and, bored and disconcerted by the tenor of the lecture, wondering whether they were not being made the victims of some obscure hoax, so too did most of the gentlemen. Only a score remained behind, among them a young student, the future novelist Camille Lemonnier, who left an unforgettable description of the poet as he remembered him that evening.

A small table occupied the middle of the platform; the speaker, wearing a white tie, stood behind it in the luminous circle projected by the reading lamp. This patch of light played over his slender, mobile hands, which he showed a certain vanity in displaying; fingering negligently and with an almost feminine grace the scattered sheets of paper as if to convey the impression he was improvising his discourse. Those aristocratic hands, accustomed to manipulate the lightest of tools, would sometimes be raised in the air to trace slow, evocative curves; or else they would float gradually down, accompanying the always musical fall of the sentences, as though the lecturer were accomplishing some mystic rite. He made one think, in fact, of a preacher and of the eloquent gestures of the pulpit; the cuffs of his limp cloth coat fluttered like the sleeves of a priest's robe in moments of pathos. . . . His pale, clean-shaven face could be discerned in semi-darkness above the shade of the lamp; I could see his eyes moving like black suns; his mouth seemed to live with a life of its own, separate from the animation and expressiveness of his face; the thin lips quivered, like a taut violin-string under the bow of the words he spoke, and the whole head rose like a tower, dominating the attentive but bewildered audience.[4]

The last of the five pre-arranged lectures was given on May 23rd, but to Baudelaire's disappointment Albert Lacroix, in spite of pressing invitations, had attended none of them. Stevens made one last effort on his friend's behalf and persuaded Prosper Crabbe, a banker and art collector, to ask Lacroix along to a party in his own house at which Baudelaire would speak; but the elusive publisher sent his apologies and indeed, the occasion turned out a complete fiasco, with only five guests present out of the fifteen that had been invited. Baudelaire started talking about his own literary career but then, realizing he was not carrying his audience, broke off, suggesting they should instead do justice to the splendid buffet supper Crabbe had provided.

This was on June 13th, 1864. The chief purpose of the trip to Brussels having failed, there seemed to be nothing for it but to cut his losses and return to Paris. But, to the astonishment of his friends, Baudelaire stayed on. He was still in Brussels at the beginning of 1865 and his affectionate friend Mme Paul Meurice wrote half-seriously, half-jokingly on January 5th: 'Come now, what are you doing in Brussels? nothing, except dying of boredom, while here everyone is dying to see you again. What thread holds you tied by the wing to that stupid Belgian cage? Tell us simply what it is. Our little circle that misses you so much wants nothing better than to cut the thread, if that can be managed. What do you need? a free pass for the railway? We'll get one for you. Do we have to put the police or the armed forces on to you? Once more, come back to us, we are missing you sorely.'[5] Baudelaire let a month pass before replying. He was, he said, 'particularly touched' by the solicitude Mme Meurice showed. As to why he was staying on in Brussels, the answer he gave was embarrassed and evasive. 'In the first place, *because this is where I am*, and in my present state, any place is as bad as any other; – secondly, because I am doing penance, until I have cured myself of my vices (it's a slow process); and also because I must wait until a certain person whom I've asked to look after my business affairs in Paris has had time to resolve certain questions.'[6] This mysterious individual who was negotiating on his behalf with the Paris publishers we know to have been Julien Lemer, who managed a bookshop on the Boulevard des Italiens and, as a side-line, acted as unpaid literary agent for impecunious authors.

At Brussels Baudelaire was safe from his creditors, and this was an important additional consideration which he could not mention to Mme Meurice. Alexandre Dumas likewise had found the Belgian capital a useful refuge when he went bankrupt, and it was here that Poulet-Malassis had moved, after serving a spell of imprisonment for debt in Paris. However, the reason Poulet-Malassis gave, in letters to their mutual friend Asselineau, why Baudelaire could not leave Brussels was that, quite simply, he never had the few hundred francs needed to settle his hotel bill. He had a room in the Hôtel du Grand Miroir which Stevens had originally booked for him, and here he stayed like a monk in his cell. The furnishings were sparse: a bed covered with a green eiderdown, a wash-stand, a threadbare sofa, one worn armchair and two other wicker chairs. There was no clock on the mantelpiece, and Baudelaire's watch was at the pawnshop, so to tell the time he had to rely on the church bells tolling the quarters. His books and papers were stacked on a table pushed against a wall. The one extraordinary item was a live bat in a cage; Baudelaire had captured the creature in a nearby churchyard and kept it fed on milk and crumbled bread.

We owe this description to Georges Barral,[7] a young journalist who was in Brussels to cover the widely publicized ascent that Nadar was preparing to make in his new balloon, *Le Géant*, on September 26th, 1864; Nadar had sent him to the Hôtel du Grand Miroir to invite Baudelaire to accompany him and the other 'aeronauts' on the trip. Seeing a chance to check on the authenticity of Poe's tales of balloon flight, Baudelaire was delighted to accept and deeply disappointed when at the last moment, Nadar having realized the nacelle would be overloaded, he was refused a place. However, he joined the rest of the party on their last night in Brussels, when they celebrated their safe return by repairing to a brothel; Barral observed that Baudelaire not only spurned the Flemish beauties displaying their ample charms, but, by reading his young companion a lecture on the virtues of chastity, persuaded him to do likewise. Though there was little merit, as he told Mme Meurice with his usual frankness, in staying chaste in this country. 'The sight of a Belgian woman almost makes me faint. The god Eros himself, if he wanted to freeze all his ardour, would only need to take one look at their faces.'[8]

Visitors such as Nadar and Barral were few, and among his compatriots domiciled in Brussels, there were only Mme Hugo, whose pressing invitations to dine with her and her family he declined at first and accepted later with a bad grace, and of course his old friend Poulet-Malassis. The resilient publisher had inaugurated a new line in reprints of eighteenth-century erotica, on which he was an expert. Seeing Baudelaire evince some interest in the venture, he suggested he might write a preface for a new edition of Laclos's *Dangerous Acquaintances*, a novel that had been banned in France since 1823; Baudelaire promised to think about it, and indeed was still thinking about it in March 1866 when Gustave Frédéric, one of Mme Hugo's circle, saw him on his sick-bed reading *Les Liaisons dangereuses* avidly and commenting on the cruel beauty and serene audacity of Laclos's masterpiece; it must have been the last book he held in his hands. Poulet-Malassis also secured his agreement to the publication, under the title *Epaves* (*Flotsam*), of an edition of his miscellaneous later verse in which were also reprinted the six poems condemned as pornographic by the judges at the 1857 trial; but the police were on the watch, and no sooner was this volume offered for sale in France than it too was seized. Baudelaire was a regular guest at Poulet-Malassis's table in the first few months of his stay in Brussels, but they saw less and less of one another as time went by, and Poulet-Malassis was not sorry about this for, as he observed in a letter to Asselineau on August 30th, 1865: 'although I am always glad to see him, on the other hand his faults – his slowness, his way of emphasizing points and rambling on – have reached such a point that it would be more than tedious to have him as a visitor every day'.[9]

The decline in Baudelaire's intellectual faculties that Poulet-Malassis hints at here was real enough; a further symptom was the 'writer's block' to which he was now subject, quite different in nature to anything he had experienced previously. There had been plenty of occasions in the past when he would stare, mesmerized, at the blank sheet in front of him, too despondent even to dip his pen in the ink. But now, although he was covering quantities of paper, nothing of what he wrote was in a form suitable for submission to a publisher. Shortly after his arrival in Belgium, the idea had occurred to him to profit from his stay in this foreign country to write up his impressions, presenting them in the form of a series of letters to a fictional correspondent. This literary device had a respectable ancestry; Voltaire had used it to put over his views on England and the English in the 1730s, De Brosses had written his *Lettres familières écrites d'Italie* a little later, and quite recently the same recipe had served Dumas for his account of a journey through Spain, *De Paris à Cadix*. The advantage, from Baudelaire's point of view, was that the separate fictional letters could be conveniently published in a journal (he had *Le Figaro* in mind) before being collected and issued as a book by, as he hoped, Michel Lévy or Hetzel.

The idea was of a kind to appeal to a newspaper editor and in fact Villemessant, the proprietor of *Le Figaro*, expressed keen interest. As time went by, Baudelaire clarified his view of the type of book it would be: satirical, iconoclastic, with a dash of sour humour; the title, *Pauvre Belgique!*, indicated that he would have little good to say about his host country. His correspondence with his friends in France is peppered with allusions to this work: it was causing him endless trouble, but he was making progress – just a few more sections to write – now it was getting unmanageably long, perhaps he ought to make a few cuts . . . When, after Baudelaire had been struck down by paralysis, Poulet-Malassis went through his papers to see if there were any marketable manuscripts, he reported to Asselineau that 'as for the famous book, *Pauvre Belgique!*, it's nothing but a jumble of notes – not one line written',[10] and Asselineau, after he had

had a chance of looking at it himself, had to agree regretfully that it was decidedly not publishable. In fact, of course, it has been published; no line, however insignificant, that Baudelaire ever wrote could fail to be published by his devoted twentieth-century editors; but as one ploughs through page after page of disjointed notes, obscure references, painfully repetitive reflections, one cannot but endorse Poulet-Malassis's verdict. The truth is that even when he was in full command of his faculties, Baudelaire had never found it possible to write a really long work; he was essentially an essayist. His development of the prose poem is an admirable instance of an invention being mothered by necessity.

The piling up of notes for *Pauvre Belgique!* did at least give him the comforting illusion that he was still engaged on productive work, while at the same time it provided him with an outlet for his passionate detestation of the country which had offered him asylum. In this self-imposed exile he felt himself an Ovid among the Scythians. His antipathy for the Belgians manifested itself almost from the moment of his arrival. They were, he told his mother, 'even more stupid than the French,' and he warned Manet: 'Never believe what you may hear about the good nature of the Belgians. Cunning, mistrust, sham affability, rudeness, deceitfulness, yes.'[11] Those he had come across wilfully misunderstood him from the start, and he was driven in self-defence to drop the mask of well-mannered reserve and bare his teeth. 'A lot of people flocked to gape curiously at the author of *Les Fleurs du Mal*,' he reported to Ancelle. 'The author of the said *Fleurs* was bound to be a weirdie. All this rabble took me for a monster and when they saw that I was discreet, quiet, gentlemanly, and that I had a strong aversion to freethinkers, progress, and all the modern fads, they spread it around, I suppose, that I was not the author of my book. . . . I have to admit that after two or three months of this I gave rein to my natural disposition and took a peculiar delight in being offensive and impertinent, something I excel at when I choose. But here, that cuts no ice. One has to be *downright rude to be understood*. What riff-raff they are! – and I thought France was an absolutely barbarous country, here I am obliged to admit there is one country more barbarous than France!'[12]

Baudelaire did find a few fellow spirits among the Belgians. In the first place there was Arthur Stevens, whom he knew already, and his brother Joseph, a painter specializing in animal portraiture, to whom he dedicated the one prose poem he ever wrote with a Belgian setting, *Les Bons Chiens*. Another good friend was Félicien Rops, '*the only true artist* (in the sense which I, and I alone perhaps, understand the word *artist*) that I have found in Belgium',[13] who would sometimes entertain Baudelaire by inviting him to his studio in Antwerp where he and Guys would sketch the voluptuous Flemish prostitutes they paid to pose for them. Finally, there was the photographer Charles Neyt, whom Baudelaire appreciated for his wit and good humour and to whom we owe the last few studio portraits ever taken of the poet.

But these occasionally enlivening social contacts were no real compensation for what he was missing. 'In Paris, there are supper parties with one's friends, there are art galleries, concerts, girls. Here, there is nothing,'[14] not even decent food; the Belgians were incapable of cooking eggs or grilling a chop decently, and they regarded wine as a luxury product reserved for special occasions; *faro*, the Belgian beer, gave him the colic, but one was never served with anything else. For a joke, and as a sort of experiment, he invited the few friends he had to sample some vintage wine, a few bottles he had laid down, he said, on his return from the Indies in 1842. They were brought in on their wickerwork baskets, black with age, covered with dust and cobwebs, 'like glass mummies', as Neyt related.[15] Everyone was hugely impressed. What bouquet! what pure ruby colour! and Baudelaire, who had amused himself pouring new claret into old bottles, was overjoyed at this display of Belgian wine-connoisseurship.

For the most part, except when he took a local train to visit one or other of the smaller, picturesque towns like Bruges, Ghent, and Malines (where he said he would willingly spend the remainder of his days were it not inhabited by Belgians), the hours limped past in purgatorial boredom. 'I am without books, living in discomfort, with no money and seeing nobody except people I loathe, who are ill-bred and seem to have invented a stupidity peculiar to themselves. Every morning my heart beats as I go downstairs to see if there are any letters for me at the porter's, if my friends are exerting themselves on my behalf, if any articles of mine have been published, if there are any remittances, if negotiations for the sale of my books have come to anything – but no, nothing, never anything. . . . I don't know what I wouldn't give to be in a tavern in Le Havre or Honfleur, clinking glasses with a seaman, even a convict, provided he wasn't a Belgian!'[16]

In fact he was to visit Honfleur once more, in July 1865, in a desperate effort to raise 2000 francs for Poulet-Malassis to whom he owed 5000 and who found himself once more in grave financial difficulties. As so often before, it was his mother who came to his rescue, but once the matter had been disposed of he was constrained, greatly against his will, to return to Brussels, his unpaid bill at the Hôtel du Grand Miroir acting as a ball-and-chain. Many years later Catulle Mendès related[17] how he ran across Baudelaire quite unexpectedly in the booking-hall of the Gare du Nord on the eve of his departure. The author of *Les Fleurs du Mal* explained he had just missed the last train to Brussels and would have to spend the night in a hotel. Mendès could not help noticing how shabby his clothes were and, guessing he might not even have the price of a room on him, offered to put him up in his own lodgings. As they walked along, exchanging the odd remark about the shop-window displays and the bar-loungers, Mendès was struck by the disjointedness of Baudelaire's speech compared with the rounded sentences he habitually used in conversation. His first action, once the young man had ushered him through the door, was to stretch himself out on the sofa and ask for something to read. A few minutes later, dropping the book, he turned to his host and asked him: 'Guess how much I have earned in the whole of my working life!' – whereupon he proceeded to list, from memory, every payment that had been made him for books, articles, poems and pamphlets, adding it up as he went along to reach the grand total of 15,892 francs 60 centimes; after which he uttered a strange sound, midway between a snort and a bark of laughter, and turned down the lamp, saying it was time to sleep. But he went on talking in the darkness about all the men he had known and admired and who had been attacked and undervalued just as he had: Wagner, Manet, Vigny, Leconte de Lisle – until finally the name of Nerval came up. In the darkness, he seemed excessively agitated over the question whether Nerval had really died by his own hand. 'No, no, he was not mad, he was not ill, he did not kill himself. No, you must make sure everyone knows, you must tell everyone that he was not mad, that he did not take his own life. Promise me you will say he did not kill himself.' Mendès, frightened, swore he would do as Baudelaire wished; he may have guessed his strange visitor was not talking about Nerval but about himself, and that in his own mind he was wrestling with the old temptation to end everything with rope or razor-blade so as to escape the insanity he fancied was creeping up on him relentlessly, day by day and night by night.

Half an hour later, hearing no further sound, Mendès thought it safe to leave the room and go to bed. He hesitated a few minutes longer, afraid of disturbing his guest if he knocked into a piece of furniture in the dark. As he sat, trembling, a sudden sound from the direction of the sofa made him catch his breath, a muffled groan or a sob, 'like a heart bursting under a heavy weight'. Then all was silence. The following morning, when Mendès woke, Baudelaire had gone, leaving a note on the table: *A bientot!*

Back in Belgium, life went on much as before, except that he felt more and more unwell. The symptoms he complained of – mainly in letters to Ancelle, whom he took into his confidence as never before over these last years – were an exhausting diarrhoea, which he attributed to the climate and the abominable Brussels beer, and insomnia; he would wake up at one or two in the morning and lie in the darkness, trembling with cold and fever, until the coming of dawn, when he would fall asleep at last, waking again a few hours later bathed in sweat and feeling more tired than when he first went to bed. Laudanum and brandy were the only remedies he thought of using, in spite of the warnings of doctors and friends, and Poulet-Malassis, worried about his excessive intake of alcohol, made a practice of keeping all spirits locked away when Baudelaire came to dine at his house.

In March 1866 he made the short journey to Namur, Félicien Rops's father-in-law having invited him to spend a few days as the guest of the family. It was not his first visit to this little town and he was insistent that Rops and Poulet-Malassis should come with him to look round the church of Saint-Loup. As he was expatiating on the ornate wood-carvings of the confessional-boxes, he suddenly reeled and sat down heavily on a stone step. His companions helped him to his feet; he laughed it off as an accident, pretending he had slipped. They accepted this explanation, but the following morning it was quite clear he was not himself. Alarmed, they thought it best to take him back to Brussels; on the way, they noticed he was already mixing up his words, asking for the carriage window to be opened when he really wanted it closed.

At Brussels they got Neyt to promise to keep an eye on him, and the photographer duly invited him to dinner. He noticed how, every now and then, as he was raising his glass to his lips, Baudelaire would hold it in mid-air, lost in thought. 'It was as though at certain moments his mind, in a trance, hesitated, hovered, silently sought its way, and circled round and round before returning to its accustomed path. He could be seen to frown then, his face darkening, while his eyes were lit for a second by a haggard gleam of terror and anxiety like a dreamer feeling himself slip down the edge of an abyss.'[18] Concerned about his condition, Neyt went out, half an hour after Baudelaire had left, to check whether he had got back to his hotel safely. Seeing his key still hanging on the rack in the vestibule, he began a search among all the late-night cafés in the centre of Brussels, and finally, at one in the morning, came across him in the Taverne Royale. A waiter was dozing against a counter, a small group of late drinkers were huddled round a table on the right of the hall and in a corner on the other side, slumped up against the upholstered back of a wall-sofa, sat Baudelaire with an empty brandy glass in front of him, lost in a nameless reverie.

Neyt helped him to his feet and guided him back to his hotel, where Baudelaire none too civilly told him to leave. Early the following morning the photographer entered his room, to find him lying fully dressed on his bed with the lamp smoking on the table. He could still speak, but the whole of the right side of his body was affected by a partial paralysis, and it was Neyt who wrote, at his dictation, Baudelaire's last few letters before a further attack, nine days later, left him incapable of articulating a word. This was on March 30th, 1866. Poulet-Malassis wired Ancelle, who arrived on April 1st and arranged for him to be removed to a private clinic in Brussels staffed by nuns, the Institut médico-chirurgical St Jean et Ste Elisabeth. Mme Aupick made the journey to Brussels a day or two later, in a state of great alarm, but was reassured once she had seen for herself how things stood. It seemed that it was only the faculty of speech that was affected; his intelligence was unimpaired, he suffered from no hallucinations, ate and drank normally and seemed to enjoy going on carriage rides with Stevens and herself or simply walking about the streets in the sunshine, bareheaded, for he obstinately refused to wear a hat despite her pleading. His will was as strong as ever, and when the nursing sisters tried to persuade him to make the sign of the cross before a meal he pretended not to understand, turning his head away or shutting his eyes. But, as his mother reflected, it was an ill wind . . . At least he could not answer back or say harsh and wounding things to her as he used to. It was some consolation too to find herself, as she imagined, once more indispensable to her son. 'I talk to him about things that happened in his childhood, he understands me and listens closely. . . . I shall not leave him, I shall keep him like a tiny baby.'[19] Life was beginning all over again for Caroline.

After a little more than a fortnight, when it was apparent that his life was not in danger and that apart from the paralysis of the speech organs he was in reasonable health and spirits, he was discharged from the clinic, much to the relief of the sisters who were profoundly unhappy at having so notorious an infidel and blasphemer to look after. He was driven back to the Hôtel du Grand Miroir, where Arthur Stevens had booked a spacious, ground-floor room for him. This change delighted Baudelaire, as they could all see, for it was not at all difficult to understand what was going on in his mind; he had no trouble in following a conversation and could participate to a limited extent, even though his active vocabulary was now reduced to a mere grunt, heard as 'Non!' or 'Cré nom!', which served equally to express assent or disagreement, depending on the tone he used.

However, a hotel room in a foreign capital was clearly not suitable for an invalid for more than a few days, and the general feeling was that Baudelaire had best be taken down to Honfleur, where his mother could look after him with the help of a male domestic. This proposal met with unexpected opposition, however, from Mme Aupick, who dreaded facing the Emons and her other friends at Honfleur with this wreck of all her hopes exhibited to their insulting compassion. Touched though she was by his helplessness, she could never reconcile herself to the deep disappointment caused her by his choice of career, his way of life, his improvidence, and his scandalous refusal to conform to the norms of bourgeois society. Only a few months earlier the seventy-year-old woman had poured her heart out in a letter to Ancelle in which she revealed as never before her sense of having been cheated by life and cheated by her child. 'I ought to have grown accustomed to his life-style,' she wrote, 'outlandish though it is and so contrary to every accepted standard, and to have resigned myself to it. But this I cannot do. I cling stupidly, obstinately to the idea that I am surely owed a little satisfaction from him before I die. And now it is becoming urgent, I am growing very old and rather feeble. He has very little time left to give me the satisfaction I want, and I fear I shall never have it. It would have been some consolation if he had attained great literary celebrity (for I realize that he has what it needs to achieve it), but there again nothing but disappoint-ments, Charles having adopted a bizarre mode of writing, as absurd as he is, which attracts very few adherents . . .'[20]

It was not only Mme Aupick's reluctance to agree to have him at Honfleur that forced a change of plan, but also the realization by Poulet-Malassis and Stevens that in spite of her maternal devotion she was not the best person to have charge of him. She vexed him unintentionally in all kinds of small ways – offering him a dirty hairbrush instead of a clean one or a coarse clothes-brush for his hat, as though she had never noticed that in matters of personal cleanliness her son had always shown the most exquisite fastidious-ness. These mistakes put him into a rage, which he could express only by throwing the offending brush across the room. It was also obvious that Baudelaire himself had not the slightest wish to be taken down to Honfleur; the alternative, which was that he should be looked after in a Paris nursing-home, appealed to him much more, as Poulet-Malassis realized as soon as he spoke to him about it.

Stevens and Mme Aupick accordingly accompanied him back to Paris on July 2nd, 1866. They were met at the station by Asselineau who, although in constant touch with Poulet-Malassis, was not sure what to expect. The prolonged burst of laughter with which Baudelaire greeted him alarmed him at first; perhaps, after all, there was some truth in the rumours that he was suffering from softening of the brain. But seeing the intelligent interest he took in conversa-tions going on around him, and the patient efforts he made to communicate his own thoughts and opinions by means of smiles, shrugs, nods and gestures, Asselineau realized that he was as rational and lucid as ever. This, in a way, made his condition the more deplorable; here was the supreme master of language tongue-tied, reduced to signs and grunts. But Baudelaire seemed unaware of, or indifferent to, this aspect of his situation. Once installed in the nursing-home, a pleasant establishment near the Arc de Triomphe, he appeared content and in good spirits, except only when irritated by some display of puerile emotion on the part of his mother. However, after a day or two, satisfied he was in good hands, she returned thankfully to Honfleur.

Curiously, the despondency and lethargy in which Baudelaire had lived for so many months prior to his seizure seemed now to have lifted. It was as though the disease, having dealt him this blow, had temporarily ceased undermining his morale. He seemed quite confident he would be cured in time, and whenever he managed to force himself to utter a name more easily pronounced than others he would repeat it triumphantly over and over again. The minor pleasures of life now took on fresh meaning for him. He revelled in the perfume and beauty of the flowers that grew profusely in the garden of the nursing-home. Music, too, entranced him, and one of his principal delights was when Manet's sister-in-law, Berthe Morisot, found time to come and play his favourite airs from Wagner on the piano. He had a constant stream of visitors, one of whom, Jules Troubat, related in a letter to Eugène Crépet[21] how Baudelaire took him into the garden to show him an exotic plant that he admired and how subsequently, when Troubat told him of the success Courbet was having in the *Salon* that year with his *Lady with the Parrot*, Baudelaire exhibited unmistakable displeasure by barking out his usual 'Non, cré non!' in a tone of vexation. Under the thick crust of the enforced silence all the old loves and antipathies simmered on.

The one friend debarred from visiting him was Poulet-Malassis, who risked arrest if he crossed the frontier. But in the days immediately preceding Baudelaire's return to Paris he had tried to get him to understand the urgent need to bring out a new edition of *Les Fleurs du Mal*, the last (1861) edition having long gone out of print. Baudelaire had signified his agreement, and accordingly Asselineau persuaded Michel Lévy to visit him in the nursing-home at the beginning of January 1867, saying he would act as his interpreter. Lévy was quite prepared to put in hand the new edition without delay, but Baudelaire proved unexpectedly reluctant to give his assent. Pointing to a calendar, he showed Asselineau a heavy line he had scored after March 31st. His friend realized that Baudelaire was giving himself until that date, three months ahead, to recover his faculties. Lévy would have to wait till then, since he was not prepared to allow *Les Fleurs du Mal* to be reprinted during his lifetime unless he could correct the proofs.

The fateful day arrived, but Baudelaire was no better, and from that time on his mood changed. He grew sombre, resigned, and rarely left his bed. He still welcomed his friends, listened to their conversations, but made no further effort to participate. 'Whenever one of us turned to look at him,' recalled Asselineau, 'we would see his eyes fixed on us with an attentive and intelligent gaze, darkened however by an expression of infinite melancholy which none of those who saw it will ever forget.'[22] Throughout that summer the flowers in the garden were as scented as ever but could not draw him out of doors as they had the previous year. He remained still and silent, lying motionless on his bed, and when Asselineau wanted to press his hand he had to grope for it under the blanket.

During this final phase a new figure appears on the scene, one we have not had occasion to mention hitherto, though Baudelaire had known him since his childhood; it is possible the two had played together, long, long ago, in the Jardin du Luxembourg. His name was Edmond Albert. Born in the same year as Baudelaire, he came of a quite humble family of booksellers and newsagents established in the Rue de Seine. In 1845 he set up as a publisher of minor poets and pamphleteers. For a short while, in the mid-1850s, he became Baudelaire's unpaid secretary and general dog's-body, as later he became Banville's, being one of those unassuming, undemanding souls, fascinated by the world of literature and only too happy to be employed on menial tasks for those demigods, the poets, the object of their discreet and ardent cult. Somehow, news got to Albert that Baudelaire was slowly dying, and so he quietly insinuated himself into the nursing-home and for the last three months of the poet's life he sat with him night after night, keeping watch, while Mme Aupick, who had returned from Honfleur, nursed him by day. It was Albert who, when Baudelaire finally breathed his last, sent telegrams to the chosen few. His only tangible reward for these services was Baudelaire's gold watch, an old-fashioned repeater, which Mme Aupick allowed him to keep.

As snatches of military music and distant cheering drifted through his windows, in those last days of the summer of 1867 when Paris was nosily celebrating Exhibition Year, step by step the dying poet was entering the realm of eternal silence. When she first moved to Paris to be by his bedside in the last stages, Mme Aupick had amused herself getting him to repeat after her a few simple words. 'When he pronounced properly, I clapped my hands; when he mispronounced, I mimicked his jabber.' But this ghastly play-acting – a fond mother trying to get her backward child to talk – lasted only a week or two. 'At present', she added, 'there is the silence of death between us.'[23] Bed-sores caused him great discomfort towards the end, but over the last forty-eight hours he appeared to be sleeping, though his eyes remained open, and he died, on the last day of August, 'very quietly,' she reported, 'with no death-agony and no pain; I held him cradled in my arms for an hour, waiting for him to draw his last breath; I was murmuring endearments to him all the time, being convinced he could hear me, prostrate and speechless though he was, and could respond . . .' He died, she said, 'with a smile on his lips'.[24] A smile of contentment, perhaps, and of thankfulness that the long damnation of earthly existence was over at last.

The funeral took place on September 2nd, attended by Asselineau and Banville, who delivered the traditional graveside orations, and by a few others out of the many who had called themselves his friends: Champfleury, Manet, Nadar, Alfred Stevens; Paul Verlaine was there too, to represent the younger generation of symbolist poets for whom he was to become a kind of god before the century was out. But there were many absentees, notably Sainte-Beuve (who was, however, in very poor health), Théophile Gautier, Barbey d'Aurevilly, Gustave Flaubert. As the coffin was carried into the Cimetière Montparnasse, there was a sudden clap of thunder and a premature gust of autumnal wind brought a shower of yellow leaves down on to the bier.

The circumstances of his last illness had made it impossible for Baudelaire to stipulate how he would have wished his remains to be disposed, and so, by a final stroke of diabolic irony, his body was laid to rest alongside his stepfather's, to the everlasting discomfiture of them both if there was any substance in Baudelaire's belief that the dead, 'entombed within their sepulchres of stone', retain memory and consciousness. The inscription on the headstone read as follows:

Jacques Aupick, divisional general, senator, former ambassador at Constantinople and at Madrid, member of the General Council of the département du Nord, grand officer of the Imperial Order of the Legion of Honour and decorated with several foreign orders, died in Paris at the age of 68, April 18th, 1857

Charles Baudelaire, his stepson, died in Paris, August 31st, 1867, at the age of 46.

No career, no distinctions, no services to his country.

Four years later Caroline joined her son and her second husband in the same tomb, and her name was engraved after Baudelaire's, at the base of the stone. And there Hamlet lies for all time, with Gertrude on one side and Claudius on the other.

NOTES

I.   CAROLINE

1 *Propos sur Baudelaire*, Paris, 1957, p. 198.
2 See J. F. Desjardins, 'Les Origines familiales de Baudelaire', *Revue des Deux Mondes*, no. 24 (1964), p. 576.
3 Baudelaire, *Œuvres complètes*, ed. Claude Pichois, Paris, Bibliothèque de la Pléiade, 1975–6, vol. I, p. 661. All references to Baudelaire's works will be to this edition in two volumes, designated hereafter: *OC*.
4 She refers to these pronunciation lessons in a letter to Poulet-Malassis, February 17th, 1867 (see *Les Derniers Mois de Charles Baudelaire ... correspondances, documents*, ed. J. Richer and M. A. Ruff, Paris, 1976, p. 90).
5 Details given in A. E. Carter, 'A propos d'une visite de Baudelaire au Château de Versailles', *Etudes baudelairiennes*, vol. III (Neuchâtel, 1973), pp. 28–9.
6 See Jean Ziegler, 'François Baudelaire, peintre et amateur d'art', *Gazette des Beaux-Arts*, vol. XCIII (1979), p. 110.
7 Maurice Kunel, 'Quatre jours avec Baudelaire', *Les Œuvres Libres*, vol. CXXXII (1932), p. 202.
8 Although the key documents were unearthed by others, it was the leading Baudelairian Marcel A. Ruff who revealed them, firstly in an article, 'Baudelaire, fils de prêtre', *La Quinzaine Littéraire*, May 16th, 1969, and subsequently in his paper 'Regards sur l'homme Baudelaire', at a colloquium held the following year in the University of Western Ontario.
9 Baudelaire, *Correspondance*, ed. Claude Pichois and Jean Ziegler, Paris, Bibliothèque de la Pléiade, 1973, vol. II, pp. 152, 304. This edition is the most recent and most comprehensive of Baudelaire's letters; subsequent references will designate it simply: *Corr*.
10 See Jean Adhémar, 'L'Education artistique de Baudelaire faite par son père', *Gazette des Beaux-Arts*, vol. XCIII (1979), p. 130.
11 According to Caroline's account in a letter to Ancelle written at the time of her son's final illness: Féli Gautier, 'Documents sur Baudelaire', *Mercure de France*, vol. LIII (1905), p. 340.
12 See W. T. Bandy, 'Les morts, les pauvres morts ...', *Revue des Sciences humaines*, vol. XXXII (1967), p. 478.
13 For the details of Aupick's early life and later career the essential reference work is Claude Pichois, *Le Vrai Visage du Général Aupick, beau-père de Baudelaire*, Paris, 1955.
14 These circumstances, which explain the hurried wedding, were not known to Pichois when he wrote the aforementioned biography of Aupick; the discovery was made only fairly recently, and revealed by J. Flavien in a note published April 1st, 1971: 'La Demi-Sœur de Baudelaire', *Le Cramérien*, 2e série, no. 3, p. 4.
15 'A soft bath fragrant with delightful perfumes'; the lines are taken from a Latin poem of Baudelaire's own composition, included in *Les Fleurs du Mal* under the title: *Franciscae meae laudes*.
16 *Un Mangeur d'Opium*, chap. VII ('Chagrins d'enfance'): *OC* I, 499.

17 Letter of May 6th, 1861: *Corr.* II, 153.
18 *Corr.* I, 445. The text of the poem ('Je n'ai pas oublié, voisine de la ville, Notre blanche maison . . .') is in *OC* I, 99.
19 *OC*, I, 556.
20 Maria Lori and Bernard Delmay ('Baudelaire et le vrai visage de sa mère', *Studi francesi*, nos. 61–2 (1977), pp. 201–2) have put forward an alternative but distinctly far-fetched interpretation of the poem, based on the hypothesis of a lesbian relationship between Caroline and Mariette.
21 *OC* I, 333.
22 *Un Mangeur d'Opium*, chap. VI ('Le Génie enfant'): *OC* I, 498. Much the same idea is found in the third chapter of Baudelaire's essay *Le Peintre de la vie moderne*: 'Le génie n'est que *l'enfance retrouvée à volonté*, l'enfance douée maintenant, pour s'exprimer, d'organes virils et de l'esprit analytique qui lui permet d'ordonner la somme de matériaux involontairement amassée' (*OC* II, 690).

II. SCHOOLDAYS

1 Nadar, *Le Monde où l'on patauge*, Paris, 1883, p. 196; quoted in *Baudelaire devant ses contemporains*: témoignages rassemblés et présentés par W. T. Bandy et Claude Pichois, Paris, 1967, pp. 47–8.
2 Claude Pichois, *Baudelaire, études et témoignages*, Neuchâtel, 1967, pp. 37–8. Pichois gives a fuller version of Buisson's recollections than is found in Eugène Crépet's *Baudelaire: étude biographique*, which must have been the source Sartre used (see his *Baudelaire*, Paris, 1947, p. 19).
3 *Corr.* I, 4 (letter of February 1st, 1832).
4 *OC* I, 334.
5 *L'Invitation au voyage* exists as a prose poem as well as being one of the most movingly melodic pieces of verse that Baudelaire ever wrote. Other prose poems that treat of this theme include *Le Port*, *Déjà!*, and *Anywhere out of the world*. In *Les Fleurs du Mal* one finds the theme in *Bohémiens en voyage*, in *Moesta et errabunda*, and most notably in the long closing poem *Le Voyage* with its opening lines which are peculiarly apposite to Baudelaire at the period we are now dealing with:
    'Pour l'enfant, amoureux de cartes et d'estampes,
    L'univers est égal à son vaste appétit.'
6 *Corr.* I, 23.
7 It is likely that he had started school before he left Paris, though at what particular establishment is still not known. See David W. H. Pellow, 'Charles Baudelaire's School Years', *Studi francesi*, no. 49 (1973), p. 30.
8 See Hélène Fredrickson, *Baudelaire, héros et fils. Dualité et problèmes du travail dans les lettres à sa mère*, Saratoga, Calif., 1977, pp. 41–2.
9 *Corr.* I, 52–3. The letter was written (June 10th, 1838) from Paris, when his mother was down at Barèges, Aupick having been advised by his doctors to take the waters.
10 *OC* I, 702, 706 (*Mon cœur mis à nu*, XLV, XXXIX). In *Les Vocations* (see above, pp. 12–13, the first of the four boys has ambitions to be an actor, while the second sees God sitting in a cloud.
11 E. and J. Crépet, *Baudelaire: étude biographique*, Paris, 1906, p. 14.
12 *OC* I, 680 (*Mon cœur mis à nu*, VII).
13 Letter of February 25th, 1834: *Corr.* I, 26.
14 In 1966, by Philippe Auserve, under the title *Lettres inédites aux siens*.

15 Letter written towards the end of August or the beginning of September 1835: *Corr.* I, 34.
16 Letters of October 21st, 1834, and June 27th, 1838: *Corr.* I, 32, 56.
17 In *Fusées* XIII: *OC* I, 662.
18 Cf. Fredrickson, *op. cit.*, p. 80.
19 Letter originally published by Georges-Emmanuel Lang, 'Charles Baudelaire et sa mère', *Le Figaro*, March 5th, 1922.
20 Letter of June 21st, 1861: *Corr.* II, 175.
21 Letter of May 6th, 1861: *Corr.* II, 153.
22 Letter probably written April 23rd, 1837: *Corr.* I, 39.
23 A play on the subject of education (Desguillon's *Les Nouveaux Adelphes*) had been objected to in 1824 on the grounds that it argued in favour of this new custom. In his report, the censor posed the question: 'Est-il bien à propos d'encourager, comme fait cette pièce, le tutoiement des enfants à l'égard de leurs parents? J'ai toujours vu blâmer cette opinion révolutionnaire par les hommes les plus modérés' (quoted in Louis Allard, *La Comédie de mœurs en France au XIXe siècle*, Cambridge, Mass., 1933, vol. II, p. 87.
24 *Corr.* I, 59, 62.
25 Letter to Asselineau quoted in Crépet, *op. cit.*, pp. 254, 258.
26 The remark occurs in the biographical sketch he provided of the actor Philibert Rouvière for the *Nouvelle Galerie des artistes dramatiques vivants* (1856): *OC* II, 60.
27 Many of the reports they wrote on him have been discovered and printed, firstly by Léon Lemonnier, *Enquêtes sur Baudelaire* (Paris, 1929), and subsequently by Jean Pommier, *Dans les chemins de Baudelaire* (Paris, 1945) and by David Pellow, *loc. cit.* (see note 7).
28 This letter has been reproduced by Pichois in his edition of Baudelaire's correspondence (*Corr.* I, 723).
29 *Corr.* I, 69. The story that he and his friend had been enacting the parts of Corydon and Alexis in Virgil's second Eclogue was reported by Charles Cousin, another former student at the Lycée Louis-le-Grand; see his *Voyage dans un grenier*, Paris, 1878, p. 11.

III. WILD OATS

1 Letter of July 16th, 1839: *Corr.* I, 75.
2 I.e. Aupick. It is noteworthy that about this period Baudelaire gave up calling him his 'father'. Later, Aupick will be 'your husband' in references to him in the letters to his mother.
3 *Corr.* I, 75–6.
4 Hignard, *Lettres de l'Ecole Normale* ..., Lyon, 1898, quoted in *Baudelaire devant ses contemporains*, ed. W. T. Bandy and Claude Pichois, Paris, 1967, pp. 52–3.
5 Renan, *Souvenirs d'enfance et de jeunesse*, ed. Jean Pommier, Paris, 1959, p. 185.
6 Quoted in Crépet, *Baudelaire: étude biographique*, Paris, 1906, p. 257.
7 'Je n'ai pas pour maîtresse une lionne illustre ...', a 12-stanza poem which has survived in manuscript. Its literary merits would certainly have justified Baudelaire in including it in *Les Fleurs du Mal* and there is no way of telling why he decided not to do so.
8 Quoted in Pichois, *Baudelaire, études et témoignages*, Neuchâtel, 1967, p. 27.
9   'Ci-gît qui, pour avoir par trop aimé les gaupes,
        Descendit jeune encore au royaume des taupes'

– a couplet cited by Auguste Dozon in a letter to Eugène Crépet and first published by Jacques Crépet in *La Plume*, April 15th, 1898.

10 Originally published in *Vers*, par G. Le Vavasseur, E. Prarond, A. Argonne [Auguste Dozon], Paris, 1843, pp. 125–6, and reprinted in *Lettres à Charles Baudelaire*, ed. Claude Pichois, Neuchâtel, 1973, p. 313.

11 'Tu mettrais l'univers entier dans ta ruelle . . .', *Les Fleurs du Mal*, XXV (*OC* I, 27–8). Although this poem was placed by Baudelaire in the middle of the cycle inspired by Jeanne Duval, we have Prarond's word for it that it was addressed not to her but to her predecessor.

12 In an article published in *La Revue fantaisiste*, August 1861, and reprinted in vol. IV of Eugène Crépet's anthology *Les Poètes français*, Paris, 1862: *OC* II, 179–81.

13 Quoted by Crépet, *op. cit.*, p. 20.

14 Cousin, *Voyage dans un grenier*, Paris, 1878, p. 12.

15 Letter to Eugène Crépet, October 1886; quoted in *Baudelaire devant ses contemporains*, pp. 27–8.

16 Letter of January 25th, 1841; reproduced by Pichois, *Corr.* I, 731–3.

17 *Corr.* I, 86 (letter of January 20th, 1841).

18 *Corr.* I, 734–5.

19 Quoted in Crépet, *op. cit.*, p. 255.

20 *Ibid.*, p. 27.

21 Baron Paul Pérignon was the son of Pierre Pérignon who had been Caroline's legal guardian before her first marriage. Labie was formerly notary at Neuilly.

22 Quoted in J. Crépet, 'Quelques documents inédits sur Baudelaire', *Mercure de France*, vol. CCLXXIV (1937), p. 631.

23 Maxime Du Camp, *Souvenirs littéraires*, Paris, 1892, vol. II, p. 59.

24 *Corr.* I, 88.

25 *Ibid.*, p. 155.

26 *Fusées*, VIII: *OC* I, 655.

27 Capt. Saliz's report, sent to Aupick, was first published by Féli Gautier, 'Documents sur Baudelaire', *Mercure de France*, vol. LIII (1905), pp. 191–4. The details furnished by the passenger (whose identity is not known) are contained in an account first printed in *La Chronique de Paris*, September 13th, 1867, and reproduced more recently in *Baudelaire devant ses contemporains*, pp. 58–9.

28 *Corr.* I, 145.

29 Banville, *Petites études. Mes souvenirs*, Paris, 1883, p. 79.

30 Baudelaire's references are to be found in his notes for the unwritten work *Pauvre Belgique!*: *OC* II, 950, 822. See Charles D. Hérisson, 'Le Voyage de Baudelaire. Le séjour au Cap de Bonne Espérance en 1841', *Mercure de France*, vol. CCCXXXV (1959), pp. 637–73.

31 *Corr.* I, 90.

IV. ON THE ILE SAINT-LOUIS

1 *Corr.* I, 105 (letter of March 3rd, 1844).

2 *Opium and the Romantic Imagination*, London, 1968, p. 156.

3 Quoted in Crépet, *Baudelaire: étude biographique*, Paris, 1906, p. 35.

4 Crépet, *op. cit.*, p. 42 and Pichois, *Baudelaire, études et témoignages*, Neuchâtel, 1967, pp. 25–6.

5 Quoted in Pichois, *op. cit.*, p. 39. It was only under the Second Empire that the Bois de Boulogne was drained, replanted, and laid out with walks and rides.

6 Chennevières, *Souvenirs d'un directeur des Beaux-Arts*, Paris, 1979, vol. V, p.

98. *Les Cariatides* was the title of Théodore de Banville's first collection of poems, published in 1842.

7 *Les Fleurs du Mal*, LXXXVII (*OC* I, 83).

8 The 'wicker shawl' was the basket in the form of an inverted cone that rag-pickers carried on their backs and into which they deposited any resaleable article they found in the refuse dumps. His 'number seven' was the wooden prong, so called from its shape, used to rake over the rubbish at the street corners.

9 *OC* I, 381. My italics.

10 According to Adolphe Boschot, who made this observation in an address to the Académie des Beaux-Arts in 1947, quoted in Jean Ziegler, 'Emile Deroy (1820–1846) et l'esthétique de Baudelaire', *Gazette des Beaux-Arts*, vol. LXXXVII (1976), p. 156.

11 *Baudelaire et Asselineau*, textes recueillis et commentés par Jacques Crépet et Claude Pichois, Paris, 1953, p. 69.

12 Auguste Vitu in *La Silhouette*, September 2nd, 1849, quoted in Ziegler, *loc. cit.*, p. 154.

13 *Mon cœur mis à nu*, XXXVIII (*OC* I, 701).

14 Quoted in Crépet, *op. cit.*, p. 70.

15 See Jacques Crépet, *Propos sur Baudelaire*, Paris, 1957, p. 155.

16 Nadar, *Charles Baudelaire intime: le poète vierge*, Paris, 1911, pp. 6–7.

17 *Ibid.*, pp. 7–8.

18 Banville, *Petites études. Mes souvenirs*, Paris, 1883, p. 75.

19 Cf. a note in *Mon cœur mis à nu* (*OC* I, 691): 'De la haine du peuple contre la beauté. Des exemples. Jeanne et Madame Muller' – the latter being supposedly someone he came across in Brussels.

20 Pichois, *op. cit.*, p. 27.

21 'Choix de maximes consolantes sur l'amour', published in *Le Corsaire-Satan*, March 3rd, 1846, over the signature 'Baudelaire-Dufays'.

22 *OC* I, 549.

23 *Parfum exotique*; cf. also *La Chevelure*: *Les Fleurs du Mal*, XXII, XXIII, *OC* I, 27.

24 *Mon cœur mis à nu*, XXXIX; *OC* I, 702.

25 'Je t'adore à l'égal de la voûte nocturne', *Les Fleurs du Mal*, XXIV; *OC* I, 27.

26 *Les Fleurs du Mal*, XXXII; *OC* I, 34.

27 Balzac's *La Fille aux yeux d'or* was published in 1834–5, Gautier's *Mademoiselle de Maupin* in 1835. Both had been anticipated by the minor novelist Hyacinthe Latouche in *Fragoletta*, published in 1829.

28 *Pièces condamnées*, III; *OC* I, 155.

29 Specifically, in *Duellum*, *Le Vampire*, *Sed non satiata*, and *Le Possédé*.

30 *Les Fleurs du Mal*, XXXIII; *OC* I, 34–5.

V. IN CHANCERY

1 See Claude Pichois, 'Baudelaire jeune collectionneur' in *Humanisme actif. Mélanges d'art et de littérature offerts à Julien Cain*, Paris, 1968, vol. I, pp. 207–11.

2 *Corr.* I, 102.

3 *Don Juan aux enfers* on September 6th, *A une Malabaraise* on December 13th.

4 *Corr.* I, 103.

5 *Ibid.*, p. 104.

6 Baudelaire changed his mind radically about the merits of this work only a few years later, to judge by the dismissive remark he makes in the *Salon de 1846*

about 'la littérature *Marion Delorme*, qui consiste à prêcher les vertus des assassins et des filles publiques' (*OC* II, 477).

7 *Corr.* I, 82.
8 Sainte-Beuve, 'La Morale et l'Art', *Le Moniteur*, February 20th, 1860.
9 Letter to Joséphin Soulary, February 28th, 1860 (*Corr.* I, 682).
10 *Corr.* II, 495.
11 Théophile Gautier, *Portraits et souvenirs littéraires*, Paris, 1875, pp. 139–41.
12 Gautier himself dated this meeting as 'some time in the middle of 1849'. But, as Armand Moss has shown (*Baudelaire et Madame Sabatier*, Paris, 1975, p. 43), there can be little doubt that it took place several years earlier.
13 This synopsis, due to Charles Cousin, has been reproduced in *OC* I, 205–6, under the title 'Cauchemar'. See also Asselineau's recollections of the contents, in Crépet, *Baudelaire: étude biographique*, Paris, 1906, p. 283.
14 *Corr.* I, 108–9.
15 *Ibid.*, pp. 110–11.
16 Quoted in Jacques Crépet, 'Quelques documents inédits sur Baudelaire', *Mercure de France*, vol. CCLXXIV (1937), p. 636.
17 See above, p. 36.
18 Edouard Clerc, *Théorie du notariat* ... (1861), quoted (in this translation) by Theodore Zeldin, *France 1848–1945*, Oxford, 1973, vol. I, p. 43.
19 Letter of December 31st, 1853: *Corr.* I, 244.
20 *Corr.* II, 163.
21 *Ibid.*, p. 164.
22 Jacques Crépet and Claude Pichois, *Baudelaire et Asselineau*, Paris, 1953, pp. 223–4.
23 *Corr.* I, 124–5.
24 This account was first given by Philippe Berthelot, in an obituary article on Ménard published in *La Revue de Paris*, June 1st, 1901, the relevant part of which has been reproduced in *Baudelaire devant ses contemporains*, ed. W. T. Bandy and Claude Pichois, Paris, 1967, p. 74. It should be said that Ménard, although very close to Baudelaire at the time (they were old schoolfellows), quarrelled with him in consequence of an unfriendly review Baudelaire published of his *Prométhée délivré* a little later (February 3rd, 1846). His account is therefore slightly suspect, particularly in respect of the motives he said Jeanne gave for the abortive suicide attempt.
25 *Corr.* I, 130.

VI.   THE ART CRITIC

1 Quoted by Léon Rosenthal, *Du romantisme au réalisme. Essai sur l'évolution de la peinture en France de 1830 à 1848*, Paris, 1914, p. 77.
2 *OC* II, 389.
3 *Ibid.*, pp. 383–4, 394.
4 *Ibid.*, pp. 351–2.
5 *Ibid.*, p. 360.
6 When André Ferran published his monumental work *L'Esthétique de Baudelaire* in 1933, he was unable to assess Baudelaire's estimate of *The Fountain of Youth* since at that time the picture was supposed lost. It did, however, turn up in a London auction-room a little before the war, and has been reproduced (in black and white) in Jonathan Mayne's translation of Baudelaire's art criticism, *Art in Paris, 1845–1862* (London, 1965). In the opinion of Henri Lemaître, 'le tableau apparaît comme très original et justifie la description élogieuse de

Baudelaire' (Baudelaire, *Curiosités esthétiques – L'Art romantique*, Paris, Garnier, 1962, p. 16).

7 *OC* II, 407.

8 *Le Nain jaune*, April 18th, 1866; quoted in W. T. Bandy, *Baudelaire judged by his contemporaries*, New York, 1933, p. 81.

9 In a letter to Banville, July 6th, 1845: *Corr.* I, 127.

10 The suggestion has been made by Lloyd Austin (Club du Meilleur Livre edition of Baudelaire, *Œuvres complètes*, Paris, 1955, vol. I, p. 44).

11 *Mon cœur mis à nu*, XXVII: *OC* I, 694.

12 See *Baudelaire et Asselineau*, ed. Crépet and Pichois, Paris, 1953, p. 81.

13 'Comment on paie ses dettes quand on a du génie', November 24th, 1845.

14 'Choix de maximes consolantes sur l'amour', March 3rd, 1846; see above, p. 52.

15 'Le Musée classique du Bazar Bonne-Nouvelle', January 21st, 1846.

16 *OC* II, 408.

17 *Ibid.*, p. 409.

18 *Ibid.*, pp. 409–10.

19 The phrase was used by Asselineau; see *Baudelaire devant ses contemporains*, ed. W. T. Bandy and Claude Pichois, Paris, 1967, p. 82.

20 *Corr.* I, 135–6.

21 *OC* II, 17–19.

22 *Corr.* I, 137.

23 The first such request, undated, was probably made in December 1846.

24 Delacroix, *Journal*, ed. André Joubin, Paris, 1932, vol. I, pp. 202, 214. Delacroix refers to Baudelaire by his pseudonym Dufays in both these diary entries (March 9th and April 4th, 1847).

25 *OC* II, 430–32.

26 Cf. Armand Moss, *Baudelaire et Delacroix*, Paris, 1973, p. 222, and Lois Hyslop, *Baudelaire, man of his time*, New Haven and London, 1980, p. 13.

27 *OC* II, 419.

28 *Ibid.*, p. 806.

29 *Ibid.*, pp. 353, 407.

30 *Ibid.*, p. 3. Jean de la Falaise was the pen-name of Philippe de Chennevières.

31 *OC* II, 496.

32 A theory oddly corroborated by the fact that the man who was later to give the word currency in a literary context, Emile Zola, was of Italian extraction and Provençal upbringing.

33 *OC* II, 433–4.

34 *OC* I, 14. In the *Salon de 1846* (*OC* II, 440), in a passage on Delacroix's 'haute et sérieuse mélancolie', Baudelaire writes that it is 'plaintive et profonde comme une mélodie de Weber'.

VII. THE REVOLUTIONARY

1 *Corr.* I, 120. In his rambling article 'Autour de *la Fanfarlo*. Baudelaire, Balzac et Marie Daubrun' (*Mercure de France*, vol. CCCXXVIII (1956), pp. 604–36), Claude Pichois came to the conclusion that the story, in its present form, must have been composed in the early months of 1846. Reopening the question in the 1975 edition of the complete works, he showed himself more prudent: '*La Fanfarlo* a pu être écrite entre 1843 et la fin de 1846' (*OC* I, 1414).

2 Thus, in his review of Champfleury's short stories (*Le Corsaire-Satan*, January 18th, 1843), Baudelaire says of Balzac: 'C'est un grand homme dans toute la force du terme; c'est un créateur de méthode et *le seul dont la méthode vaille la*

peine d'être étudiée' (*OC* II, 22; my italics). Baudelaire appears to have appreciated Stendhal much more for his writings on art and for the treatise *De l'Amour* than for his novels.

3 The idea of this 'imitation' was first mooted by Jean Prévost in the chapter, 'L'Influence de Balzac', of his *Baudelaire: essai sur l'inspiration et la création poétiques*, Paris, 1953. The main difference between the plot of *Béatrix* and that of *La Fanfarlo* is that in Baudelaire's story, Cramer agrees to seduce La Fanfarlo only in the hope of being rewarded by the favours of Mme de Cosmelly; in Balzac's version, La Palférine performs a similar service for Sabine du Guénic without any corresponding expectation.

4 *OC* I, 553.

5 Gautier, *Portraits et souvenirs littéraires*, Paris, 1875, p. 133.

6 *OC* I, 553.

7 C. A. Hackett, 'Baudelaire and Samuel Cramer', *Australian Journal of French Studies*, vol. VI (1969), p. 319.

8 *OC* I, 554, 555.

9 *Ibid.*, p. 580.

10 Quoted in *Baudelaire devant ses contemporains*, ed. W. T. Bandy and Claude Pichois, Paris, 1967, p. 34.

11 Jean Rousseau, 'M. Baudelaire et Edgar Poe', *Gazette de Paris*, July 27th, 1856; quoted in W. T. Bandy, *Baudelaire judged by his contemporaries*, New York, 1933, p. 27.

12 Quoted in E. and J. Crépet, *Baudelaire: étude biographique*, Paris, 1906, p. 48.

13 *Corr.* I, 145.

14 *OC* II, 14.

15 *Le Chien et le Flacon*, *OC* I, 284. The same idea, phrased more directly, occurs in *Mon cœur mis à nu*, XXXIV: 'Le Français est un animal de basse-cour . . . ; l'ordure ne lui déplaît pas dans son domicile, et en littérature, il est scatophage. Il raffole des excréments' (*OC* I, 698).

16 *OC* II, 18.

17 Delacroix, *Journal*, ed. André Joubin, Paris, 1932, vol. I, p. 197.

18 Jules Mouquet and W. T. Bandy, *Baudelaire en 1848*, Paris, 1946, p. 11. The authors are drawing on Toubin's *Souvenirs d'un septuagénaire*, originally serialized in the *Revue de France*, 1925–6.

19 E. and J. Crépet, *op. cit.*, p. 79.

20 *Ibid.*, p. 76.

21 *OC* I, 676, 709. The first of these maxims occurs in *Mon cœur mis à nu*, the second is a reflection contributed by Baudelaire to an album kept by Philoxène Boyer.

22 Barrès, preface to the 1909 edition of Ménard's *Rêveries d'un païen mystique*; quoted in *Baudelaire devant ses contemporains*, p. 138.

23 Preface to the 1851 edition of Pierre Dupont, *Chants et chansons*: *OC* II, 31. The phrases in inverted commas represent actual quotations from Dupont's songs.

24 *OC* I, 357–8.

25 Toubin, *Souvenirs d'un septuagénaire*, quoted in Mouquet and Bandy, *op. cit.*, pp. 20–21.

26 See T. J. Clark's discussion of the question in *The Absolute Bourgeois: artists and politics in France, 1848–1851*, London, 1973, pp. 141–77.

27 Baudelaire related the incident in a letter to Poulet-Malassis, at the time of Proudhon's death in 1865; see *Corr.* II, 470.

28 Quoted in *Baudelaire devant ses contemporains*, p. 98.

29 A re-examination of the question, based on an analysis of the 12 issues of *La*

Tribune nationale, was undertaken by Marcel Ruff, 'La Pensée politique et sociale de Baudelaire', pp. 65–75 in *Littérature et société. Recueil d'études en l'honneur de Bernard Guyon*, Paris, 1975.

30 Paul de Flotte (1817–1860), a naval officer, a friend of Leconte de Lisle and a lifelong revolutionary. He was eventually killed in Italy, fighting under Garibaldi.

31 Quoted in E. and J. Crépet, *op. cit.*, p. 82.

32 *OC* I, 679.

33 *Mon cœur mis à nu*, XXV: *OC* I, 692.

34 *Corr.* II, 41.

35 *Corr.* I, 188.

36 Letter dated May 16th, 1859: *Corr.* I, 578.

37 Besides *Assommons les pauvres!*, already mentioned, one may cite among these *Le Miroir*, *Le Joujou du pauvre*, *Le Gâteau*, and *Les Yeux des pauvres*.

38 *Mon cœur mis à nu*, V: *OC* I, 679.

39 Letter to Alphonse Toussenel, January 21st, 1856: *Corr.* I, 337.

40 *OC* I, 677.

41 On a railway journey to Versailles in May 1853, one of the two friends Baudelaire was travelling with exclaimed in admiration at the magnificent golden hair worn by an Englishwoman on the station platform. Baudelaire looked at her carefully, saw that her hair was her own, a product of nature, not of art, and pronounced her 'atrocious'. (The story, told by Francis Magnard in *La Chronique de Paris*, September 27th, 1867, is also found, with minor variations, in Maxime Rude, *Confidences d'un journaliste*, Paris, 1876, pp. 170–1.)

42 *OC* I, 684.

43 Swinburne, *Complete Works* (Bonchurch edition), London and New York, 1926, vol. XIII, p. 426.

44 *OC* I, 961. These remarks occur in the notes Baudelaire made for his book on Belgium, *Pauvre Belgique!*, in the last years of his life.

VIII. AN ELECTIVE AFFINITY

1 Prarond, quoted in Claude Pichois, *Baudelaire, études et témoignages*, Neuchâtel, 1967, p. 24.

2 'Je vais apprendre l'anglais et j'espère bien être bientôt en état d'entamer quelques conversations' (letter to Alphonse Baudelaire, November 9th, 1832: *Corr.* I, 11).

3 See Edmond Estève, *Byron et le romantisme français*, Paris, 1929, pp. 65–6.

4 Gautier, *Histoire du romantisme*, Paris, 1884, pp. 40–41.

5 *Le Guignon*: *OC* I, 17.

6 In the *Notes nouvelles sur Edgar Poe*, published in 1857, Baudelaire contrasts 'la mélancolie molle, harmonieuse, distinguée de Tennyson' with 'l'effusion ardente de Byron' (*OC* II, 336). In 1865, drafting an indignant rebuttal of an attack by Jules Janin on Heine and his 'satanic' following in France, he cites 'Byron, Tennyson, Poe and Co.' (the 'and Co.' obviously stands for himself) as 'stars of the first magnitude' shining in 'the melancholy sky of modern poetry' (*ibid.*, p. 237).

7 It was W. T. Bandy who first located the original, in *The Forget Me Not* of 1836, and announced his discovery in 'Baudelaire et Croly: la vérité sur *le Jeune Enchanteur*', *Mercure de France*, vol. CCCVIII (1950), pp. 233–47. In his article, Bandy gives instances of the occasional 'howlers' that Baudelaire committed, and also speculates that the author of *The Young Enchanter* may have been the Dublin-born clergyman-poet and polygraph George Croly,

referred to ironically by Byron in a stanza of *Don Juan* as 'the very Reverend Rowley-Powley'.

8 *OC* II, 248.

9 Quoted in Arthur H. Quinn, *Edgar Allan Poe, a critical biography*, New York, 1941, p. 466.

10 *Corr.* I, 180.

11 *Baudelaire et Asselineau*, ed. Jacques Crépet and Claude Pichois, Paris, 1953, pp. 94–5.

12 By the time he came to write this introduction, Baudelaire had a little extra material at his disposal of which he made some slight use: Rufus Griswold's defamatory *Memoir*, published in the third volume of the Redfield edition of Poe's works, and also the preface written by James Hannay for the charming illustrated pocket edition of *Poe's Poetical Works*, published by Addey in London in 1853.

13 A comparison between Baudelaire's 1852 essay and his American sources has been undertaken by Henry Haswell: 'Baudelaire's self-portrait of Poe: *Edgar Allan Poe, sa vie et ses ouvrages*', *Romance Notes*, vol. X (1968–9), pp. 253–60. The text of the articles by J. M. Daniel and J. R. Thompson that Baudelaire used can be read in W. T. Bandy's edition of *Edgar Allan Poe, sa vie et ses ouvrages*, Toronto, 1973, pp. 55–93.

14 Quoted in A. H. Quinn, *op. cit.*, p. 341.

15 *OC* II, 272.

16 *Ibid.*, pp. 249–50.

17 *Ibid.*, p. 254. In fact, it is not known what Poe's father died of, nor when he died; what is certain is that he abandoned his wife and family and that Poe's mother died in straitened circumstances, probably through illness brought on by poverty and strain (she was a professional actress).

18 'He became, and was, an Ishmaelite', as Daniel wrote of Poe (see Bandy's aforementioned edition of Baudelaire's essay, p. 74).

19 *Corr.* I, 676.

20 'Ce qu'il y a d'assez singulier, et ce qu'il m'est impossible de ne pas remarquer, c'est la ressemblance intime, quoique non positivement accentuée, entre mes poésies propres et celles de cet homme [Poe], déduction faite du tempérament et du climat' (Baudelaire to his mother, March 8th, 1854: *Corr.* I, 269).

21 *Corr.* I, 191, 214.

22 *Ibid.*, pp. 142–5.

23 *Ibid.*, pp. 191–2 (letter to his mother dated March 27th, 1852).

24 *Ibid.*, pp. 237, 242.

25 *Ibid.*, pp. 264, 302.

26 *Ibid.*, pp. 326–7.

27 *OC* I, 16; first published in *La Revue des Deux Mondes*, June 1st, 1855, and believed to have been composed only shortly before.

28 *Baudelaire et Asselineau*, pp. 96–7. Banville relates how 'lorsqu'il traduisit Edgar Poe, on put le voir ... se servant d'atlas, de cartes, d'instruments de mathématiques nettoyés avec soin, car toujours pour l'amour de la perfection (qui fut son unique règle) il vérifiait les calculs nautiques de Gordon Pym, et voulait s'assurer personnellement de leur exactitude' (*Petites études. Mes Souvenirs*, Paris, 1883, p. 81).

29 Letter to Alphonse Baudelaire, May 7th, 1858; quoted in *Baudelaire devant ses contemporains*, ed. W. T. Bandy and Claude Pichois, Paris, 1967, p. 111.

30 *Le Salut public*, May 4th, 1869; reprinted in *Armand Fraisse sur Baudelaire, 1857–1869*, ed. Claude and Vincenette Pichois, Gembloux, 1973, p. 55. The

question whether Baudelaire, in translating Poe, improved on him, has been carefully examined in a chapter of Patrick F. Quinn's *The French Face of Edgar Poe*, Carbondale, 1957. Quinn concludes that although occasionally Baudelaire did express better than Poe what Poe would have liked to express, in general he translated very faithfully: 'the Poe of Baudelaire is the Poe we know in English ... there is no full-scale transmutation'.

31 Letter dated February 18th, 1865: *Corr.* II, 466–7.

32 Henry James felt that 'an enthusiasm for Poe is the mark of a decidedly primitive stage of reflection'. Paul Elmer More put it more epigrammatically: 'Poe is the poet of unripe boys and unsound men'. T. S. Eliot judged Poe to be suffering from arrested development; his intellect was 'powerful', but it was 'the intellect of a highly gifted young person before puberty'. The mystery how this 'boys' author' could have so deeply impressed not just Baudelaire, but Mallarmé and Valéry too, none of whom can be accused of intellectual or critical immaturity, remains entire.

IX. HARPOCRATES' FOREFINGER

1 Lamartine, *History of the French Revolution of 1848* ..., translated from the French, London, 1905, pp. 362–3.

2 Letter to Edouard Thouvenel, chargé d'affaires at Athens; quoted in Claude Pichois, *Le Vrai Visage du général Aupick, beau-père de Baudelaire*, Paris, 1955, p. 28.

3 Letter of December 8th, 1848: *Corr.* I, 153–4.

4 The exact date is provided in a letter Flaubert wrote to his mother on December 4th, 1850: 'nous dînons après-demain à l'ambassade chez le général' (Flaubert, *Correspondance*, ed. Jean Bruneau, vol. I (Paris, 1973), p. 718.

5 Du Camp, *Souvenirs littéraires*, Paris, 1892, vol. II, pp. 57–8.

6 *Corr.* I, 173–4.

7 *Ibid.*, p. 193.

8 *Ibid.*, p. 194.

9 *OC* I, 33. *Le Vampire* was first published in *La Revue des Deux Mondes*, June 1st, 1855.

10 Judith Gautier, *Le Collier des jours. Le Second Rang du collier*, Paris, n.d., pp. 182–3.

11 *Sisina, OC* I, 60–61; it was first published in *La Revue française*, April 10th, 1859. There are biographical sketches of both 'Bébé' and Elisa Neri in Jean Ziegler, *Gautier – Baudelaire: un carré de dames*, Paris, 1970.

12 *Jean-Louis-Ernest Meissonier, ses souvenirs, ses entretiens*, Paris, 1897, quoted in André Billy, *La Présidente et ses amis*, Paris, 1945, p. 80.

13 *Les Fleurs du Mal*, XLI: *OC* I, 42.

14 Gautier, *Portraits et souvenirs littéraires*, Paris, 1875, p. 219.

15 *Corr.* I, 205.

16 *Les Fleurs du Mal*, XLVI: *OC* I, 46. The setting (the newly risen sun shining through the windows on to the aftermath of an orgy) may have been drawn from real life but may also have been affected by Baudelaire's memory of similar scenes described in different works of Balzac, notably *La Peau de chagrin* and *L'Elixir de longue vie*. Cf. also Baudelaire's notes for a short story, to be called *La Maîtresse vierge*: 'Ce qui rend la maîtresse plus chère, c'est la débauche avec d'autres femmes. Ce qu'elle perd en jouissances sexuelles, elle le gagne en adoration' (*OC* I, 597).

17 *Corr.* I, 276.

18 *Ibid.*, p. 241 (letter dated December 26th, 1853).

19 *Ibid.*, p. 246.

20 In *La Revue des Deux Mondes*, June 1st, 1855.

21 The birth-certificate was traced by Yvon Boureau, who reproduced it in his article 'L'Etat-civil de Marie Daubrun', *Revue d'Histoire Littéraire de la France*, vol. LVIII (1958), pp. 59–61.

22 Quoted in Claude Pichois, 'Autour de *la Fanfarlo*: Baudelaire, Balzac et Marie Daubrun', *Mercure de France*, vol. CCCXXVIII (1956), p. 613.

23 Letters of October 14th and 22nd, 1854: *Corr.* I, 294, 297.

24 In *Le Beau Navire* (*Les Fleurs du Mal*, LII) Baudelaire refers to 'ta beauté, Où l'enfance s'allie à la maturité'; in *Inviolata*, one of the poems in his collection *Améthystes*, Banville similarly declared:

> 'Ta beauté, lys exalté, vêtement
> Joyeux, que rien n'offense,
> Garde, malgré l'épanouissement
> Comme un duvet d'enfance.'

25 *Ciel brouillé* (*Les Fleurs du Mal*, L): *OC* I, 49.

26 *Corr.* I, 182.

27 *Ibid.* In the original, the last sentence runs: 'Soyez mon ange gardien, ma Muse et ma Madone, et conduisez-moi dans la route du Beau.' This is a conflation of two lines from separate poems written for Apollonie Sabatier:

> 'Je suis l'Ange gardien, la Muse et la Madone'

(*Que diras-tu ce soir . . ., Les Fleurs du Mal*, XLII) and

> 'Ils [i.e. ces Yeux] conduisent mes pas dans la route du Beau'

(*Le Flambeau vivant, Les Fleurs du Mal*, XLIII).

28 *Conseils aux jeunes littérateurs*, *OC* II, 19–20.

29 We are following here the sequence of events as reconstructed by Albert Feuillerat, *Baudelaire et la Belle aux cheveux d'or*, Paris and New Haven, 1941, pp. 37–43.

30 See Léon Cellier, 'Baudelaire et George Sand', *Revue d'Histoire Littéraire de la France*, vol. LXVII (1967), p. 240, and George Sand's letters to Vaëz of August 16th and 23rd, 1855, in her *Correspondance*, ed. Georges Lubin, vol. XIII (Paris, 1978), pp. 295 and 320.

31 *Corr.* I, 279 (letter of May 18th, 1854).

32 See Alan Bowness, 'Courbet and Baudelaire', *Gazette des Beaux-Arts*, vol. XC (1977), pp. 197–8.

33 *Corr.* I, 356–7.

34 *Les Fleurs du Mal*, XXXVI: *OC* I, 36–7.

X. MISUNDERSTANDINGS

1 *OC* II, 358.

2 *Baudelaire et Asselineau*, ed. J. Crépet and C. Pichois, Paris, 1953, pp. 64–5.

3 This was the so-called *limbo patrum*. There was also a *limbo infantum* or *puerorum*, reserved for babies born to Christian parents who died before there had been an opportunity to christen them.

4 *Inferno*, canto IV, Melville B. Anderson's translation. In the remainder of this canto Dante is introduced by Virgil to his fellow poets dwelling in limbo: Homer, Horace, Ovid and Lucan. This passage gave Delacroix the subject for his ceiling painting in the Library of the Luxembourg Palace, described by Baudelaire in the *Salon de 1846* (*OC* II, 437–8), together with a long quotation from the relevant part of the *Inferno*.

5   'Un de ces *limbes* noires qui circonscrivent l'âme,
      Quand l'atmosphère est grise et le soleil sans flamme!
      Névrose, maladie, hallucination,
      Velléité de *spleen* et de consomption.'
      Quoted in Léon Cellier, 'Baudelaire et les Limbes', *Studi francesi*, vol. VIII (1964), pp. 432–41.

6 *Indiana*, chap. XIII; *Stello*, chap. II.

7 'De l'essence du rire et généralement du comique dans les arts plastiques', *Le Portefeuille*, July 8th, 1855: *OC* II, 538. A line in Gautier's *Après le bal* puts particular emphasis on the Anglo-Saxon resonance of the word:
      'Quand sur nos fronts blêmis le spleen anglais s'assied.'

8 *Les Fleurs du Mal*, LXXVIII: *OC* I, 74–5.

9 Baudelaire used the word 'flower', meaning 'poem', in a letter sent to his mother shortly before his departure for the East: 'je t'enverrai dans ma prochaine lettre des fleurs qui te paraîtront singulières' (*Corr.* I, 88).

10 See above, pp. 56–7 and 123.

11 *Les Fleurs du Mal*, CXVI. The other two were *La Destruction* (CIX) and *L'Amour et le crâne* (CXVII).

12 *Corr.* I, 314 (dated June 13th, 1855).

13 The description, by Alfred Delvau, is quoted in Pierre Dufay, *Autour de Baudelaire. Poulet-Malassis, l'éditeur et l'ami...*, Paris, 1931, p. 26.

14 'Epouvanté moi-même de l'horreur que j'allais inspirer, j'en ai retranché un tiers aux épreuves': *Corr.* I, 411.

15 *Corr.* II, 344.

16 The complete text of Barbey d'Aurevilly's article has been reproduced by Pichois, *OC* I, 1191–6.

17 Letter to Vigny, accompanying a copy of the second edition, December 16th, 1861 (*Corr.* II, 196). Cf. also the less frequently quoted statement to his mother: 'J'avais pris soin de noter, à la table des matières, tous les morceaux nouveaux. Il t'était facile de vérifier qu'ils étaient tous faits pour le cadre' (*Corr.* II, 141).

18 See above, p. 2.

19 See above, p. 39.

20 See, *inter alia*, Colin Burns, '"Architecture secrète": notes on the second edition of *Les Fleurs du Mal*', *Nottingham French Studies*, vol. V (1966), pp. 67–79.

21 *Corr.* II, 27, 67.

22 *Corr.* I, 382–93, *passim*.

23 *Ibid.*, pp. 408, 364.

24 This poem, with its ending 'Peter denied the Christ – and he did well', was always regarded as the most overtly blasphemous in the collection. After Baudelaire's death, his mother tried to persuade the editors of the posthumous edition of *Les Fleurs du Mal* to excise it, and only desisted when they threatened to withdraw their services entirely.

25 Quoted in H. Patry, 'L'Epilogue du procès des *Fleurs du Mal* ...', *Revue d'Histoire Littéraire de la France*, vol. XXIX (1922), pp. 67–8.

26 *Corr.* I, 411.

27 Jean Pommier, *Autour de l'édition originale des 'Fleurs du Mal'*, Geneva, 1968, pp. 65–6.

28 Letter to Mme de La Rochejaquelin, August 29th, 1857; Prosper Mérimée, *Correspondance générale*, 2e série, Toulouse, 1955, vol. II, p. 365.

29 *Corr.* I, 418.

30 *Ibid.*, p. 422.

31 *Lettres à Charles Baudelaire*, ed. Claude Pichois, Neuchâtel, 1973, p. 322.

32 *Corr.* I, 425.
33 It was first published in *Le Boulevard*, June 14th, 1863. At this date her liaison with Mosselman had ended and she had moved out of the Rue Frochot apartment; if she was still seeing Baudelaire, it would have been at Gautier's house.
34 *Laquelle est la vraie?*, *Le Spleen de Paris*, XXXVIII: *OC* I, 342.
35 *Lettres à Charles Baudelaire*, p. 323.
36 *Ibid.*, pp. 323–4.
37 *Baudelaire et Asselineau*, p. 114.
38 *OC* I, 1186.
39 The autobiographical *Mon cœur mis à nu* was to have included an 'histoire des *Fleurs du Mal*, humiliation par le malentendu' (*OC* I, 658).

XI.   'O JUST, SUBTLE, AND MIGHTY OPIUM!'

1 *OC* II, 125.
2 Letter to his mother, July 9th, 1857: *Corr.* I, 411.
3 'Du vin et du hachisch comparés comme moyens de multiplication de l'individualité', *Le Messager de l'Assemblée*, March 7th–12th, 1851.
4 *OC* I, 397.
5 *Corr.* I, 666.
6 *Du hachisch et de l'aliénation mentale, études psychologiques*, Paris, 1845.
7 Balzac, *Lettres à Madame Hanska*, vol. III, Paris, 1969, pp. 112–13.
8 *OC* I, 438–9. The hero of Balzac's story *Louis Lambert* (1832) started writing a *Treatise on the Will* at school, in which he tried to prove that the will was a substance, a fluid as electricity was then supposed to be.
9 *OC* I, 396–7.
10 Gautier, *Portraits et souvenirs littéraires*, Paris, 1875, p. 268.
11 F. L. M. Dorvault, *L'Officine, ou Répertoire général de pharmacie pratique* (first edition 1844). See Robert Kopp and Claude Pichois, 'Baudelaire et le haschisch. Expérience et documentation', *Revue des Sciences humaines*, vol. XXXII (1967), pp. 467–76.
12 *OC* I, 403.
13 Léon Lemonnier spoke to Mme Allais, the widow of the pharmacist in business at Honfleur when Baudelaire was staying there in 1859. She mentioned that the poet 'avait pris l'habitude de l'opium, et il suppliait mon mari de lui en fournir. Mais M. Allais ne lui en a jamais donné qu'autant que le pouvait un pharmacien consciencieux' (Lemonnier, *Enquêtes sur Baudelaire*, Paris, 1929, p. 21).
14 *Corr.* II, 603.
15 See Marcel Monnier, 'La Maladie de Baudelaire', in Claude Pichois, *Baudelaire, études et témoignages*, Neuchâtel, 1967.
16 The two extremes are represented respectively by Emanuel J. Mickel, *The Artificial Paradises in French Literature*, Chapel Hill, 1969 (last chapter); and Alethea Hayter, *Opium and the Romantic Imagination*, London, 1968, pp. 154–5.
17 *OC* I, 280–2.
18 Letter of November 10th, 1858: *Corr.* I, 522.
19 Letter of December 11th, 1858: *Corr.* I, 532.
20 See the introduction written by Michèle Stäuble to her invaluable 'parallel text' edition of Baudelaire's *Un Mangeur d'opium*, Neuchâtel, 1976.
21 Letter of February 16th, 1860: *Corr.* I, 669.
22 *OC* I, 403, 438–40.
23 *Lettres à Charles Baudelaire*, ed. Claude Pichois, Neuchâtel, 1973, p. 155.

24 *Corr.* II, 53. This exchange of letters between Flaubert and Baudelaire took place on June 25th–26th, 1860.
25 *OC* I, 440.
26 *Fusées*, XI: *OC* I, 658–9.
27 *A Tale of the Ragged Mountains*. Quoted here from *The Complete Works of Edgar Allan Poe*, ed. James A. Harrison, New York, 1902, vol. V, p. 167.
28 *Exposition Universelle – 1855*: *OC* II, 596.

XII.   THE WIDOW AND HER SON

1 *Corr.* I, 403.
2 Letter of May 7th, 1858, originally published by Georges-Emmanuel Lang, 'Charles Baudelaire et sa mère', *Le Figaro*, March 2nd, 1922.
3 *Corr.* I, 438–9.
4 *Ibid.*, p. 450.
5 *Ibid.*, p. 460.
6 *Ibid.*, p. 469.
7 *OC* I, 668.
8 Letter of February 10th, 1858: *Corr.* I, 457–8.
9 *Le Port*, *Le Spleen de Paris*, XLI: *OC* I, 580.
10 *OC* I, 132–3.
11 *Exposition Universelle – 1855*: *OC* II, 580.
12 *Mon cœur mis à nu*, XXXII: *OC* I, 697. The reference to table turning may have been intended as a gibe at Hugo, who was known to have interested himself in spiritualist phenomena at Guernsey.
13 *Ibid.*, XLIV: *OC* I, 705–6.
14 *Corr.* I, 441, 451.
15 *Ibid.*, pp. 437–8, 450–1.
16 *Ibid.*, pp. 522–3.
17 *OC* I, 1196. See above, p. 147.
18 Prarond, however, stated that he remembered hearing Baudelaire declaim *Le Rebelle* as early as 1843.
19 *Tableaux parisiens* does not consist entirely of poems written after 1857. Baudelaire made up the cycle partly by displacing certain poems which in the original *Les Fleurs du Mal* had been allocated to other cycles.
20 *OC* I, 141.
21 *Corr.* I, 568, 576.
22 *Corr.* II, 67.
23 See Jean-Paul Bouillon, 'Artiste et éditeur: correspondance de Bracquemond et de Poulet-Malassis', *Bulletin du Bibliophile*, 1975, pp. 49–66.
24 Quoted in Jean Pommier, *Autour de l'édition originale des 'Fleurs du Mal'*, Geneva, 1968, p. 138.
25 Asselineau, *Charles Baudelaire, sa vie et son œuvre*, Paris, 1869, quoted in *Baudelaire et Asselineau*, ed. Jacques Crépet and Claude Pichois, Paris, 1973, pp. 129–30.
26 Léon Cladel, 'Chez feu mon maître', *Musée des Deux Mondes*, September 1st, 1876; quoted in *Baudelaire devant ses contemporains*, ed. W. T. Bandy and Claude Pichois, Paris, 1967, pp. 180–1. Cladel was visiting Baudelaire in the summer of 1861, the poet having offered to write a preface for his maiden novel *Les Martyrs ridicules*.
27 *Corr.* II, 140–1.
28 *Corr.* I, 661.
29 *Ibid.*, p. 609.

30 *Corr.* II, 122.
31 *Ibid.*, p. 233.

XIII.   PARIS SPLEEN

1 *Un Plaisant, Le Spleen de Paris* IV : *OC* I, 279.
2 See above, p. 150.
3 Quoted by Robert Kopp in the introduction to his critical edition of the *Petits Poèmes en Prose* (Paris, Corti, 1969, p. lxiii).
4 *La Chevelure* was the title first used (in *Le Présent*, August 24th, 1857) for the prose poem subsequently retitled *Un hémisphère dans une chevelure*.
5 *OC* I, 312.
6 A. Proust, 'Edouard Manet: souvenirs', *Revue Blanche*, February 15th, 1897, p. 168. For some reason, Proust did not include the story in the biography of Manet he published in 1913; it is, however, told (with a few supplementary details) in E. Moreau-Nélaton, *Manet raconté par lui-même* (1926).
7 *OC* I, 328.
8 In a letter to Alphonse de Calonne, the editor of the *Revue contemporaine*, dated January 8th, 1859, Baudelaire writes: 'Si je me sentais plus appuyé et plus soutenu par vous, je pourrais vous donner une série de *nouvelles* d'une nature surprenante, et qui ne seraient ni du Balzac, ni de l'Hoffmann, ni du Gautier, ni même du Poe, qui est le plus fort de tous' (*Corr.* I, 537). He was still toying with the idea in 1865; writing from Brussels to Julien Lemer, and giving him a list of works in progress, he includes 'une série de *Nouvelles*, toutes apparentées entre elles' (*Corr.* II, 443). All he ever did, as far as is known, towards this project was to compile lists of titles and in one instance to sketch out an incomplete scenario.
9 See above, pp. 154, 174.
10 *OC* I, 339.
11 *Un Mangeur d'opium*, III : *OC* I, 468.
12 *OC* I, 291.
13 *Le Peintre de la vie moderne*, III : *OC* II, 691–2.
14 *Corr.* I, 667, 671.
15 *Ibid.*, pp. 672–3.
16 See above, p. 110, and, in a letter to the art critic Théophile Thoré: 'Savez-vous pourquoi j'ai si patiemment traduit Poe? Parce qu'il me ressemblait. La première fois que j'ai ouvert un livre de lui, j'ai vu, avec épouvante et ravissement, non seulement des sujets rêvés par moi, mais des PHRASES pensées par moi, et écrites par lui vingt ans auparavant' (*Corr.* II, 386).
17 'La musique creuse le ciel' (*Fusées*, VI : *OC* I, 653); 'la musique donne l'idée de l'espace' (*Mon cœur mis à nu*, XXXIX : *ibid.*, p. 702).
18 *OC* II, 785.
19 *Corr.* II, 202.
20 *Ibid.*, pp. 142, 151–2.
21 The most disastrous of these was the so-called 'shuttle system', whereby he gave Poulet-Malassis a note-of-hand, payable in, say, six months, which the publisher discounted to settle some pressing debt; when the six months were up, Poulet-Malassis gave Baudelaire his note-of-hand which Baudelaire then discounted to pay the earlier one. Eventually the system broke down and Poulet-Malassis was landed in a debtors' prison.
22 *Corr.* I, 598 and II, 492.
23 *Corr.* II, 225. Cf. also his statement to Arsène Houssaye (*ibid.*, p. 207): 'étant, personnellement, sans espérances, j'ai *pris plaisir* à me faire *bouc* pour tous les infortunés hommes de lettres.'

24 Robert Stoepel, the German-American composer, approached Baudelaire in November 1860 with a request to translate parts of Longfellow's *Hiawatha* for use as a libretto in a choral symphony of his composition. Baudelaire worked for several months on this project before learning that Stoepel had sailed for New York without paying him a cent. See W. T. Bandy and Claude Pichois, 'Un inédit: *Hiawatha, légende indienne*, adaptation de Charles Baudelaire', pp. 7–68 in *Etudes baudelairiennes*, II, Neuchâtel, 1971.

25 *OC* I, 668.

26 *Corr.* II, 135–6.

27 Letter to his mother, April 1st, 1861: *Corr.* II, 140.

28 *Fusées*, XI: *OC* I, 660.

29 *Mon cœur mis à nu*, XI: *ibid.*, p. 683.

30 *Fusées*, III: *ibid.*, p. 652.

31 *Mon cœur mis à nu*, XXX: *ibid.*, p. 696.

32 *OC* I, 318–19.

XIV.   FLIGHT INTO SILENCE

1 See Gustave Charlier, *Passages*, Brussels, 1947, pp. 144 ff. and Jean Adhémar, 'Baudelaire, les frères Stevens, la modernité', *Gazette des Beaux-Arts*, vol. LI (1958), pp. 123–6.

2 Reproduced in Maurice Kunel, *Baudelaire en Belgique*, Liège, 1944, p. 29. The author was Gustave Frédérix, a friend of the Hugo family.

3 Nadar, *Charles Baudelaire intime* ..., Paris, 1911, pp. 119–20. Baudelaire's catastrophic faux-pas was reported at the time in *La Petite Revue*; see *Baudelaire devant ses contemporains*, ed. W. T. Bandy and Claude Pichois, Paris, 1967, p. 185.

4 Lemonnier, *La Vie belge*, Paris, 1905, pp. 70–72.

5 *Lettres à Charles Baudelaire*, ed. Claude Pichois, Neuchâtel, 1973, pp. 262–3.

6 *Corr.* II, 448.

7 Barral's account has been reproduced in Maurice Kunel, 'Quatre jours avec Baudelaire', *Les Œuvres Libres*, vol. CXXXII (1932), pp. 193–244.

8 *Corr.* II, 408.

9 Quoted in *Les Derniers Mois de Charles Baudelaire ... correspondances, documents*, ed. Jean Richer and Marcel A. Ruff, Paris, 1976, p. 19.

10 *Ibid.*, p. 54.

11 *Corr.* II, 362, 370 (letters of May 6th and 27th, 1864).

12 Letter of October 13th, 1864: *ibid.*, p. 409.

13 Letter to Manet, May 11th, 1865: *ibid.*, p. 496.

14 *Ibid.*, p. 449 (letter to Mme Meurice).

15 See Kunel, *Baudelaire en Belgique*, p. 139.

16 Letter to his mother, February 3rd, 1865: *Corr.* II, 446.

17 In an article in *Le Figaro*, November 2nd, 1902, reproduced in *Baudelaire devant ses contemporains*, ed. W. T. Bandy and Claude Pichois, Paris, 1967, pp. 141–6.

18 Kunel, *op. cit.*, p. 155. An abridged version of Neyt's account was given in Pierre Dufay, *Autour de Baudelaire* ..., Paris, 1931, pp. 140–1.

19 Letter from Mme Aupick to Ancelle, quoted in E. and J. Crépet, *Baudelaire: étude biographique*, Paris, 1906, pp. 197–8.

20 *Ibid.*, p. 163.

21 Published by Jacques Crépet in *Le Bulletin du Bibliophile*, February 1946, pp. 63–4. Troubat also related this visit in his *Souvenirs du dernier secrétaire de Sainte-Beuve*, Paris, 1890, pp. 208–9.

22 *Baudelaire et Asselineau*, ed. Jacques Crépet and Claude Pichois, Paris, 1953, pp. 149–50.

23 Letter to an unknown correspondent, first published by G. E. Lang, 'Charles Baudelaire et sa mère', *Le Figaro*, March 5th, 1922, and reproduced in *Baudelaire devant ses contemporains*, p. 197.

24 Letters to Poulet-Malassis of September 18th, 1867, January 12th and April 20th, 1868; the first quoted in E. and J. Crépet, *op. cit.*, p. 206, the other two in *Les Derniers Mois de Charles Baudelaire*, pp. 153, 170.

APPENDIX

French texts of poems and fragments quoted in translation.

1. *Le Rebelle* p. xiii

Un Ange furieux fond du ciel comme un aigle,
Du Mécréant saisit à plein poing les cheveux,
Et dit, le secouant: 'Tu connaîtras la règle!
(Car je suis ton bon Ange, entends-tu?) je le veux!

Sache qu'il faut aimer, sans faire la grimace,
Le pauvre, le méchant, le tortu, l'hébété,
Pour que tu puisses faire à Jésus, quand il passe,
Un tapis triomphal avec ta charité.

Tel est l'Amour! Avant que ton cœur ne se blase,
A la gloire de Dieu rallume ton extase;
C'est la Volupté vraie aux durables appas!'

Et l'Ange, châtiant autant, ma foi! qu'il aime,
De ses poings de géant torture l'anathème;
Mais le damné répond toujours: 'Je ne veux pas!'

2. from *Bénédiction* p. 2

Lorsque, par un décret des puissances suprêmes,
Le Poète apparaît en ce monde ennuyé,
Sa mère épouvantée et pleine de blasphèmes
Crispe ses poings vers Dieu, qui la prend en pitié:

– 'Ah! que n'ai-je mis bas tout un nœud de vipères,
Plutôt que de nourrir cette dérision!
Maudite soit la nuit aux plaisirs éphémères
Où mon ventre a conçu mon expiation!

Puisque tu m'as choisie entre toutes les femmes
Pour être le dégoût de mon triste mari,
Et que je ne puis pas rejeter dans les flammes,
Comme un billet d'amour, ce monstre rabougri,

Je ferai rejaillir ta haine qui m'accable
Sur l'instrument maudit de tes méchancetés,
Et je tordrai si bien cet arbre misérable,
Qu'il ne pourra pousser ses boutons empestés!'

Elle ravale ainsi l'écume de sa haine,
Et, ne comprenant pas les desseins éternels,
Elle-même prépare au fond de la Géhenne
Les bûchers consacrés aux crimes maternels.

3.   from   *'La servante au grand cœur . . .'*   p. 12

Si, par une nuit bleue et froide de décembre
Je la trouvais tapie en un coin de ma chambre,
Grave, et venant du fond de son lit éternel
Couver l'enfant grandi de son œil maternel,
Que pourrais-je répondre à cette âme pieuse,
Voyant tomber des pleurs de sa paupière creuse?

4.   from   *L'Albatros*   p. 38

Le Poète est semblable au prince des nuées
Qui hante la tempête et se rit de l'archer;
Exilé sur le sol au milieu des huées,
Ses ailes de géant l'empêchent de marcher.

5.   from   *Le Voyage*   pp. 41–2

Amer savoir, celui qu'on tire du voyage!
Le monde, monotone et petit, aujourd'hui,
Hier, demain, toujours, nous fait voir notre image:
Une oasis d'horreur dans un désert d'ennui!

        *   *   *

O Mort, vieux capitaine, il est temps! levons l'ancre!
Ce pays nous ennuie, ô Mort! Appareillons!
Si le ciel et la mer sont noirs comme de l'encre,
Nos cœurs que tu connais sont remplis de rayons!

Verse-nous ton poison pour qu'il nous réconforte!
Nous voulons, tant ce feu nous brûle le cerveau,
Plonger au fond du gouffre, Enfer ou Ciel, qu'importe?
Au fond de l'Inconnu pour trouver du *nouveau*!

6.   from   *Le Soleil*   p. 46

Quand le soleil cruel frappe à traits redoublés
Sur la ville et les champs, sur les toits et les blés,
Je vais m'exercer seul à ma fantasque escrime,
Flairant dans tous les coins les hasards de la rime,
Trébuchant sur les mots comme sur les pavés,
Heurtant parfois des vers depuis longtemps rêvés.

7.   *Parfum exotique*   p. 53

Quand, les deux yeux fermés, en un soir chaud d'automne,
Je respire l'odeur de ton sein chaleureux,
Je vois se dérouler des rivages heureux
Qu'éblouissent les feux d'un soleil monotone;

Une île paresseuse où la nature donne
Des arbres singuliers et des fruits savoureux;
Des hommes dont le corps est mince et vigoureux,
Et des femmes dont l'œil par sa franchise étonne.

Guidé par ton odeur vers de charmants climats,
Je vois un port rempli de voiles et de mâts
Encor tout fatigués par la vague marine,

Pendant que le parfum des verts tamariniers,
Qui circule dans l'air et m'enfle la narine,
Se mêle dans mon âme au chant des mariniers.

8.   '*Je t'adore à l'égal de la voûte nocturne* . . .'   p. 54

Je t'adore à l'égal de la voûte nocturne,
O vase de tristesse, ô grande taciturne,

Et t'aime d'autant plus, belle, que tu me fuis,
Et que tu me parais, ornement de mes nuits,
Plus ironiquement accumuler les lieues
Qui séparent mes bras des immensités bleues.

Je m'avance à l'attaque, et je grimpe aux assauts,
Comme après un cadavre un chœur de vermisseaux,
Et je chéris, ô bête implacable et cruelle!
Jusqu'à cette froideur par où tu m'es plus belle!

9. *'Une nuit que j'étais près d'une affreuse Juive . . .'* pp. 54-5

Une nuit que j'étais près d'une affreuse Juive,
Comme au long d'un cadavre un cadavre étendu
Je me pris à songer près de ce corps vendu
A la triste beauté dont mon désir se prive.

Je me représentai sa majesté native,
Son regard de vigueur et de grâces armé,
Ses cheveux qui lui font un casque parfumé,
Et dont le souvenir pour l'amour me ravive.

Car j'eusse avec ferveur baisé ton noble corps,
Et depuis tes pieds frais jusqu'à tes noires tresses
Déroulé le trésor des profondes caresses,

Si, quelque soir, d'un pleur obtenu sans effort
Tu pouvais seulement, ô reine des cruelles!
Obscurcir la splendeur de tes froides prunelles.

10.   from   *Femmes damnées*   p. 56

Loin des peuples vivants, errantes, condamnées,
A travers les déserts courez comme les loups;
Faites votre destin, âmes désordonnées,
Et fuyez l'infini que vous portez en vous!

11.   *Remords posthume*   pp. 56-7

Lorsque tu dormiras, ma belle ténébreuse,
Au fond d'un monument construit en marbre noir,

Et lorsque tu n'auras pour alcôve et manoir
Qu'un caveau pluvieux et qu'une fosse creuse;

Quand la pierre, opprimant ta poitrine peureuse
Et tes flancs qu'assouplit un charmant nonchaloir,
Empêchera ton cœur de battre et de vouloir,
Et tes pieds de courir leur course aventureuse,

Le tombeau, confident de mon rêve infini
(Car le tombeau toujours comprendra le poète),
Durant ces grandes nuits d'où le somme est banni,

Te dira : 'Que vous sert, courtisane imparfaite,
De n'avoir pas connu ce que pleurent les morts?'
– Et le ver rongera ta peau comme un remords.

12. from   *Les Phares*   p. 84

Delacroix, lac de sang hanté des mauvais anges,
Ombragé par un bois de sapins toujours vert,
Où, sous un ciel chagrin, des fanfares étranges
Passent, comme un soupir étouffé de Weber.

13.   *L'Ennemi*   p. 114

Ma jeunesse ne fut qu'un ténébreux orage,
Traversé çà et là par de brillants soleils;
Le tonnerre et la pluie ont fait un tel ravage,
Qu'il reste en mon jardin bien peu de fruits vermeils.

Voilà que j'ai touché l'automne des idées,
Et qu'il faut employer la pelle et les râteaux
Pour rassembler à neuf les terres inondées,
Où l'eau creuse des trous grands comme des tombeaux.

Et qui sait si les fleurs nouvelles que je rêve
Trouveront dans ce sol lavé comme une grève
Le mystique aliment qui ferait leur vigueur?

– O douleur! ô douleur! Le Temps mange la vie,
Et l'obscur Ennemi qui nous ronge le cœur
Du sang que nous perdons croît et se fortifie!

Toi qui, comme un coup de couteau,
Dans mon cœur plaintif es entrée;
Toi qui, forte comme un troupeau
De démons, vins, folle et parée,

De mon esprit humilié
Faire ton lit et ton domaine;
– Infâme à qui je suis lié
Comme le forçat à la chaîne,

Comme au jeu le joueur têtu,
Comme à la bouteille l'ivrogne,
Comme aux vermines la charogne,
– Maudite, maudite sois-tu!

J'ai prié le glaive rapide
De conquérir ma liberté,
Et j'ai dit au poison perfide
De secourir ma lâcheté.

Hélas! le poison et le glaive
M'ont pris en dédain et m'ont dit:
'Tu n'es pas digne qu'on t'enlève
A ton esclavage maudit,

Imbécile! – de son empire
Si nos efforts te délivraient,
Tes baisers ressusciteraient
Le cadavre de ton vampire!'

Le Démon, dans ma chambre haute,
Ce matin est venu me voir,
Et, tâchant à me prendre en faute,
Me dit: 'Je voudrais bien savoir,

Parmi toutes les belles choses
Dont est fait son enchantement,
Parmi les objets noirs ou roses
Qui composent son corps charmant,

Quel est le plus doux.' – O mon âme!
Tu répondis à l'Abhorré:
'Puisqu'en Elle tout est dictame,
Rien ne peut être préféré.

Lorsque tout me ravit, j'ignore
Si quelque chose me séduit.
Elle éblouit comme l'Aurore
Et console comme la Nuit;

Et l'harmonie est trop exquise,
Qui gouverne tout son beau corps,
Pour que l'impuissante analyse
En note les nombreux accords.

O métamorphose mystique
De tous mes sens fondus en un!
Son haleine fait la musique,
Comme sa voix fait le parfum!'

16.   *L'Aube spirituelle*   p. 130

Quand chez les débauchés l'aube blanche et vermeille
Entre en société de l'Idéal rongeur,
Par l'opération d'un mystère vengeur
Dans la brute assoupie un ange se réveille.

Des Cieux Spirituels l'inaccessible azur,
Pour l'homme terrassé qui rêve encore et souffre,
S'ouvre et s'enfonce avec l'attirance du gouffre.
Ainsi, chère Déesse, Etre lucide et pur,

Sur les débris fumeux des stupides orgies
Ton souvenir plus clair, plus rose, plus charmant,
A mes yeux agrandis voltige incessamment.

Le soleil a noirci la flamme des bougies;
Ainsi, toujours vainqueur, ton fantôme est pareil,
Ame resplendissante, à l'immortel soleil!

243

17. from *Ciel brouillé* p. 133

On dirait ton regard d'une vapeur couvert;
Ton œil mystérieux (est-il bleu, gris ou vert?)
Alternativement tendre, rêveur, cruel,
Réfléchit l'indolence et la pâleur du ciel.

18. *Le Balcon* pp. 138–9

Mère des souvenirs, maîtresse des maîtresses,
O toi, tous mes plaisirs! ô toi, tous mes devoirs!
Tu te rappelleras la beauté des caresses,
La douceur du foyer et le charme des soirs,
Mère des souvenirs, maîtresse des maîtresses!

Les soirs illuminés par l'ardeur du charbon,
Et les soirs au balcon, voilés de vapeurs roses,
Que ton sein m'était doux! que ton cœur m'était bon!
Nous avons dit souvent d'impérissables choses
Les soirs illuminés par l'ardeur du charbon.

Que les soleils sont beaux dans les chaudes soirées!
Que l'espace est profond! que le cœur est puissant!
En me penchant vers toi, reine des adorées,
Je croyais respirer le parfum de ton sang.
Que les soleils sont beaux dans les chaudes soirées!

La nuit s'épaississait ainsi qu'une cloison,
Et mes yeux dans le noir devinaient tes prunelles,
Et je buvais ton souffle, ô douceur! ô poison!
Et tes pieds s'endormaient dans mes mains fraternelles.
La nuit s'épaississait ainsi qu'une cloison.

Je sais l'art d'évoquer les minutes heureuses,
Et revis mon passé blotti dans tes genoux.
Car à quoi bon chercher tes beautés langoureuses
Ailleurs qu'en ton cher corps et qu'en ton cœur si doux?
Je sais l'art d'évoquer les minutes heureuses!

Ces serments, ces parfums, ces baisers infinis,
Renaîtront-ils d'un gouffre interdit à nos sondes,
Comme montent au ciel les soleils rajeunis
Après s'être lavés au fond des mers profondes?
– O serments! ô parfums! ô baisers infinis!

Quand le ciel bas et lourd pèse comme un couvercle
Sur l'esprit gémissant en proie aux longs ennuis,
Et que de l'horizon embrassant tout le cercle
Il nous verse un jour noir plus triste que les nuits;

Quand la terre est changée en un cachot humide,
Où l'Espérance, comme une chauve-souris,
S'en va battant les murs de son aile timide
Et se cognant la tête à des plafonds pourris;

Quand la pluie étalant ses immenses traînées
D'une vaste prison imite les barreaux,
Et qu'un peuple muet d'infâmes araignées
Vient tendre ses filets au fond de nos cerveaux,

Des cloches tout à coup sautent avec furie
Et lancent vers le ciel un affreux hurlement,
Ainsi que des esprits errants et sans patrie
Qui se mettent à geindre opiniâtrement.

– Et de longs corbillards, sans tambours ni musique,
Défilent lentement dans mon âme; l'Espoir,
Vaincu, pleure, et l'Angoisse atroce, despotique,
Sur mon crâne incliné plante son drapeau noir.

La sottise, l'erreur, le péché, la lésine,
Occupent nos esprits et travaillent nos corps,
Et nous alimentons nos aimables remords,
Comme les mendiants nourrissent leur vermine.

*   *   *

C'est le Diable qui tient les fils qui nous remuent!
Aux objets répugnants nous trouvons des appas;
Chaque jour vers l'Enfer nous descendons d'un pas,
Sans horreur, à travers des ténèbres qui puent.

Pour ne pas oublier la chose capitale,
Nous avons vu partout, et sans l'avoir cherché,
Du haut jusques en bas de l'échelle fatale,
Le spectacle ennuyeux de l'immortel péché:

La femme, esclave vile, orgueilleuse et stupide,
Sans rire s'adorant et s'aimant sans dégoût;
L'homme, tyran goulu, paillard, dur et cupide,
Esclave de l'esclave et ruisseau dans l'égout;

Le bourreau qui jouit, le martyr qui sanglote;
Le fête qu'assaisonne et parfume le sang;
Le poison du pouvoir énervant le despote,
Et le peuple amoureux du fouet abrutissant;

Plusieurs religions semblables à la nôtre,
Toutes escaladant le ciel; la Sainteté,
Comme en un lit de plume un délicat se vautre,
Dans les clous et le crin cherchant la volupté;

L'Humanité bavarde, ivre de son génie,
Et folle maintenant comme elle était jadis,
Criant à Dieu, dans sa furibonde agonie:
'O mon semblable, ô mon maître, je te maudis!'

Et les moins sots, hardis amants de la Démence,
Fuyant le grand troupeau parqué par le Destin,
Et se réfugiant dans l'opium immense!
— Tel est du globe entier l'éternel bulletin.

Viens par ici,

Loin d'eux. Vois se pencher les défuntes Années,
Sur les balcons du ciel, en robes surannées;
Surgir du fond des eaux le Regret souriant;

Le Soleil moribond s'endormir sous une arche,
Et, comme un long linceul traînant à l'Orient,
Entends, ma chère, entends la douce Nuit qui marche.

INDEX

Albert, Edmond, 216
Allan, John, 110
Ampère, Jean-Jacques, 103
Ancelle, Narcisse-Désiré, 58, 65, 67–70, 99, 111, 118, 136, 171–3, 184, 197, 209, 211, 213–14
Arondel, Antoine, 59
L'Artiste, 59–60, 167
Asselineau, Charles, 30, 35, 49, 69, 108, 115, 140, 152, 155, 206, 208, 214–17
Aupick, Jacques, 9–10, 12, 14–20, 22–4, 26, 27, 34–7, 41, 43–4, 65, 70–1, 92, 117–20, 130, 169–70, 182, 217
Aupick, Mme. *See* Defayis, Caroline Archenbaut
Autard de Bragard, Mme, 39, 148

Babou, Hippolyte, 143
Bailly, Emmanuel, 33–4
Balzac, Honoré de, 5, 10, 55, 59, 78, 83, 85–6, 88, 89, 106, 110, 160
Banville, Théodore de, 40, 47–8, 49, 51, 60, 107, 133, 136, 140, 146, 198, 216, 217
Barbey d'Aurevilly, Jules, 147–8, 151, 178, 217
Barbier, Auguste, 73, 198
Barral, Georges, 6, 207
Barrès, Maurice, 93
Barrot, Odilon, 91
Baudard, Louis, 9
Baudelaire, Charles-Pierre
    Art, interest in, 49, 73–4; Belgians, antipathy towards, 209–10; birthplace, 5–6; as conversationalist, 64–5, 128; dandyism, dress, 33, 65, 87–8, 100, 200; education, 17–26; English, knowledge of, 102–3, 105–6; financial affairs, 34–5, 58–9, 65–7, 69, 80, 171–3, 196–7, 211; French Academy, candidacy for, 196–8; as lecturer, 204–6; lesbianism, interest in, 55–6; mother's remarriage, reaction to, 14–15; music,

interest in, 195; novels, plans to write, 60–1, 89; poetry, method of composition, 46, 88; political views, 92–101; poverty, experience of, 88, 111–14; recitations of poetry, 45–6, 65; religion, attitude to, x, 18, 29, 166–7, 175, 177–8; sex, attitude to, 53, 201–3; spleen, attacks of, 28, 141–3, 177; suicide, thoughts of, 70, 199–200; travel, love of, 16, 37; venereal disease, progress of, 30–1, 86, 144, 161–2, 198–9, 211–12
    Works: *L'Art romantique*, 204; *Conseils aux jeunes littérateurs*, 80, 89–90; *Curiosités esthétiques*, 204; *Edgar Allan Poe, sa vie et ses ouvrages*, 108, 111; *Épaves* 207; *Exposition universelle, 1855*, 167, 175; *La Fanfarlo*, 11–12, 85–7;
    Les Fleurs du Mal, xii, 2, 11, 39, 45–6, 55–6, 60, 84, 88, 90, 100, 104, 115, 126, 127, 132, 140–52, 155, 157–8, 162, 170–1, 176–82, 187–9, 195, 204, 209, 215–16; component poems: *Abel et Caïn*, 100; *L'Albatros*, 38; *L'Ame du vin*, 158; *L'Aube spirituelle*, 130, 144; *Au lecteur*, 145; *A une dame créole*, 39, 148; *A une Madone*, 134; *A une mendiante rousse*, 148; *L'Avertisseur*, 178; *Le Balcon*, 138–9; *Le Beau Navire*, 134; *Bénédiction*, 2, 148; *Les Bijoux*, 53, 134; *Chant d'automne*, 133; *La Chevelure*, 188; *Confession*, 144; *Crépuscule du soir*, 188; *L'Ennemi*, 114; *L'Examen de minuit*, 178; *Femmes damnées*, 56; *Hymne*, 127, 130; *L'Imprévu*, 178; *L'Irréparable*, 132, 144; *L'Invitation au voyage*, 134, 144, 188; 'Je t'aime à l'égal de la voûte nocturne', 54; *Les Litanies de Satan*, 96, 100; *Moesta et errabunda*, 144; *La Mort des artistes*, 148; *La Musique*, 195; *Parfum exotique*, 53;

Baudelaire, Charles-Pierre—*cont.*
Les Phares, 84; *La Rançon*, 96; *Le Rebelle*, xii–xiii, 178; *Recueillement*, 179; *Remords posthume*, 56–7, 144; *Le Reniement de Saint-Pierre*, 100, 150; *Rêve parisien*, 162; *Réversibilité*, 144; *Sed non satiata*, 55; 'La servante au grand cœur dont vous étiez jalouse', 12; *Le Soleil*, 46; *Spleen*, 142–3; *Tout entière*, 127–8; *Une charogne*, 56; 'Une nuit que j'étais près d'une affreuse Juive', 54–5; *Le Vampire*, 123, 144; *Le Vin de l'assassin*, 135, 148; *Le Vin des chiffonniers*, 158; *Le Vin du solitaire*, 158; *Le Voyage*, 41, 105, 174–6; *Voyage à Cythère*, 144;
   Histoires extraordinaires (tr.), 108, 114–15; *L'Ivrogne*, 135; *Le Jeune Enchanteur* (tr.), 105–6; *Les Limbes*, 141, 143; *Mon cœur mis à nu*, 98–100, 175; *Nouvelles histoires extraordinaires* (tr.), 115; *Les Paradis artificiels*, 158, 160, 162, 164, 166, 204; *Pauvre Belgique!*, 208–9; *Le Peintre de la vie moderne*, 193;
   Petits poèmes en prose, 94, 187–93; component prose poems: *Assommons les pauvres!*, 94–5; *Les Bons Chiens*, 209; *La Chambre double*, 162–4; *Le Chien et le flacon*, 90; *La Corde*, 189–91; *Crépuscule du soir*, 188–9; *Les Fenêtres*, 192; *Les Foules*, 192–3; *Laquelle est la vraie?*, 154, 191; *Le Port*, 174, 191; *Un plaisant*, 187; *Les Vocations*, 12, 16; *Les Yeux des pauvres*, 202–3;
   Richard Wagner et 'Tannhäuser' à Paris, 195–6; *Salon de 1845*, 72–7, 81, 88, 140; *Salon de 1846*, 55, 77, 80–4, 89, 92; *Salon de 1859*, 81; *Le Spleen de Paris*: see *Petits Poèmes en prose*
Baudelaire, Claude-Alphonse (the poet's half-brother), 5, 7, 8, 11, 16, 20, 22, 29, 31, 34–6, 43, 65, 69, 115, 170
Baudelaire, Edmond (the poet's nephew), 34
Baudelaire, Joseph-François (the poet's father), 4–8, 11, 43
Beauvoir, Roger de, 47

Beethoven, 195
Béranger, Jean-Pierre de, 151
Berlioz, Hector, 194–5
Bernard, Thalès, 93, 107
Bertin, Armand, 61
Bertrand, Aloysius, 188
Billault, Adolphe, 151
Blanqui, Louis-Auguste, 96
Bloch, Joséphine ('Maryx'), 125, 153
Boissard, Fernand, 47, 64, 125, 159
Bonjour, Abel, 115
Bossuet, Jacques-Bénigne, 25
Bouilhet, Louis, 18, 126
Bourdaloue, Louis, 25
Bourdin, Gustave, 150, 187
Boyer, Philoxène, 129
Bracquemond, Félix, 180
Broise, Eugène de, 150, 180
Brosses, Charles de, 208
Browning, Robert, 148
Brunod, Aimé, 132
Buisson, Jules, 14, 32, 45, 92
Le Bulletin de l'Ami des Arts, 59
Buloz, François, 144–5
Byron, 103–5

Cabanis, P. J. G., 4
Calonne, Alphonse de, 147, 158, 165, 177–8
Cavaignac, Eugène, 97
Cézanne, Paul, 18, 49, 74
Champfleury (Jules Husson), 77, 87, 89, 91, 96, 217
Champsaur, Félicien, 201
Chateaubriand, François-René de, xi, 36
Chatterton, Thomas, xi
Chenavard, Paul, 126, 160
Chénier, André, xi
Chennevières, Philippe de, 45, 77, 83, 97
Choiseul-Praslin, Duc de, 4
Cladel, Léon, 200–1
Clésinger, Jean-Baptiste, 125–6
Condorcet, Antoine-Nicolas de, 4
Constant, Benjamin, 85
Corday, Charlotte, 79
Cormenin, Louis de, 119
Corot, Camille, 74, 76
Le Corsaire-Satan, 77–8, 80
Courbet, Gustave, 74, 77, 78, 91, 101, 136–7, 194, 215
Cousin, Charles, 33, 44

Crabbe, Prosper, 205–6
Crépet, Eugène, 98, 172, 215
Crépet, Jacques, 1

Daniel, John Moncure, 108–11
Dante, x, 56, 141, 151
Daubrun, Marie, 131–6, 144, 148, 183
Daumier, Honoré, 49
David, Jacques-Louis, 78–9, 108
Debussy, Claude, 188
Decamps, Alexandre-Gabriel, 76
Defayis, Caroline Archenbaut
    (Baudelaire's mother), 1–15, 20–4,
    27–8, 30, 35–6, 43–4, 58–61, 63,
    65–9, 72, 111, 115, 117–22, 130–1,
    136–8, 169–73, 181–4, 191, 196, 199–
    200, 213–18
Defayis, Charles (Baudelaire's
    grandfather), 3
Delacroix, Eugène, 24, 48, 49, 60, 76,
    78, 81, 83–4, 90, 104, 126, 160, 168,
    194, 204
Delécluze, Etienne, 103
La Démocratie pacifique, 60, 106–7
De Quincey, Thomas, 10, 157–8, 161–
    2, 164–6, 192
Deroy, Emile, 48–9, 73, 86, 148
Devéria, Jacques, 47
Diaz de la Peña, Narcisse, 125
Diderot, Denis, 81, 106
Dozon, Auguste, 32
Drouet, Juliette, 134
Du Camp, Maxime, 37, 119, 126, 175
Dumas fils, Alexandre, 59
Dumas père, Alexandre, 61, 132, 134,
    159, 206, 208
Dupont, Pierre, 93, 97–8
Duval, Jeanne, 50–7, 58, 69–70, 87,
    107, 112, 118, 121–3, 127, 131, 136,
    144, 148, 183–5, 197, 199
Duval, Jeanne-Marie-Marthe (Jeanne's
    mother), 50, 58, 131

Eliot, T. S., 145, 176
Emon, Louis, 170–1, 182, 214
L'Esprit public, 80, 105
Esquiros, Alphonse, 95–6
Eugénie, Empress (Eugénia de
    Montijo), 151, 169, 196
Eveleth, George, 107

Ferrier, Ida, 134
Feuchères, Jean, 64, 125

Féval, Paul, 89
Le Figaro, 150, 187, 208
Flaubert, Gustave, x, 10, 18, 101, 105,
    119, 126, 151–2, 155, 166–7, 173,
    198, 217
Flotte, Paul de, 98
Fourier, Charles, 106, 141
Foyot, Louise-Julie, 3
Fraisse, Armand, 110, 115, 195
Frédérix, Gustave, 207

Galigniani, John Anthony, 103
Gautier, Féli, 134
Gautier, Judith, 125–6
Gautier, Théophile, 26, 46, 55, 64, 73,
    84, 86, 88, 89, 104, 125–6, 128, 140,
    151–2, 157, 159–61, 194, 198, 204,
    217
Gavarni (Sulpice-Guillaume
    Chevalier), 49
Genevray, Louis de la, 32
Géricault, Jean-Louis, 41
Gilbert, Laurent, xi
Girardin, Emile de, 61, 91, 97
Girodet (Anne-Louis Girodet de
    Roussy), 78
Goethe, ix, 106, 157
Goncourt, Edmond and Jules de, 126
Gray, Thomas, 104
Grisi, Ernesta, 126
Guérin, Pierre, 78
Guizot, François, 73, 91, 95
Guys, Constantin, x, 100, 193–4, 210

Haussmann, Baron, 179, 186
Haussoulier, William, 76
Hayter, Anthea, 44
Helvétius, Mme, 4
Hignard, Henri, 28
Hoffmann, E. T. A., 106, 109
Hohenlohe, Prince de, 9–10
Hostein, Hippolyte, 135
Houssaye, Arsène, 60, 187
Hugo, Mme Victor, 134, 207
Hugo, Victor, xi, 24–6, 30, 36, 62, 98–9,
    134, 140, 157, 197, 204

Ingres, Jean-Auguste-Dominique, 78

Janin, Jeanne-Justine-Rosalie, 5–6
Janin, Jules, 24, 59–60, 73
Jacquotot, Antoine, 169, 173

Jean Paul (Johann Paul Richter), 106
Jouve, Nicole Ward, xii
Joyant, Jules, 75
Juvenal, 55

Keats, John, 179

Labie, Jean, 36, 67
Laclos, Choderlos de, 106, 207
Lacroix, Albert, 204–6
La Fizelière, Albert de, 59–60
La Madelène, Henri de, 77
Lamartine, Alphonse de, xi, 10, 24, 30, 36, 72, 91, 117, 120
Landor, Walter Savage, 157
Lanier, (bookseller), 150–1
Lasègue, Charles, 27–8
Laurent, Marie, 136
Lebrun, Pierre, 47, 103
Leconte de Lisle, Charles-Marie, 60, 93, 101, 106–7, 140, 198, 211
Le Hon, Charles, 124
Leleux, Adolphe and Armand, 75
Lemaître, Frédérick, 88
Lemer, Julien, 206
Lemonnier, Camille, 205
Leopold I (of Belgium), 204
Le Poittevin, Eugène, 75
Leroux, Pierre, 97
Lesseps, Ferdinand de, 39
Le Vavasseur, Gustave, 32–3, 35, 45, 77, 97
Lévy, Michel, 108, 114, 146, 204, 208, 215–16
Lewis, Wyndham, x
Liszt, Franz, 195
Longfellow, Henry Wadsworth, 104, 109, 198
Louis-Napoléon, see Napoleon III
Louis-Philippe, 15, 27, 65, 95, 117

Maistre, Joseph de, 99–100
Mallarmé, Stéphane, 105
Manet, Edouard, xi, 77–8, 189–90, 194, 204, 209, 211, 215, 217
Mann, William Wilberforce, 108
Marat, Jean-Paul, 79, 108
Mariette, (servant girl), 11–13, 57
Marlowe, Christopher, ix
Maryx, see Bloch, Joséphine
Mathilde, Princess, 152
Maturin, Charles Robert, 106

Maupassant, Guy de, 190, 199
Meissonier, Jean-Louis-Ernest, 126–7, 160
Ménard, Louis, 33, 60, 70, 93, 107, 159–60
Mendès, Catulle, 193, 210–11
Mérimée, Prosper, 103, 151, 169
Le Messager de l'Assemblée, 140–1, 143
Meunier, Isabelle, 106–7
Meurice, Mme Paul, 115, 206–7
Meyerbeer, Giacomo, 194
Michelet, Jules, 103
Molière, 25
Monnier, Henry, 126
Moreau de Tours, Dr Joseph, 159
Morisot, Berthe, 215
Mosselman, Alfred, 124–6, 130, 153
Musset, Alfred de, 73, 157, 200

Nadar (Félix Tournachon), 14, 48, 50–1, 55, 99, 128, 180, 184, 194, 205, 207, 217
Napoleon I, 5, 8, 159, 169
Napoleon III, 98–100, 120, 186, 196
Neri, Elisa, 126
Nerval, Gérard de, 88, 144, 159–60, 194, 199, 211
Neyt, Charles, 210, 212–13

Offenbach, Jacques, 186
O'Neddy, Philothée (Théophile Dondey), 141
Orléans, Duc d', 29

Palmerston, Henry John Temple, 119
Pascal, Blaise, 25
Le Pays, 114, 147, 151
Peacock, Thomas Love, 157
Pelletan, Eugène, 73
Pérignon, Paul, 36, 43
Pérignon, Pierre, 3–5
Picasso, Pablo, 79
Pichot, Amédée, 107
Planche, Gustave, 73
Poe, Edgar Allan, xi, 3, 11, 62, 102, 105–11, 114–16, 129, 146, 157, 167–8, 191, 195, 198, 204, 207
Poulet-Malassis, Auguste, 68, 146–7, 149–50, 158, 165, 176, 178, 180, 183–4, 194–5, 199, 204, 206–10, 212–15
Prarond, Ernest, 12, 31–3, 35, 44–5, 49, 51–2, 62, 77, 92, 172

Préault, Auguste, 88, 126
La Presse, 61, 80, 90, 91, 187
Privat d'Anglemont, Alexandre, 40, 70
Proudhon, Pierre-Joseph, 95–7, 118, 119
Proust, Antonin, 189
Proust, Marcel, 61
Prudhon, Pierre, 78
Pushkin, A. S., 103
Puvis de Chavannes, Pierre, 125
Pyat, Félix, 73

Racine, Jean, x
Regnault, Jean-Baptiste, 7
Renan, Ernest, 29
Le Représentant de la Loire, 107
La Revue contemporaine, 158, 164–5
La Revue de Paris, 108, 111
La Revue des Deux Mondes, 81, 143–5
La Revue européenne, 178–9, 196
La Revue fantaisiste, 193
Reyer, Ernest, 126
Rodin, Auguste, 184
Ronsard, Pierre de, 34, 44, 63
Rops, Félicien, 209, 212
Rousseau, Théodore, 74, 78
Rouvière, Philibert, 135

Sabatier, Apollonie, 124–31, 133–4, 144, 148, 152–5, 160, 183, 202
Sacy, Silvestre de, 159
Sainte-Beuve, Charles-Augustin, 62–4, 89, 115, 151–2, 197–8, 200, 217
Saint-Pierre, Bernardin de, 39
Saint-Victor, Paul de, 132
Saliz, Capt., 37, 39–41
Le Salut public, 96–7
Sand, George, 94, 135–6, 141–2
Sara (prostitute), 31–2, 54
Sartre, Jean-Paul, xii, 14
Savatier, Aglaé. *see* Sabatier, Apollonie
Savatier, André, 124
Savatier, Irma-Adèle ('Bébé'), 124, 126, 152
Schiller, 103
Schmeltz, Jules, 97

Shakespeare, 48, 104, 157, 198
Shelley, Percy Bysshe, 197
Soulié, Frédéric, 61, 132
Soult, Marshal, 27
Staël, Mme de, 83
Stendhal (Henri Beyle), 10, 52, 74, 104
Stevens, Arthur, 204–6, 209, 213–14, 217
Stevens, Joseph, 209
Sue, Eugène, 61, 89–90, 155
Swinburne, Algernon, 100

Tennyson, Lord, 105, 148, 158
Théot, Céleste, 29
Thierry, Edouard, 151
Thiers, Adolphe, 73
Thomas, Frederick, 109
Thompson, John R., 108–9
Thoré, Théophile, 195
Tisserant, Jean-Hippolyte, 135, 148
Tolstoy, L. N., 202
Toubin, Charles, 87–8, 91–2, 96
La Tribune nationale, 97
Troubat, Jules, 200, 215

Vabre, Jules, 104
Vaëz, Gustave, 136
Vallès, Jules, 101
Verlaine, Paul, xi, 217
Vernet, Horace, 75
Véron, Dr Louis-Désiré, 61
Vigny, Alfred de, xi, 30, 142, 148, 198, 211
Villemain, Abel, 196–7
Villemessant, Henri de, 208
Villon, François, 33
Virgil, 141
Vitu, Auguste, 77
Voltaire, 208

Wagner, Richard, 82, 194–6, 200, 202, 211, 215
Watteau, Jean-Antoine, 47
Weber, Carl Maria von, 195
Wilkin, Charles James, 103

Zola, Emile, 18, 49, 82, 135